The Bird and the Cage

Nicholas Borst

The Bird and the Cage

China's Economic Contradictions

Nicholas Borst
Novato, CA, USA

ISBN 978-981-96-3996-0   ISBN 978-981-96-3997-7 (eBook)
https://doi.org/10.1007/978-981-96-3997-7

© The Editor(s) (if applicable) and The Author(s), under exclusive license to Springer Nature Singapore Pte Ltd. 2025

This work is subject to copyright. All rights are solely and exclusively licensed by the Publisher, whether the whole or part of the material is concerned, specifically the rights of translation, reprinting, reuse of illustrations, recitation, broadcasting, reproduction on microfilms or in any other physical way, and transmission or information storage and retrieval, electronic adaptation, computer software, or by similar or dissimilar methodology now known or hereafter developed.

The use of general descriptive names, registered names, trademarks, service marks, etc. in this publication does not imply, even in the absence of a specific statement, that such names are exempt from the relevant protective laws and regulations and therefore free for general use.

The publisher, the authors and the editors are safe to assume that the advice and information in this book are believed to be true and accurate at the date of publication. Neither the publisher nor the authors or the editors give a warranty, expressed or implied, with respect to the material contained herein or for any errors or omissions that may have been made. The publisher remains neutral with regard to jurisdictional claims in published maps and institutional affiliations.

Cover credit: Grant Faint

This Palgrave Macmillan imprint is published by the registered company Springer Nature Singapore Pte Ltd.
The registered company address is: 152 Beach Road, #21-01/04 Gateway East, Singapore 189721, Singapore

If disposing of this product, please recycle the paper.

This book is dedicated to Alden and Rosie

Acknowledgments

I am deeply grateful to the many people who helped make this book possible.

First, I am thankful to my family, especially my wife Julia, for their love and support throughout the long process of writing a book.

I am grateful to my colleagues at Seafarer Capital Partners, who provided me with a supportive and encouraging environment to write this book.

I thank Andrew Foster for encouraging me to turn these ideas into a book and for showing me how companies can serve as a prism for understanding the Chinese economy.

I am thankful to Nicholas Lardy, who has been an incredible mentor and a model for fact-driven, objective analysis of the Chinese economy.

Many thanks go to my editor, Jacob Dreyer, for seeing the book's potential while it was still in its early stages, and to Amanda Cassano for her thoughtful work improving the text and sharpening the arguments.

I appreciate Gou Shuang's help in reviewing several translations.

Lastly, I am grateful to my friends and colleagues, both in China and beyond, who have helped shape my understanding of the Chinese economy over the years.

Contents

1 Introduction   1
2 State and Market Tensions Throughout China's Economic Reforms   7
   1 The Era of Central Planning and Economic Disaster (1949–1976)   8
   2 Early Reforms and the Private Sector's Struggle for Recognition (1977–1988)   13
   3 Rebooting Reform and Saving the State Economy (1988–2000)   25
   4 The Rise of the Private Sector and the Global Financial Crisis (2000–2011)   45
   5 Conclusion   56
3 Xi Jinping's New Era for the Economy   73
   1 Xi's Rise to Power   74
   2 Xi's Early Economic Agenda   78
   3 Grey Rhinos and Black Swans   85
   4 Strengthening SOEs and Guiding the Market   98
   5 Trade and Technology Conflict with the United States   119
   6 Putting the Bird Back in the Cage   128
   7 Conclusion   133

4	**China's Economic Contradictions**	**163**
	1 *Growth vs. Stability*	165
	1.1 Case Studies of Government Intervention for Stability	167
	2 *Innovation vs. Control*	182
	2.1 Case Studies of Government Intervention for Control	183
	3 *Global Integration vs. Self-Reliance*	197
	3.1 Case Studies of Government Intervention for Self-Reliance	199
5	**Conclusion**	**233**
	1 *Xi's Economic Evolution*	236
	2 *China's Economic Trajectory*	237
	3 *How to Respond to China*	241
Index		**245**

ABOUT THE AUTHOR

Nicholas Borst is Vice President and Director of China Research at Seafarer Capital Partners. Prior to joining Seafarer, Nicholas was a senior analyst at the Federal Reserve Bank of San Francisco covering financial and economic developments in Greater China. Previously, he was the China Program Manager and a research associate at the Peterson Institute for International Economics. Nicholas has also worked as an analyst at the World Bank.

Nicholas' research and commentary has been featured in the *Financial Times, The Wall Street Journal, The Economist, Bloomberg,* and *South China Morning Post*. Nicholas was a 2021–2023 Public Intellectuals Program Fellow at the National Committee on U.S.-China Relations and has testified before the U.S.-China Economic and Security Review Commission on multiple occasions.

Nicholas holds a Bachelor's degree from the University of Arizona, a Graduate Certificate from the Johns Hopkins University—Nanjing University Center for Chinese and American Studies, and a Master's degree from the Johns Hopkins University School of Advanced International Studies (SAIS). He speaks Chinese and has lived and worked in China. Nicholas is a CFA charterholder and a member of the CFA Institute.

List of Figures

Chapter 2

Fig. 1	China's share of global GDP	12
Fig. 2	Return on assets of private and state holding industrial firms	37
Fig. 3	SOE share of total exports	47
Fig. 4	SOE fixed asset investment growth (YoY, YTD)	54
Fig. 5	Private vs. state industrial enterprises, growth of sales revenues (YoY, YTD.)	56

Chapter 3

Fig. 1	Growth of shadow banking products in China, 2006–2013	79
Fig. 2	Investment and household consumption share of GDP, 2006–2013	80
Fig. 3	SHIBOR overnight rate, May 15–July 16, 2013	86
Fig. 4	Growth residential floor space under construction, 2012–2017(YoY, YTD)	87
Fig. 5	Shanghai stock exchange composite index and margin lending outstanding, 2014–2016	89
Fig. 6	RMB/USD Central parity rate	91
Fig. 7	China capital outlfows, 2012–2016	92
Fig. 8	Changes in Vanke's major shareholders, 2014–2020	98
Fig. 9	China Unicom change shareholder structure	102
Fig. 10	Share of private companies in China with Communist Party Committees	115
Fig. 11	Share of Chinese exports to the U.S. subject to tariffs	120

Fig. 12	Sales volume of property developers	132

Chapter 4

Fig. 1	China coal price producer price index, 2020–2022	169
Fig. 2	Real estate developer major source of funds, June 2020–September 2024 (YoY, YTD)	172
Fig. 3	Chinese private education stock prices, January–December 2021	174
Fig. 4	China CSI 300 index, 2015–2017	177
Fig. 5	Bank price-to-book ratios, 2015–2023	181
Fig. 6	Tencent market capitalization, 2019–2023	187
Fig. 7	Value and transaction volume of non-bank payments	188
Fig. 8	Total assets and return on assets of central SOEs	191
Fig. 9	Freight transportation in China	192
Fig. 10	China's exports of battery electric passenger cars, January 2018–September 2024	202
Fig. 11	Huawei overseas revenue growth	206
Fig. 12	Share of global payments by currency (September 2024)	210

List of Tables

Chapter 2

Table 1	Foreign strategic investments in China's largest banks (2004–2006)	40
Table 2	Sectors targeted for state control	51

Chapter 3

Table 1	Categorization of state-owned enterprises	100
Table 2	Made in China 2025 priority sectors	107
Table 3	Select national state-guided investment funds	108
Table 4	Excerpts from the Constitution of the Communist Party of China related to party committee in state-owned enterprises	114
Table 5	Known golden share stakes held by the Chinese government	118

Chapter 4

Table 1	Primary contradictions of chinese economic policy	165
Table 2	China national team members	176
Table 3	Levels of Party organizations within companies	185

CHAPTER 1

Introduction

China's economic policies have long been perplexing due to their seemingly contradictory nature. In the late 1970s, China shocked the world by adopting market reforms and opening up to global trade. Foreign businesses were invited to invest and establish factories in China. Collective farms, a cornerstone of Mao Zedong's economic vision, were dismantled in favor of household plots. Private businesses began to spread across both rural and urban China, bypassing state economic planning. It was a remarkable transformation for a nation that had been engulfed by class struggle and anti-capitalist denunciations only a few years earlier during the Cultural Revolution.

In the first three decades after reforms began, China's ruling Communist Party appeared to be guiding the country toward greater economic liberalization and openness. Private firms and market forces gained increasing influence, with the government closing thousands of state-owned enterprises. China established stock markets, listing shares of state companies for public purchase, and even admitted private entrepreneurs into the Party. Yet, despite this outward embrace of market economics, the Party continually reaffirmed its commitment to socialism.

In 2012, Xi Jinping assumed leadership over China, bringing with him experience from provinces that thrived under economic reforms. His father, Xi Zhongxun, was one of China's chief reformers in the 1980s.

Initially, many economists interpreted Xi Jinping's early economic policies as indicative of his desire for a stronger role for market forces in China's economy. However, after more than a decade of his rule, China has shifted toward even greater state intervention in the economy and tighter control over private enterprises. As a result of these policies, the Chinese economy has slowed substantially.

What explains the contradictions that define Chinese economic policy-making? Why did the Chinese Communist Party, dedicated to achieving socialism, allow an economy characterized by markets, private enterprises, and trade with the capitalist world to develop? And why, under Xi Jinping, has China seemingly moved to undo the economic reforms that powered its rapid economic development over the past four decades?

Many analysts have grappled with these contradictions. When China's leaders reaffirmed their commitment to Marxism and state economic control, it was often dismissed as outdated rhetoric. Although Chinese leaders paid lip service to socialism, the country's actual economic policies increasingly relied on markets and other key elements of capitalism.

China's economic reforms led many foreign observers to believe the country would gradually embrace a more open, market-based economy. Certainly, as many analysts would acknowledge, China would always be unique due to its history and size. Yet trade, investment, and the spread of ideas would lead the country toward a greater convergence with the Western capitalist economies.

This assumption was shattered by Xi Jinping's large-scale economic crackdowns and interventions starting in 2015, making it clear that the Party aimed to reinforce its control and bolster state-owned enterprises. China was not on an inevitable path toward economic liberalization, leaving foreign observers with a profound sense of whiplash and uncertainty about China's true direction.

Based on careful observation of the Chinese economy over many years, this book is an effort to unravel the complexities and contradictions of China's economic policies. While Chinese economic statistics offer valuable insights into general trends, many economists have underestimated the significance of speeches and statements from Party leaders, which provide a deeper understanding of the leadership's underlying motivations. This is essential because the government wields so much power over economic outcomes, and China's leadership is often explicit in declaring its goals. The book will explore the economic objectives outlined by China's leaders and analyze how these goals have been translated into policy. This approach not only clarifies many of China's economic contradictions, but also highlights a persistent tension at the core of the Party's management of the economy: the uneasy balance between state and market forces.

Metaphors can often illuminate complex political and economic ideas. Chen Yun, one of China's most influential reformers of the late 1970s and 1980s—second only to Deng Xiaoping in stature—had a talent for using vivid imagery to convey the Party's goals. In 1982, as new reforms swept across China at a breakneck pace, Chen offered a powerful metaphor to frame the Party's approach to economic reform.

"Liberalizing the economy should be done under the guidance of a plan, not independent of it," according to Chen.[1] The Party might embrace market reforms, but it was not relinquishing control. "This is like the relationship between a bird and a cage," Chen explained. "A bird cannot be held tightly in your hand, otherwise it will die. It must be allowed to fly, but only within the cage. Without a cage, the bird will fly away."

Chen likened economic liberalization to a bird that needed space to "fly" for China's economy to grow. The "cage" was the Party's national development plan—the policies designed to shape China's economic path. Chen believed the "cage" could be expanded as needed, allowing reforms to extend across all provinces and even internationally. The structure of the "cage" could also adapt to changing circumstances. However, Chen emphasized, "no matter what, there always must be a cage."

Chen's bird-and-cage analogy captured the Party's approach to managing the economy. The Party recognized the necessity of reforms—market forces needed room to grow and propel China's economic progress toward the goal of national rejuvenation. Yet these forces had to be closely controlled to prevent them from "flying" beyond reach. For Chen, this control was essential to guard against risks like corruption, inflation, and foreign capital threatening China's socialist system. At its heart, the bird and the cage theory highlighted the Party's conflicted relationship with the market economy. The market was necessary but also dangerous. Therefore, the Party must retain strong control over the economy and guide it in the proper direction.

Metaphors have their limits, and Chen's bird-and-cage comparison was never universally accepted within the Party. No single framework can capture every economic decision made in China—a country too vast and complex for generalized explanations. Yet, as this book will show, the tension symbolized by the bird and the cage has influenced many major economic policies over the past half-century, from Deng Xiaoping to Xi Jinping. The Party has struggled to find the right balance between allowing market forces to shape the economy and maintaining its control.

Over time, the cage for the economy has grown larger, giving rise to an economy that is primarily driven by markets and private enterprise. Yet the cage has also gone through periods of contraction. During these periods, China adopted restrictions on markets and private companies to rein in the bird before it flew away. After a few years, these restrictions would begin to stifle the economy and the Party would adjust course and provide more space for market forces to once again drive forward growth.

This book is organized into three main sections, followed by a conclusion. Chapter 2 covers China's initial reform period, beginning in 1978 and extending through Hu Jintao's leadership in the 2000s. It argues that the economic crises of the Mao years created an opening for the Party to embrace market-driven reforms. Recognizing the potential of market forces to rejuvenate the economy and advance national goals, the Party nonetheless feared that unchecked capitalism could threaten China's socialist foundations. As a result, reforms were often contentious, marked by cycles of greater opening followed by tighter restrictions, as the Party continually reassessed the "cage" needed to contain the economy.

Chapter 3 examines Xi Jinping's rise to power and his evolving economic policies. This chapter argues that Xi initially adopted economic policies consistent with his predecessors. Xi pursued modest economic reforms during his initial years in office. However, a series of economic crises led him to shift course back toward tightening controls on the market. Xi's economic crackdown further accelerated due to a deteriorating relationship with the United States. As Xi increasingly viewed China as locked in a geostrategic competition with the United States, he sought to create a tighter cage for the economy to control risks and to direct resources toward competition with the United States.

Chapter 4 delves into recent examples of the Party's attempts to direct the economy across various sectors. This chapter highlights the Party's conflicting economic objectives: stability versus growth, control versus innovation, and self-reliance versus global integration. As China has prioritized stability, control, and self-reliance, these efforts have come at the expense of economic growth and strained relations with the rest of the world.

The book's conclusion considers what the Party's goals suggest for China's future economic trajectory and its relationship with the United States. It argues that a shift in China's approach is unlikely amidst ongoing U.S.-China tensions. Consequently, with limited leverage over the Party's policies, U.S. policymakers should adopt a strategy of strategic prudence, protecting U.S. economic interests while awaiting potential moderation in China's policies.

Note

1. Chen Yun's full quote: "Liberalizing the economy should be done under the guidance of a plan, not independent of it. This is like the relationship between a bird and a cage. A bird cannot be held tightly in your hand, otherwise it will die. It must be allowed to fly, but only within the cage. Without a cage, the bird will fly away. If we say that the bird represents the liberalization of the economy, then the cage represents our national economic development plan. Of course, the size of the 'cage' should be suitable. It can be whatever size it needs to be. Economic activities are not necessarily limited to one province or one region. Under the guidance of the plan, economic activities can cross provinces and regions, even cross continents and countries. Additionally, the 'cage' can be frequently adjusted. For example, the adjustments we make to our Five-Year Plans. However, no matter what, there always must be a cage." 搞活经济是在计划指导下搞活，不是离开计划的指导搞活。这就像鸟和笼子的关系一样， 鸟不能捏在手里，捏在手里会死，要让它飞，但只能让它在笼子里飞。没有笼子，它就飞 跑了。如果说鸟是搞活经济的话，那末，笼子就是国家计划。当然， '笼子'大小要适当， 该多大就多大。经济活动不一定限于一个省、一个地区，在国家计划指导下，也可以跨省 跨地区，甚至不一定限于国内，也可以跨国跨洲。另外， '笼子'本身也要经常调整，比如 对五年计划进行修改。但无论如何，总得有个 '笼子'。See Jiamu Zhu, "*Chen Yun's Thoughts on Reform and Opening Up - in Memory of the 110th Anniversary of Comrade Chen Yun's Birth* (陈云的改革开放思想——纪念陈云同志诞辰110周年)," *Chinese Communist Party News Network* (中国共产党新闻网), August 10, 2015, http://theory.people.com.cn/n/2015/0810/c83854-27437051.html.

CHAPTER 2

State and Market Tensions Throughout China's Economic Reforms

The conventional account of China's economic reforms describes a dramatic ideological shift within the Communist Party in the late 1970s. According to this narrative, the Party jettisoned the extreme ideologies of Mao Zedong and embraced market forces and openness to international trade. Deng Xiaoping was the grand architect of these reforms. He pushed China toward a freer and more open economy, successfully defeating the anti-reform faction within the Party. Deng's successors, Jiang Zemin and Hu Jintao, carried on Deng's vision of economic reform through the 1980s to the late 2000s, albeit with less vigor than he did. China's economic reforms then began to reverse under Xi Jinping as he attempted to reassert the state's power over the economy.

This chapter argues that China's economic reforms were far more politically contentious and complex than the simplistic account outlined above. Rather than Deng and the Party being the grand architects of reform, in many instances, they were reacting to developments occurring at the grassroots level. While some reforms were implemented top-down by the leadership, others started as experiments started by local governments officials or through the initiative of farmers, taking Beijing by surprise. As reforms started in the late 1970s, the Party viewed selective economic liberalization as a tool to advance its goals. The market could play a greater role in the economy as long as it did not threaten the Party's monopoly on power. At several key moments during these decades, the

Party intervened to curtail economic reforms in order to reestablish its control. This tension between the market and the state began in the reform era and has since become the defining feature of Chinese economic policymaking over the past fifty years.

To outside observers, the shift in economic policy seems puzzling for a political party that had been dedicated to Marxism since its founding in 1921. However, the shift becomes more comprehensible after recognizing that the Party's goals remained the same, but its evaluation of the best tools to achieve them had changed. Since its founding, the Party has been engaged in a project of "national restoration" for China, seeking to return the country to its former wealth, power, and prestige. After the policies of collectivization and class struggle had thoroughly failed to advance these goals, the post-Mao leadership was willing to change tactics, even if it meant departing from communist orthodoxy. Market-based economic reform emerged as the most viable strategy to address China's backwardness and isolation.

Rather than a sudden ideological shift toward markets and openness, China's economic reforms can better be understood as a new set of tools to achieve the same goal: national rejuvenation. The Party, however, never lost sight of the danger that these tools, markets, and other economic reforms, would threaten its control over China. This chapter will recount the history of China's economic reforms, focusing on the struggles between the Party and the Market.

1 THE ERA OF CENTRAL PLANNING AND ECONOMIC DISASTER (1949–1976)

To understand the Party's motivations in embracing new economic policies, it is first necessary to set the context for China's pre-reform economy. Strengthening China and raising the living standards of its people have been core motivating factors for the Chinese Communist Party since its founding. The Party's earliest origins trace back to the May Fourth Movement in 1919, where students protested the Treaty of Versailles in Tiananmen Square. The protests developed into a mass movement in cities across China. The protestors were outraged at the continued violation of China's sovereignty by foreign powers and the backwardness of China's living standards compared to the rest of the world. The nationalist movements in China during this period were driven by a strong sense that China had fallen from grace. Previously among the wealthiest and most powerful states in the world, China was now being picked apart by foreign imperialist powers. After the loss of the Opium War, Western powers set up foreign concessions in China's most important port cities, including Guangzhou, Shanghai, Tianjin, where their citizens would be immune to Chinese law. Furthermore, China fought and lost a disastrous war with Japan between 1894–1895, known as the First Sino-Japanese War, that resulted in China losing Korea as a tributary state and relinquishing the territory of Taiwan. Moreover, Beijing was occupied by a foreign military coalition, made up of Japanese, Russian, American, British, German, French, Austro-Hungarian, and Italian forces during the Boxer Rebellion in 1900. To settle the conflict, China was forced to pay large indemnities to the foreign occupying powers for its support of the violent uprising. Following the fall of the Qing Dynasty in 1911, China fractured into political chaos and was ruled by warlords, each vying to control portions of the country as personal fiefdoms. These events strongly motivated young Chinese nationalists who were seeking solutions to the country's weakness and disorder.

For a group of radical students and academics, Marxism, an ideology which had recently gained traction in China's northern neighbor Russia, was seen as the answer to China's struggles. Two of the Party's founding leaders, Chen Duxiu and Li Dazhao, were affiliated with Peking University, China's premier university and one that would play a pivotal role in Chinese politics in subsequent decades. The students and intellectuals saw Marxism as a method of analyzing the problems that plagued China, such as poverty and vulnerability to foreign exploitation. The example of the Soviet Union loomed large for the early Chinese Communist Party. Leninism, as developed by Vladimir Lenin during the Russian Revolution, was seen as a plan of action for implementing Marxism under the leadership of a communist party. However, the interpretations of Marxism by the founders of the Chinese Communist Party were relatively flexible and adapted to the specific history and circumstances of China at that time.[1] Most notably, China lacked a large industrial working class that Marx believed was essential to a revolution. Regardless, the Party's early members, including Mao Zedong, believed that centralized leadership under a communist party could mobilize society to achieve its goal of national rejuvenation. In doing so, China could overcome its national backwardness and free itself from domination by foreign powers. While Marxism and Leninism provided a diagnosis and a plan for action, the goal of national rejuvenation would not be held hostage to strict interpretations of these ideologies. In pursuit of national greatness, ideology could and would be adapted as necessary to the unique challenges facing China.

Although the Party was officially established in 1921, it remained largely a fragmented underground organization due to suppression by the ruling Nationalist regime. Circumstances began to change for the Party in the late 1930s as the Nationalist government became engaged in a large-scale war with Japan. The chaos of war and the weakening of Nationalist control over much of the country gave the Party the opportunity to expand. As the Party gained control over more territories, it began to implement economic policies that were heavily influenced by socialist beliefs. One such policy was "land reform" which involved the violent redistribution of land away from landlords to the peasantry. This helped garner popularity for the Party as peasants could see a direct and tangible benefit from Communist rule (e.g., an increase to their land holdings). The implementation of communist policies in regions controlled by the Party varied in severity depending on which CCP leader was in charge and the extent to which they had to accommodate existing local groups.

After the Communist Party seized power in 1949, it was had the ability to implement its policies on a nationwide scale. Over the next decade, the Party would centralize economic planning, force farmers into communal farm brigades, and nationalize industry and place it under the control of state-owned enterprises. However, the Party moved slowly in the first few years it took power, offering the nation a welcome respite from the turmoil and destruction of World War II and China's Civil War. China's new communist leaders recognized the need for a period of reconstruction and economic recovery. As a result, the Party did not immediately move to implement the most radical of its policies, such as the collectivization of agriculture or the abolition of private property.

However, the Party did expand its land reform campaign nationwide. The countryside was divided into social classes ranging from laborer and poor peasant (considered "good") to landlords and rich peasants (considered "bad"). Millions of those classified as landlords or rich peasants were beaten and murdered and their land was redistributed to peasants in their local community. Despite the turmoil of the land redistribution campaign, China was able to enjoy a period of relative economic stability in the early and mid-1950s. This was largely due to the cessation of large-scale conflicts, such as the Japanese invasion and the civil war, and the end of hyperinflation which had occurred under the Nationalist regime due to excessive currency printing to pay for war expenses.

However, this period of relative calm and economic recovery was short-lived. In the early 1950s, China began to implement the collectivization of agriculture. Peasant farmers were assigned, often through violent coercion, to collective farming units. Private property and businesses were nationalized and converted into state-owned enterprises. The few foreign businesspeople that had not left the country were expelled. In 1957, Mao Zedong launched the Anti-Rightist Campaign to attack those critical of the Party and who were suspected of supporting capitalism. Mao turned to Deng Xiaoping to implement key parts of the crackdown which ultimately targeted more than 500,000 people, with many being imprisoned, beaten, or killed during public struggle sessions ordered by the Party.

China's implementation of radical economic policies accelerated in 1958 with the launch of the Great Leap Forward, initiated by Mao Zedong. Motivated by a desire to rapidly increase China's national power, Mao sought to supercharge the country's industrial development through this nationwide campaign. Mao believed that through mass mobilization and absolute obedience to national economic planning, China could catch up to the Western Powers, primarily the United States and United Kingdom, in terms of steel and other industrial output. However, the movement was characterized by reckless and wasteful policies. Peasants were forced into large-scale farming communes. Party leaders ordered farmers to abandon their crops and focus on operating backyard smelters to boost China's steel production. The steel produced by these backyard smelters was worthless and the resources diverted away from agricultural production toward steel production led to a massive famine that is estimated to have killed tens of millions of people.

Facing economic devastation, the Party attempted to backtrack from the disastrous Great Leap Forward in the early 1960s. Facing pressure and criticism, Mao Zedong stepped away from day-to-day governance but retained his leadership over the Party. Liu Shaoqi and Deng Xiaoping implemented more moderate economic policies designed to undo the excesses of the Great Leap Forward. As economic policy tacked back away from ideological extremism, China experienced a brief period of stability and recovery in the early to mid-1960s. However, before China could completely recover from the disastrous Great Leap Forward, Mao Zedong unleashed the Cultural Revolution. Mao was concerned that he was being quietly shunted aside by others in the Party. In response, he used his status as the leader of China's revolution to mobilize millions of young supporters to attack the Party and had his political rivals arrested. For the next several years, China was beset by waves of political violence that closed universities, killed or imprisoned many government officials, persecuted and exiled the educated, and created widespread economic disruption.

The chaos and turmoil of the Cultural Revolution left deep scars upon the Party and the millions of people who suffered abuse during its campaigns. It also created tremendous dislocation within Chinese society and the economy. Figure 1 shows China's precipitous economic decline. In the early nineteenth century, China accounted for around a third of all global economic activity. Civil war and foreign invasion over the next century caused China's share of global GDP to plummet. The Party's victory in 1949 did little to reverse this. In 1978, after nearly 30 years of communist rule, China had fallen to 5% of global GDP despite more than a fifth of the world's population.

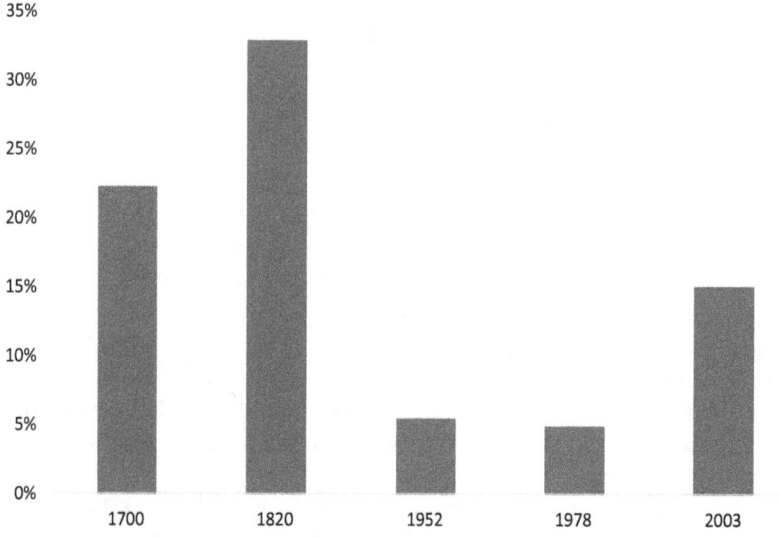

Fig. 1 China's share of global GDP (*Source* OECD)[2]

Not only had China's global economic influence declined, its people remained desperately poor. While the Party styled itself as the champion of rural peasants, the majority of Chinese society experienced little or no improvement in their living standards during the two decades between 1957 and 1978.[3] In 1970, China and Sub-Saharan African countries had equivalent levels of GDP per capita.[4] The Mao period came to a close with China far away from achieving its goal of wealth and power. Instead, China was economically backward and isolated from the rest of the world.

2 Early Reforms and the Private Sector's Struggle for Recognition (1977–1988)

The death of Mao Zedong in 1976 and the imprisonment of his most radical supporters paved the way for a major change in China's economic policy. Contrary to popular perception, China's economic reforms did not begin with Deng Xiaoping. Mao's immediate successor, Hua Guofeng, supported economic reform and opening to a degree but lacked the political strength to make a sharp break with the policies of Mao. Hua supported greater foreign trade and investment and sent senior Party leaders on inspection tours of Western Europe and Japan to learn about foreign technology and production methods.[5] He called for China to "absorb foreign technology and capital in order to greatly speed up our development and catch up with the world's achievements."[6]

Compared to Deng and other senior leaders who had helped lead China's revolution in 1949, Hua's base of support within the Party was weak due to his youth and relative inexperience. As such, Hua still exercised considerable caution in pursuing economic reforms, especially those that might provoke backlash from conservatives in the Party. While advocating for new economic policies, Hua also hewed closely to Mao's legacy and promulgated the "Two Whatevers" Policy, a public declaration to follow all policies and instructions given by Mao.

Hua's power was quickly eroded by the changing political environment in China. There was a strong backlash against the extreme policies of the Cultural Revolution within the Party and the foreign study trips contributed to a growing realization of how far China lagged behind the rest of the world. The country was eager for a shift away from the chaos of the Mao Era and to focus on improving living standards. Within the Party, there was a hunger for rehabilitation of the thousands of officials that had been purged by Mao during his numerous campaigns. Hua was cautious in meeting this demand, concerned that bringing back senior officials would undermine his already fragile power. His suspicions proved correct, the rehabilitations paved the way for Deng Xiaoping, the most senior of the purged officials, to return to power and sideline Hua. In doing so, Deng would create the conditions for a wholesale shift from the radical policies of the Mao Era.

Deng's Views on Economic Reform: As with other early communist revolutionaries in China, Deng was a firm believer in the Party's historical mission of delivering wealth and power to the country. For much of his life, he had been a trusted acolyte of Mao, believing that Mao's policies would guide China toward these goals. However, as the failures and human costs of Mao's leadership became undeniable, Deng broke with Mao and began to advocate for more pragmatic policies. The most notable example of this was following the Great Leap Forward when Deng and Liu Shaoqi attempted to undo the worst excesses of Mao's radical policies by restoring the focus of economic policy to agricultural development and consumption.[7] He would pay for this "disloyalty" by being removed from his positions by Mao and subjected to brutal criticism campaigns. Deng's critics, urged on by Mao, branded him a "capitalist roader" who was secretly working to restore capitalism in China. Despite this abuse, Deng never publicly opposed Mao, and Mao never permanently exiled Deng. At his core, Deng remained firmly committed to Party and the necessity of its unchallenged leadership of China.

In the wake of failed experiments in collectivization and highly centralized planning, Deng had become an enthusiastic supporter of economic reform. Deng's overarching framework was that of the "Four Modernizations," which called for reforms in agriculture, industry, defense, and science. Deng believed that by pursuing advances in these areas, China's economy could be revived and its national power increased. The Four Modernizations were not initially formulated by Deng. China's first Premier, Zhou Enlai advocated for them in the early 1960s and Hua Guofeng revived the idea in the late 1970s. The Four Modernizations was an acknowledgment that China had fallen desperately behind in many key areas that are the core of national power. Deng argued that China lagged the rest of the world in science and technology, by as much as 50 years in some areas.[8] To catch up, China must open up to foreign trade and investment and experiment with economic reforms at home. One early example of this was reactivating student exchanges. China would begin sending thousands of students abroad to study new concepts and technology. Yet Deng firmly stated that China's adoption of foreign technology was not an embrace of capitalism, but rather a necessary step to transform China into a powerful socialist state capable of defending its system against foreign aggression.[9]

Despite becoming China's paramount leader, Deng faced deep constraints on his power. The most immediate challenge Deng faced was pushing aside Hua Guofeng, who still wielded the legitimacy of being Mao's handpicked successor. Deng gradually weakened Hua's influence without directly opposing him, advancing his own policies and placing his allies in key positions. By 1981, Hua had been sidelined and replaced by Deng's ally, Hu Yaobang. In the early years of Deng's leadership, he also faced opposition from a faction Mao loyalists, who remained influential within the Party and resisted economic reforms. This faction was still influential in the years immediately after Mao's death, but the rehabilitation of purged Party officials eventually undermined their power. However, the most significant and longest-lasting challenge Deng faced throughout his leadership was opposition from conservative economic reformers.

The most prominent of the conservative reformers was Chen Yun, a veteran Party member who served as Vice Chairman under Mao in the 1950s and 1960s. Chen had tried to moderate the worst of Mao's economic policies and advocated for a more cautious approach. Like Deng, he had been purged from power during the Cultural Revolution. In the wake of Mao's death, Chen and the other conservative reformers knew the economy was in desperate need of reform. However, they also harbored deep suspicions that proceeding too rapidly would lead to inflation and economic disorder. In 1979, only a few years into economic reform, the conservative reformers pushed for a period of economic retrenchment, reducing foreign borrowing and lowering investment targets. Chen and the other conservative reformers believed strongly in the need for centralized planning of the economy. In a phrase that he would become well known for, Chen argued that the economy was "like a bird" that cannot be held too tight but also cannot be allowed to fly away. Thus a cage was required to maintain control over the bird while giving it enough space to grow and develop. During the 1980s, Deng and Chen would frequently clash over the correct size of the cage for the market economy in China.

One area where Deng and the conservative reformers agreed was that China's embrace of economic reforms did not mean an embrace of capitalism. Deng was explicit in his views that market forces were a tool to advance the goals of raising living standards and strengthening China. Reforms would need guardrails, however, to prevent the exploitation of Chinese workers and the undue influence of foreign businesses. Deng might disagree with Chen Yun and other conservative reformers about the amount of latitude to give policy experiments. Despite these frictions, they were in agreement about several core principles—the Party should continue to exercise a strong guiding hand over the economy, public ownership of land should be retained, there should be a significant role for the state in economic planning, and state-owned enterprises would continue to play an influential role in the economy.[10]

Deng was an active supporter of experimentation and could be flexible in the interpretation of introducing capitalist mechanisms into a socialist economy. However, he was correspondingly inflexible on the issue of political reform. In March 1979, Deng laid out the Four Cardinal Principals, his political bottom line from which he and other top Chinese leaders would not waver. Deng declared that China:

1. Must keep to the socialist road.
2. Must uphold the dictatorship of the proletariat.
3. Must uphold the leadership of the Communist Party.
4. Must uphold Marxism-Leninism and Mao Zedong Thought.

The message behind the Four Cardinal Principals was twofold. First, China would remain socialist even as it liberalized the economy across a variety of fronts. Second, the Party would not accept any challenges to its rule and economic reforms would not crossover to political reforms. Deng's successors would all reaffirm their commitment to the Four Cardinal Principals as the core bedrock of the Party's political ideology.

While he was in favor of economic reform, Deng himself was not the progenitor of many of the most significant breakthroughs that occurred during this period. Throughout his tenure at the top of the Party, he never immersed himself in the details of economic policy. Moreover, as will be discussed below, many of the most important economic reforms occurred at the grassroots level, contravening the official policies put in place by Beijing. Much of China's economic progress in the early years of reform was driven by people outmaneuvering the state and finding economic opportunities in legal gray areas.[11] Deng maneuvered to create political space to allow many of these reforms to continue and grow. However, he never saw them as the precursor for China's transition to capitalism. Deng was committed to putting "capitalist tools in socialist hands," meaning that China should use the methods of capitalism to reform and strengthen socialism.[12] Experiments with capitalism could proceed as long as the Party remained China's sole governing body and that these efforts furthered the Party's mission of transforming the country into a wealthy and powerful socialist country.[13]

Household Farming: While the death of Mao had created space for the deradicalization of economic policy in China, some of the most important initial steps toward reform actually came from the countryside rather than Beijing. In 1978, a small group of farmers in Anhui Province decided in secret to divide the land among themselves, a reform that would eventually become known as the household responsibility system. This was an explicit rejection of the collective farming system that had been responsible for so much economic and social misery in China. With land divided among the households of the villages, each farmer had more incentive to increase production to benefit his or her family. This act was dangerous for those involved as it could easily lead to their arrest and imprisonment. When it was discovered by Beijing, instead of suppressing it with force, as Mao Zedong likely would have, China's new generation of leaders cautiously allowed it to continue. As the experiment proved successful in dramatically raising agricultural output, Beijing allowed it to expand across the country.

This shift was politically sensitive and threatened to undo one of the core principles of Maoist economics—collective agriculture. The 1978 Third Plenum Communique, the landmark document that is commonly cited as marking the start of China's economic reforms, called for the continuation of the commune system and did not endorse dividing land among households. This was likely done to avoid upsetting the leftist Mao supporters still prominent in the government at that time. Deng himself displayed no ideological commitment to private farming, viewing it as another tool for raising living standards.[14]

Gradually, the experiment was officially blessed and allowed to expand to other localities. Ownership of the land was still owned by the state, but effective control of land plots was delegated to households. There were also reforms to the agricultural quota system for farmers. Instead of having to deliver all their output at fixed prices, farmers were permitted to sell a portion on the market after meeting a quota. This led to a proliferation of small private marketplaces across China. Within a few short years, these changes to agricultural production would lead to a dramatic increase in output and solve China's frequent food shortages. Famine in China was virtually eliminated by giving farmers better incentives to produce. Food insecurity, however, would remain a threat in many of China's poorer regions for years to come.

Town and Village Enterprises: As household farming spread, other aspects of the collective economy were gradually dismantled from the bottom-up by Chinese peasants and local officials eager to embrace reforms. On the other hand, the legal and policy environment remained hostile toward private enterprises.[15] While private businesses were still illegal in China, entrepreneurial former collectives began experimenting with new forms of corporate organization in the early 1980s. China's agricultural collectives were being shut down, and replaced by household contract farming. Commune and brigade enterprises, small-scale manufacturing outfits associated with collectives, were being shut down or abandoned by local officials with the end of the collective system. However, instead of being shut down, some commune and brigade enterprises were transformed into companies, known later as Town and Village Enterprises (TVEs).

TVEs initially engaged in light industry and the production of consumer goods. As they grew, TVEs soon expanded into new industries, operating hotels, restaurants, and other business areas that had been neglected for decades during Mao's monomaniacal focus on industrialization. While TVEs were technically owned by the town or village where they operated, they were in reality a forerunner of private enterprises in China. TVEs were freed of the geographical restrictions of the communes, allowing them to sell goods throughout the country, and unlike SOEs, were not bound to production quotas and central planning.[16] This provided TVE managers with incentive to grow and adapt to market trends. Moreover, both managers and employees were incentivized to work hard because they stood to profit from the enterprise's success. The expansion of TVEs was also a testament to the entrepreneurial instinct of many local government officials, who actively encouraged their development as a way to develop their villages. TVEs were most developed in the coastal provinces, driven by the opportunities for them to engage in trade and receive foreign investment.

TVEs were another example of bottom-up economic reform that was not orchestrated by Beijing. It took several years for TVEs to be officially recognized and deemed by the Party as compatible with socialism.[17] In 1987, Deng freely admitted that he and other central leaders had not thought to create the TVEs and commended them for employing rural workers.[18] Like with household farming, the Party embraced these reforms when it was clear they could help solve economic problems, such as rural unemployment. The number of TVEs soon proliferated far beyond the number of the precursor commune and brigade enterprises.[19]

Private entrepreneurs took advantage of the legal protections offered by TVEs at a time when private businesses were still largely illegal. In a process that would come to be known as "wearing a red hat," entrepreneurs registered their businesses as TVEs.[20] Because TVEs were deemed collectives and therefore not capitalist in nature, they were afforded greater legal protections and the opportunity to operate at a larger scale than private businesses (as will be discussed below). This loophole would allow TVEs to proliferate rapidly and became one of the key drivers of economic growth and employment in China during the 1980s. Some in the Party reacted negatively to TVEs, with Chen Yun and other conservative economic reformers repeatedly criticizing TVEs for siphoning resources and labor away from SOEs.[21] Yet the success of TVEs in promoting rural development and employment led Deng and other reformers to protect them.

Household and Private Businesses: The expansion of the private sector, businesses without any trappings of public ownership, occurred despite significant legal restrictions. Household businesses and small-scale enterprises providing services such as tailoring, restaurants, and barbershops, proliferated in China's towns and cities. During Mao's tenure, these everyday services were provided through the collective or the government bodies. However, after the Great Leap Forward, businesses with no ties to the state began to expand, despite significant legal restrictions. These private businesses were still technically illegal. However, after jumping through some significant ideological gymnastics, the Party decided that they could be permitted so long as they did not employ more than seven employees.[22] Additionally, the owner had to work in the business themselves to avoid being classified as a capitalist. Again, the reality on the ground was quite different as many household businesses grew and expanded beyond these limitations.

Household businesses were even more politically contentious than TVEs as they lacked any pretense of being socialist enterprises. Beijing was forced by necessity to acknowledge and eventually bless household businesses due to their role in employing surplus labor and provided services demanded by Chinese consumers. The millions of urban Chinese youth who had been sent down to work in the countryside during the Cultural Revolution were returning to the cities during the late 1970s and early 1980s.[23] There was a shortage of jobs for these returning youth. SOEs were cash-strapped and unable to provide them with employment. Chinese leaders were concerned that the returnees might become a source of social unrest or crime. Household businesses thus emerged as a critical source of jobs. They also provided consumer-oriented services for urban dwellers that were key to improving perceptions of living standards.

Despite the beneficial role played by household businesses, they continued to exist in legal ambiguity during most of the 1980s. In 1988, the Chinese government formally acknowledged the existence of private firms and approved some of the large private ownership structures that existed. Private enterprises were finally allowed to employ more than eight people. Corporate structures such as partnerships and limited liability companies were recognized, albeit with restrictions such as limiting the total number of investors.[24] The Party recognized private enterprises as a "supplement to the socialist publicly owned economy," a significant breakthrough compared to their prior status. However, private companies continued to face discriminatory taxes, fees, and restrictions compared to state-owned enterprises.[25]

State-Owned Enterprise Reform: China's traditional state-owned enterprises (SOEs), often concentrated in mining, petrochemicals, and manufacturing, also began to reform during this period. However, their transition toward a more market-oriented approach lagged behind the progress of TVEs. In early 1980s, the Chinese government granted more autonomy to SOEs, allowing them to begin selling their production at market prices after fulfilling a quota under a policy called the Contract Responsibility System.[26] SOEs could earn a profit after meeting their quota, offering incentives to the managers of SOEs to increase production and do so more efficiently. SOEs were also given more flexibility than before to reduce over staffing and adjust pay for merit. All of these reforms provided incentives for SOEs to become more efficient and adapt to market conditions. While some SOEs used these changes to boost productivity, others saw them as opportunities for corruption, with dishonest managers diverting profits for personal gain.

In the 1980s, SOEs began their first steps toward separation and direct control from the government ministries that supervised them. In 1983, the Interim Ordinances on State-Owned Enterprises established SOES as separate legal entities with a limited degree of operating autonomy.[27] SOEs began to have increased control over production planning, purchases, worker compensation, recruiting, and retention of profits.[28] While these reforms were significant, the operations of SOEs were still a far departure from market-driven private firms in terms of efficiency and profitability. State economic planning largely directed the activities of SOEs, with the selection of management for important enterprises tightly controlled by the Party. The Party's cadre system rotated individuals between government and SOE posts, reinforcing the strong connection between the state and these companies. Moreover, SOEs operated large social service programs, providing housing, medical care, and education services to workers and their families. Throughout the 1980s, SOEs could be best classified as quasi-corporatized arms of the government that had been granted important, but limited degrees of autonomy.

Beijing viewed reform as a method for strengthening SOEs and making them more efficient. Deng called for greater separation between the functions of the government and those of SOEs, in order to focus and strengthen them as enterprises.[29] However, SOE restructuring was not a precursor for privatization. China's top leadership during this period continued to view SOEs as the "backbone" of the economy and public ownership as a "core pillar" of socialism. Market incentives, new corporate structures, and foreign joint ventures were tools to strengthen SOEs and reinforce the primary role of public ownership within China's economic system. Deng declared that even as China imported managerial techniques and technology from the capitalist world, the state apparatus was so powerful that it could fend off any threats to socialism.[30] The Party would continue to play a key role in SOEs. In the 1980s, some reformers in the Party, such as Zhao Ziyang, pushed for even greater separation of the Party from enterprises and the government's administrative structures.[31] However, Deng nixed these ideas and after the turmoil of the Tiananmen Massacre in 1989 they were fully abandoned.

Foreign Trade and Investment and the Special Economic Zones (SEZs): Opening up to foreign trade and investment was one of the most important, and most politically contentious reforms during this period. Hua Guofeng, Mao's chosen successor, eagerly embraced importing foreign industrial equipment. Eager to reengage with the rest of the world after the isolationism of the Mao Era, the Party organized foreign study tours for officials to Europe, Japan, and the United States. These trips during the early days of reform reinforced the notion in the Party that China's industrial sector was extremely backward in terms of production methods and efficiency. Chinese officials found eager partners in Western and Japanese corporations who were willing to sell equipment in exchange for a toehold into the Chinese market. The governments of the capitalist countries, with whom China had strained relations since the 1949 revolution, were willing to provide financial support and technical assistance in hopes of establishing better relations with China.

Given the green light from Beijing, local governments and SOEs signed so many foreign contracts in the years immediately after Mao's death that Chen Yun and the other conservative reformers were worried the country would have a debt crisis given rapidly growing levels of foreign borrowing. During the economic readjustment of the late 1970s and early 1980s, Chen reigned in local officials and forced them to cancel many foreign projects that were underway, such as the Baoshan Steel Plant that was being built with help from West German and Japanese companies. The retrenchment proved temporary as local governments eagerly resumed foreign cooperation as soon as Beijing relaxed its stance.

Party leaders were interested in importing more than just manufacturing equipment. They also wanted to attract foreign enterprises to set up operations in the country to share management techniques and train Chinese factory workers in modern production. However, inviting foreign investment, particularly from former adversaries like Japan and the United States, was politically sensitive. The Party viewed the ending of the treaty ports and foreign concession zones within China as one of its core achievements. However, attracting foreign companies to China would require a radically different set of rules for business. Foreign firms would need flexibility in hiring and firing workers and protections for private property in order to run their businesses profitably. China's legal system and the Party's ideology were both major barriers to these types of changes. The solution to this problem was to establish special economic zones where foreign companies could set up factories and hire Chinese workers. These zones were contained from the rest of China, allowing for easier monitoring by the Party. In 1980, the first SEZs were established in Shenzhen, Shantou, and Zhuhai in Guangdong Province. Shenzhen and Shekou were located near the British-governed territory of Hong Kong. Zhuhai was near the Portuguese-governed territory of Macao. Soon after, another zone was established in the city of Xiamen, directly opposite Taiwan via the Taiwan Strait. The hope was that by establishing the SEZs in close geographic proximity to Hong Kong and Taiwan, businesspeople from those localities would be more inclined to set up operations there.

In the early years of the SEZs, much of the investment came from Hong Kong businesspeople and other overseas Chinese. Deng personally sought to recruit overseas Chinese businesspeople to invest in and establish businesses within the SEZs. Many overseas Chinese business people had left China to escape war in the 1940s, the confiscation of their assets in the 1950s, or political persecution during the 1960s. The Party renounced many of its former policies, including branding overseas Chinese and their family members remaining in China as foreign conspirators.[32] It began to slowly return some of the land, personal property, and residences that it had expropriated from the businesspeople that had fled China. The Party appealed to these businesspeople on patriotic grounds, telling them that they could play a major role in rebuilding China. At first glance, it might appear odd that many overseas Chinese businesspeople whose families had been brutalized by the Party would willingly return to the mainland. However, the dream of profits and helping to rebuild China held great appeal among overseas Chinese, even those who had a troubled history with the Party. An example of which was Yue-Kong Pao, a mainland born shipping magnate who had fled to Hong Kong ahead of the Communist takeover in 1949. During the 1980s, Pao became an enthusiastic supporter of China's modernization efforts and was frequently invited to Beijing by Deng to consult on rebuilding China's shipping industry.[33]

Later on, the SEZs were successful in attracting investment from Western and Japanese businesses because of substantial tax and regulatory incentives. Foreign-invested companies operating in the SEZs received considerable tax breaks, often paying less than half the prevailing rate applied to domestic companies.[34] The SEZs also sought to promote the transfer of advanced technology, providing even more tax incentives for companies operating in high-tech industries. While labor relations were tightly controlled in China during this period, companies operating within the SEZs were granted greater flexibility to apply market-oriented practices such as incentive-based compensation for employees and managers. These policies were more attractive to workers compared to conditions offered elsewhere in China and hundreds of thousands of workers began migrating to the SEZs each year.[35] This, in turn, provided foreign companies with a large labor force that could be employed cheaply. The SEZs were also attractive to foreign companies due to their potential to serve as an entry point into the Chinese domestic market.

The SEZs became a focal point of tension between liberal and conservative reformers within the Party. Throughout the 1980s, Chen Yun and other conservative economic reformers remained skeptical of the SEZs and their impact on the rest of the country. Chen frequently attacked the SEZs, complaining that local officials were allowing the establishment of foreign economic concessions and were engaged in illegal activities. He used his role as Chair of the Party's Central Commission for Discipline Inspection, the body tasked with addressing corruption within the Party, to punish Guangdong officials engaged in smuggling, bribery, and corruption linked to the SEZs.[36] He notably refused to visit the special economic zones and later resisted making his home city of Shanghai into a SEZ.[37] At Chen's demand, Guangdong officials were beckoned to Beijing several times to receive severe criticism. To mollify the critics of the SEZ, both Guangdong and Fujian officials were forced to make self-criticisms and implement campaigns to crack down on corruption and other economic crimes. Despite their efforts, the conservative reformers were unsuccessful in containing the SEZs because of their success. Exceeding expectations, the SEZs attracted billions of dollars of foreign investment in their first few years of operation. The Shenzhen SEZ grew at an annual rate of 58% between 1980 and 1984, many times faster than the national economy.[38] In response, cities across China began clamoring for Beijing to grant them the same privileges as the four SEZs. In 1984, 14 more cities, largely concentrated in China's coast to facilitate trade, were granted permission to receive foreign investment.

Socialism with Chinese Characteristics: The reforms outlined above represented a sharp break from the policies of the Party during the Mao Era, especially the radical years of the Great Leap Forward and the Cultural Revolution. Mao had tried to rapidly transform China into a communist society through large-scale collectivization, centralized economic planning, and breaking off economic relations with the capitalist world. After his death, the Party abandoned these policies and began embracing reforms that would have been fiercely opposed by Mao and his allies. However, Deng was unwilling to fully repudiate Mao. China's leaders viewed Khruschev's denunciation of Stalin in 1956 as a critical mistake that significantly weakened the Soviet Communist Party. Unwilling to make the same mistake, Deng instead produced the formulation that allowed him to abandon Mao's policies without rejecting his legacy and by extension the Party's own legitimacy. According to Deng, Mao was 70% correct, and his errors were secondary to his achievements.

However, the Party still faced a paradox. It had never abandoned its goal of transforming China into a socialist utopia, yet it was implementing economic reforms that were reintroducing elements of capitalism. The way to square the circle was a new ideological formulation—Socialism with Chinese Characteristics. The key idea embedded in this phrase was that as a poor country, China was still in an early phase of socialism. The mistake of the Mao Era had been to move too quickly into full communism. China needed time to develop its productive capacities. In this "primary" stage of socialism, China could use both techniques and capital from the capitalist world to grow its economy, preparing for the ultimate transition to communism at a later date. Despite embracing many aspects of capitalism, China would remain socialist because of public ownership over the means of production (SOEs) and the Party's monopoly on political power. Deng and the liberal reformers in the government genuinely believed that economic reforms were a way to strengthen socialism, not replace it with capitalism. During most of the 1980s, socialism with Chinese characteristics was a convincing enough formulation to keep the party members more skeptical of reform at bay, buying time and space for more economic experiments.

3 Rebooting Reform and Saving the State Economy (1988–2000)

The second decade of economic reform in China was as volatile and contentious as the first. The period between the late 1980s and the late 1990s was bookended by two major crises—Tiananmen and the SOE debt crisis. During this time, significant new reforms were enacted, yet these reforms were underpinned by a renewed emphasis on maintaining the Party's primacy over the economy and preserving the state-owned sector.

Reform Begins to Falter: Throughout the tumultuous 1980s, the forces in favor of economic reform had generally succeeded in enacting their policies. While there were fierce debates within the Party on the scope and the pace of reforms, there was a broad-based consensus that Mao-era economic policies needed to change. Conservative reformers had deep-seated skepticism toward opening the country up to foreign investment and trade and wanted to limit the role of market forces in the economy. For example, Chen Yun implemented a period of readjustment in 1979–81 when the economy was on the verge of overheating. Chen was able to rein in several economic experiments, such as the SEZs, when he felt they crossed political red lines of what could be allowed. Despite these "victories," Deng and his allies, such as Zhao Ziyang, were able to advance economic reforms throughout much of the 1980s. Economic experiments, whether occurring spontaneously among the populace or directed by entrepreneurial local leaders, were cultivated and given space to develop. The first half of the 1980s was a period when the cage around the economy was relaxed significantly.

However, a series of setbacks in the late 1980s brought the momentum behind economic reforms to a grinding halt. The first major stumble was the implementation of price reforms in 1988. In 1984, the Party implemented a system called "dual-track" pricing whereby enterprises had to supply a set quota of their goods at a fixed price, and then production above the quota could be sold at market prices. The dual-track system was an improvement from the prior rigid reliance on quotas for production. However, it was still far from ideal because it disincentivized the production of many consumer goods, leading to shortages, corruption, and distortions in the economy. Deng and Zhao pushed for the relaxation of price controls across a variety of different goods. China's liberal economic reformers anticipated that removing price controls would lead to significant price increases, but believed that the rapid economic growth China was experiencing would boost household incomes enough to offset inflation.[39]

Instead, the removal of price controls led to rapid inflation and social discontent. The price increases brought back painful memories of the hyperinflation under the Nationalist Government in the 1940s. Inflation is unpopular everywhere, but it was likely especially jarring for Chinese consumers who had been used to decades of fixed prices. People hoarded items in anticipation of inflation and soon there were nationwide shortages of basic necessities. The price reforms were quickly rolled back, and controls were reimplemented. Much of the goodwill garnered by Deng among the populace for his earlier reforms was eroded by the debacle, severely weakening the position of ambitious reformers. The conservative faction, led by Chen Yun, stepped in to implement another round of economic retrenchment policies. This included slashing investment and spending, lowering growth targets, raising interest rates, ordering SOEs not to raise prices, and generally slowing the implementation of new economic reforms.

Tiananmen and its Aftermath: Inflation, outrage at growing corruption, and a sense of dislocation from an economy that was rapidly changing combined to create a volatile situation in the late 1980s. In December 1986, China had seen student demonstrations demanding reform at universities across the country. While those demands had been denied, the pressures within Chinese society continued to build. Events came to a head during the Tiananmen Square Protests of 1989. The showdown with the students represented the most significant threat to the CCP's monopoly on power since it took over the country in 1949. In their calls for further political and economic reforms, the students attracted support from a wide swathe of Chinese society and some within the Party itself. However, their calls for reform went too far for Deng and the Party elders as they worried it would challenge the Party's monopoly on political power. Deng would brand the protestors as counterrevolutionaries seeking to overthrow the Party and destroy socialism.[40] After those protests were violently crushed, the conservative political faction of the Party took control. More liberal reformers lost influence over policy as their policies were blamed for creating the social discontent that led to the protests. Key reformers, such as general secretary Zhao Ziyang, were deposed from power and put under house arrest. While Deng supported the crackdown, his stature within the Party was significantly reduced after Tiananmen.

As a result of the conservative takeover in the wake of Tiananmen, economic reform in China went into a deep freeze. The hardliners that had taken control of the Party viewed rapid economic reform as one of the key causes of social instability. Deng and Zhao had moved too aggressively in dismantling large parts of the command economy. Reforms had led to inflation, corruption, and instability as agriculture and industry changed rapidly. Most Chinese citizens were better off than they had been prior to reforms, as measured by income and access to food and consumer goods.

However, many were still angry at the Party for its failure to address many of the problems created by a rapidly growing, but volatile and unequal economy. Premier Li Peng pushed for an austerity program in late 1989 and called for the strengthening of the Party's ideological and political controls.[41] The new economic plan sought to restrict lighter industries, which were linked to the town and village enterprises, in favor of heavy industries which were dominated by SOEs.[42] Chen Yun criticized the idea that the market should guide the economy and called for reversing excessive decentralization and restoring government control.[43] The Party slowed the implementation of new reforms, and pressure intensified on private sector actors operating within the many legal gray areas of that time. Many entrepreneurs were harassed and imprisoned for violating ill-defined laws and regulations and some private businesses registered as collective enterprises to avoid further scrutiny.[44] The future of the SEZs was thrown into jeopardy by the economic sanctions by the United States and many European countries for Tiananmen.

The conservative reformers pushed for a reorientation of the Party's priorities after the chaos of Tiananmen. The economic reforms of the 1980s successfully accelerated China's economic growth and improved living standards. However, it also unleashed forces that challenged the Party's leadership and threatened to derail the national restoration project. Adding to these concerns was turmoil in the rest of the communist world. Shortly after Tiananmen, demonstrations in East Germany led to the fall of the Berlin Wall. By 1991, the Soviet Union had collapsed, leaving China as the only major global power still under communist party rule. Sanctioned by the Western world and with the Soviet bloc in shambles, China was isolated and vulnerable. In a move that would shape Chinese economic policymaking for decades to come, reform was made subordinate to political and economic stability. Reforms could proceed, but the freewheeling economic and political experimentation of the 1980s was over. Concurrently, there would be a huge push for "patriotic education" in an effort to counteract the ideological loosening that had occurred due to economic reforms. The bird had nearly escaped the cage and almost brought down the entire house in the process.

Deng Xiaoping Revives Economic Reform: In the early 1990s, it was very possible that China's economic reforms had reached their high watermark. With the fall of Zhao Ziyang, conservative reformers such as Chen Yun and Premier Li Peng were firmly in control of economic policy. Deng's influence was diminished for two reasons. First, due to his age, Deng stepped back from his day-to-day responsibilities after Tiananmen. Second, Deng's status was diminished because some blamed him for the price reform debacle and other reforms that were seen as contributing factors to the social discontent behind the Tiananmen Protests, Deng faced increasing pressure to adhere to the views of the political conservatives within the Party. However, Deng had not given up on economic reform. In his view, the Party's continued existence could only be preserved through delivering rapid economic growth and raising living standards.[45] The ongoing collapse of much of the communist world only reinforced this belief.[46] As before, Deng did not view capitalism or economic pluralism as a goal itself. Rather, economic reforms and experiments with market forces were tools to achieve the goals of the Party—preserving its own rule and making China wealthy and powerful. The conservatives within the Party, in contrast, thought that reforms had gone too far and was threatening the Party's rule. Some even called for rolling back policies such as the special economic zones.[47]

In 1990 and 1991, Deng made repeated efforts to restart economic reforms. For example, he strongly advocated for developing the Pudong area of Shanghai as an SEZ. Once the economic heart of China, the Yangtze River Delta region, with Shanghai as its largest metropolis, had fallen behind the SEZs in the South. However, Deng's influence on policymaking was constrained because many within the Party blamed his policies for the economic and political difficulties China now faced. Chen Yun, a Shanghai native, opposed the establishment of an SEZ in the city over concerns the city would become a bulwark of capitalism and foreign influence.[48] Deng published comments advocating for a return to economic reform under a thinly veiled pseudonym. In a testament to his diminished influence and the strength of the conservatives, his remarks were attacked by the People's Daily and other state media outlets.[49]

Deng was undeterred and formulated a dramatic plan to restart economic reform in 1992. By then, Deng was in his late eighties, yet still undertook a major initiative to shape Chinese economic policy. In what would later come to be called the Southern Tour, Deng organized a vacation with his family to the south of China, which was a convenient cover to explain his travel to suspicious rivals within the Party. During this so-called vacation, Deng visited the areas of the country that had been the biggest beneficiaries of reform, including the SEZs. He spoke with local officials about the success of China's economic reforms in the 1980s and the need for them to continue. These speeches were picked up by local and Hong Kong media and were soon being reported across the country. Deng purposefully visited the most pro-reform areas of the country and campaigned for support for his policies at the grassroots level. Though his stature had been weakened by the events of the late 1980s, Deng's open campaign for reform helped reenergize supporters of reform who had been cowed by the events of the past few years. The public display of support for reform, evident by the crowds and media coverage Deng's tour attracted, created a counterweight to the dominance of the economic conservatives and opened the door for reforms to resume.

Deng's Southern Tour was the breakthrough necessary to restart economic reforms in China. The policies that followed, however, were not a continuation of the freewheeling experimentation of the 1980s. Whereas the first decade of reform had been about decentralization and grassroots experiments, the reforms of the 1990s were focused on recentralization, improved regulation, ownership reform, and market unification.[50] In the post-Tiananmen era, the hand of the state would play a greater role in guiding economic reform and would more tightly manage economic volatility to head off future political disturbances. Both Deng and Chen largely exited the political scene after 1992, but Deng ensured that his successor Jiang Zemin was committed to continuing economic reforms, albeit reforms that were more carefully controlled by the Party.

One of the first major reforms the Party undertook in the 1990s was fiscal. For years, Beijing's revenues had been declining relative to local revenues. This was a byproduct of China's economic reforms. SOE profits, a major source of central government revenue, failed to keep pace with GDP growth. In contrast, local governments were the prime beneficiaries of tax revenues from the new industries created by TVEs and private businesses. This increase in revenue was a significant factor behind the ardent support for reform by many local officials. The coaster provinces that had most aggressively embraced reforms saw the highest increase in tax revenues, creating a gap not only between them and Beijing, but also compared to China's less developed inland provinces.

From Beijing's perspective, these fiscal imbalances were unacceptable. The central government's declining fiscal strength was especially concerning after Tiananmen when there was a significant focus on bolstering the central government's domestic security apparatus. In 1993, a major tax reform directed revenues away from the provinces and toward the central government. This shift in funds toward Beijing would solve many of the central government's financial issues, but it would create new problems for local governments. The bulk of spending responsibility for social services continued to reside with local governments. With lower revenues, local governments would chronically face significant budget shortfalls. Nonetheless, the fiscal reform was indicative of the Party's new priorities, seeking reforms that undid many of the "excesses" of the 1980s and strengthened the central government.

The Socialist Market Economy: With the reinvigoration of economic reform after Deng's Southern Tour, the Party's ideological framework once again required updating. In 1992, Jiang Zemin put forward the concept of a "Socialist Market Economy." Under Jiang's formulation, the core of the economy would continue to be state-owned, but SOEs would be given greater flexibility and autonomy to run their operations. The market's role in guiding the economy was to be expanded to guide the allocation of capital, labor, information, and housing.[51] At its core, the Socialist Market Economy concept was meant to defuse criticism that increased adoption of market forces was incompatible with socialism. As before, the Party believed that China could continue to experiment with capitalism without becoming capitalist itself as long as the state-owned sector of the economy was dominant, and the Party retained absolute political control over the country. According to Jiang's formulation, markets were not incompatible with socialism. On the contrary, further reform and opening were necessary to strengthen socialism and the Party.

The Company Law: The major economic reforms of the 1990s were focused on restructuring SOEs and banks to look and act more like companies. SOEs had long operated as quasi-arms of the government, operating according to the instructions of government ministries and providing their workers with a wide variety of social services. In the 1980s, SOEs had undertaken steps toward restructuring, establishing separate legal identities and taking on limited degrees of autonomy from the government. These reforms were taken further with the 1994 Company Law which set forth a set of restructuring guidelines for SOEs called corporatization. This process involved SOEs adopting more traditional corporate structures, such as shareholding and limited liability. Procedures for paying dividends, establishing subsidiaries, and bankruptcy were put into place. It also established a clear separation of responsibilities between management, workers, and directors. Some smaller SOES were privatized by selling their shares to the management and workers.[52] SOEs were also theoretically made responsible for their profits and losses, an attempt to reduce the reliance on soft budget constraints and subsidies they received from the government.

The mechanisms of Party and government control over SOES were reformed but not abandoned by the Company Law. The Law specified that supervisory appointments for SOEs would continue to be made by the government, although workers would be consulted.[53] Workers could form a trade union, but all unions would be forced to operate as part of the Party's national trade union, which controlled all union activity and prevented unions from operating as competing sources of power. Party committees would continue to play an important role as the Party's eyes and ears inside of companies. The Party also set out new rules during this period that required party committees in foreign firms.[54] Article 14 of the Company Law specifically requires that all companies must "strengthen the construction of socialist culture and ideology and accept the supervision of the government and public."[55]

The Company Law also gave legal space to TVEs. For years, TVEs had to labor under the fiction that they were "sponsored" by a local government and collectively owned. This gave them political protection in an era where private enterprise was still illegal. The passage of the Company Law finally enshrined the legal status of private companies, allowing many TVEs to "take off the red hat." More than one million TVEs would reorganize as private enterprises following the passage of the Law.[56] Previously limited to sole proprietorships and private partnerships, private firms were also granted the ability to structure themselves as limited liability companies.[57] This provided private firms with a legal structure that was more appropriate for large firms, reducing the direct liability of entrepreneurs.

The Crisis of the State-Owned Economy: The restructuring reforms of the 1990s were not enough to arrest a decline in the financial condition of SOEs. By the mid and late 1990s, SOEs began to sink under the crushing weight of large non-performing loans and poor profitability. The problems stemmed from the fact that SOEs had only been partially modernized and reformed. SOEs still operated according to the direction of the government and made business decisions based on policy priorities rather than market considerations. There were limited mechanisms to force poorly performing SOEs to improve because they were subject to soft budget constraints, meaning that they were able to continually borrow from the banks to offset operational losses. In turn, banks were incentivized to loan to SOEs via implicit guarantees by the government that it would financially support SOEs if necessary. Regulators did not force banks to recognize bad loans. Instead, banks could "extend and pretend" to avoid loan losses by lending more to SOEs to repay their existing loans, a process called evergreening. Adding to their financial challenges, corruption at SOEs was widespread, with managers taking advantage of their increased autonomy to embezzle assets from their enterprises.[58] In one notable example, Chu Shijian, known as China's tobacco king, managed to divert more than $145 million in profits from Hongta Group, the state-owned cigarette factory he ran.[59]

As the 1990s progressed, conditions for SOEs continued to deteriorate. The amount of bad loans to SOEs had grown to massive proportions. A contemporary analysis concluded that the state banks had unrecognized losses greater than their new worth, rending them technically insolvent.[60] While banks might be able to continue making loans to loss-making SOEs loans for a while longer, financial losses of this scale were unsustainable over the long run. Eventually the bad debt would grow so large that the banks themselves would be unable to continue lending. This could precipitate a major financial crisis that would derail China's economic growth and lead to widespread unemployment.

The Party's sense of concern over the domestic economic situation was heightened due to a major global financial crisis unfolding at that time. The Asian Financial Crisis was a watershed event where many of Asia's rapidly growing economies, previously exemplars of successful development, were devastated by debt crises and currency depreciation, leading to a period of economic and political instability. Starting with the sharp depreciation of the Thai Baht in July 1997, the crisis rapidly spread to South Korea, Malaysia, Indonesia, and Thailand. These countries experienced volatile exchange rates, debt defaults, and rapid capital outflows. Korea, Thailand, and Indonesia were forced to seek bailouts from the International Monetary Fund, agreeing to painful economic restructuring that included cuts to social services and other government spending. These cuts were politically unpopular and fomented social discontent across the region. In Indonesia, backlash to these economic measures led to the downfall of Indonesia's longtime dictator, Suharto. Zhu Rongji, China's premier at the time, was explicit that China might suffer the same fate as other Asian economies if it did not get its economic house in order.[61]

The Asian Financial Crisis reinforced doubts within China's leadership about fully embracing market reforms. The "guided capitalism" of many East Asian economies had appealed to many in the Party. It offered an alternative model to the laissez-faire economics of the United States and other Western countries by preserving a large role for the government to guide economic policy. Some policymakers in China sought to emulate Korea's chaebol system, impressed with how quickly South Korea had modernized and produced large multinational companies.[62] The chaebol system is characterized by large conglomerates that dominate the economy and work in tandem with the government through industrial policy to develop key industries. The hope was that through government guidance, China's SOEs could replicate the success of Korea's chaebols and emerge as powerful and efficient national champions in strategic industries. However, in contrast to the chaebol, which were controlled by private families, China's SOEs would remain controlled by the government. Many Western economists believed that the Asian Financial Crisis was an indictment of East Asia's model of guided capitalism, revealing the problems from close connections between enterprises and the government, such as in the case of South Korea. The Party drew a different conclusion—the crisis highlighted the dangers of insufficient supervision of market forces. Rather than further liberalization, the proper response was to exert more control over the economy and a government which actively intervened in markets to mitigate economic risks.

Fixing the State Sector: Faced with both internal and external economic pressures, China's leaders undertook a massive SOE reform campaign in the late 1990s. In his report to the 15th Party Congress in 1997, Jiang Zemin called for reforming large state enterprises and merging them into larger groups in order to strengthen them.[63] By contrast, for smaller enterprises the Party could loosen control and allow them to be restructured or sold off. If that resulted in a smaller state share of the economy, that was fine according to Jiang, as long as public ownership remained dominant, the state-controlled strategic industries, and the remaining SOEs grew more competitive and influential. The policy would become known as "grasp the large, let go of the small," in which the Party would attempt to resuscitate the state sector via a triage approach. Small and inefficient SOEs would be systematically shutdown or privatized to reallocate resources to larger, more strategic SOEs. The "letting go" of small enterprises was massive in scale. The Chinese government forced thousands of small and inefficient SOEs, mostly operating at the city and county level, to close and sell off their assets. As a result of the closures, millions of SOE workers became unemployed. It represented a fundamental break from prior notions of lifetime employment for workers at state firms. The central government and local governments were forced to provide support for the millions of workers who no longer had jobs. Additionally, SOEs reduced many of the social services they had previously provided to workers and their families, such as operating schools and hospitals. This led to growing gaps in China's social safety net as local governments struggled to provide these services and support unemployed workers.

For the larger and more strategic SOEs, the Party worked to "grasp" them more tightly. The policy represented increased government intervention aimed at bringing the state sector to heel and ultimately enhancing its viability. The Party was taking control of the wild and dysfunctional state sector to save it from collapse. Reforms were intended to revitalize the state economy, reinforcing SOE's "dominant status in key industries" and role in "materializing the goals" of the government's economic controls.[64] The hope was that post-restructuring, the remaining SOEs would control the commanding heights of the economy, be internationally competitive, market-conforming, and closely tied to the Party.[65] At an operational level, this meant merging SOEs into large-scale industrial conglomerates and centralizing state ownership at the local or central level.[66] Around 1,000 large SOEs were chosen to receive government support and subsidies, with the aim of transforming them into national champions.[67] One notable example is Baowu Steel Group, China's largest steel company, which formed through the merger of several smaller steel firms into a single mega conglomerate.

For the SOEs that it intended to retain, the Party accelerated the corporate restructuring efforts. SOEs were transformed into limited liability companies or joint-stock companies that could list on the domestic stock exchanges. The restructuring was not a cover for large-scale privatization, but rather an effort to make SOES more profitable and efficient by adopting modern corporate structures. Throughout the process, the Party was focused on maintaining its influence over the remaining SOEs. In 1998, hundreds of "special inspectors" were sent to large SOEs to supervise them, although the inspectors lacked the accounting knowledge and business experience necessary to address the deep-rooted problems faced by SOEs.[68] When this did not achieve the desired level of control, the Party's Central Committee set up a new body, the Large Enterprise Working Committee, to directly appoint top SOE managers.[69]

SOE restructuring had two significant economic impacts. The first was an improvement in overall SOE efficiency. This was achieved largely by shutting down the worst-performing firms rather than through operational improvements at the surviving firms. From the late 1990s to around the mid-2000s, the productivity difference between SOEs and private enterprises narrowed considerably (Fig. 2). However, an even more important impact was that the closure of numerous SOEs created space for private enterprises to take on a larger role in the economy. In many sectors, private companies struggled to compete with SOEs due to the latter's government subsidies and preferential access to credit. With so many moribund SOEs shut down in the late 1990s, private companies finally had an opportunity to enter many new industries in the manufacturing and service sectors. Given the higher productivity of private firms relative to SOEs, this would prove to be a major driver of growth for the economy going forward. Faced with a large number of unemployed workers, government attitudes toward the private sector began to improve during this period because they could help absorb the excess workers. As private companies grew and expanded, they began to emerge as a major source of new employment, hiring many workers that had been laid off from the state sector.

Financial Sector Bailout: The 1990s were a period of intense financial reform in China in response to growing risks. By the end of the decade, high debt levels and low profitability in the SOE sector would pushed the financial system into full-blown crisis. In 1993, the State Council passed the Resolution on Financial System Reform in an effort to establish a more modern financial sector. The reforms included assigning the People's Bank of China, the country's central bank, the responsibilities of managing the currency and preserving macroeconomic and financial stability. The large state-owned banks, which dominated the financial system, were reorganized to focus on commercial lending. Policy-based lending, which makes loans to support government-led initiatives, was the purview of the newly created policy banks, the China Development Bank, the Agricultural Development Bank of China, and the Export-Import Bank of China.

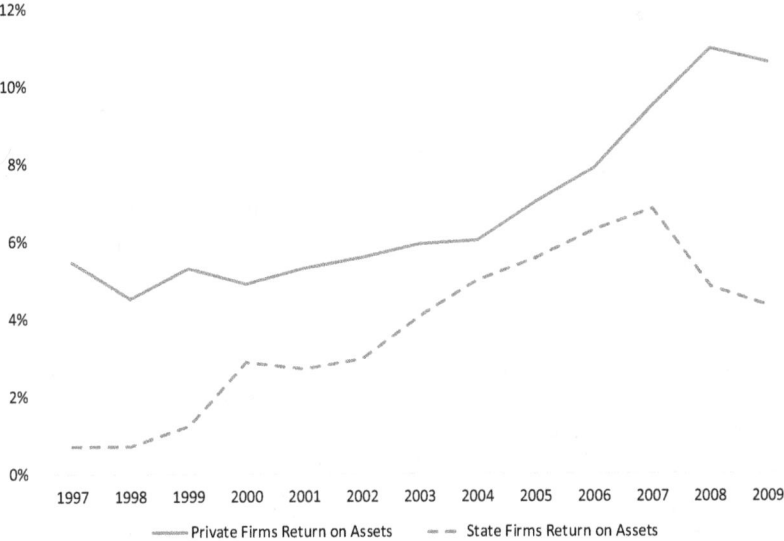

Fig. 2 Return on assets of private and state holding industrial firms (*Source* China National Bureau of Statistics)

In 1995, further reforms were passed to improve the efficiency of the banking sector and implement stronger supervision to prevent financial risks. The newly passed Commercial Banking Law formally set out a basic framework for state-owned commercial banks to operate. Notably, it called for commercial banks to operate on the principles of efficiency and safety, taking responsibility for their profits and losses, while at the same time stating that banks should lend "with the need for the development of the national economy and social progress and under the guidance of the state industrial policy."[70]

The impact of the Asian Financial Crisis on China's neighbors motived Chinese policymakers to take bolder steps to clean up the financial system. In late 1997, the State Council passed the *Notice Concerning Deepening Financial Reform, Rectifying Financial Order, and Preventing Financial Risks*. The new policy set forth a major effort to strengthen banks and eliminate some of the worst practices between banks and SOEs. In a speech at the time, Premier Zhu Rongji painted a picture of a financial sector in crisis, declaring that the most prominent problem facing the economy was that "hidden financial dangers and financial risks are constantly growing."[71] State-owned banks were facing high levels of nonperforming loans, many non-financial institutions such as trusts were in financial distress, and there were widespread supervision gaps in the banking sector and financial markets. According to Zhu, China avoided the fate of Thailand—one of the countries most affected by the Asian Financial Crisis—thanks to stricter macroeconomic controls. The solution for China's financial system outlined by Zhu was emblematic of the government's approach to reform during this period—economic liberalization combined with greater control. New rules were to be put into place to "allow banks to be banks," reducing the influence of local government and SOEs on lending decisions. At the same time, the Party made a push to increase its control over the financial system, establishing new oversight bodies for the financial system and increasing the role of party committees within financial institutions.

However, the problems within the financial system were too big to be solved without new resources and drastic policy changes. In 1998, the governor of the central bank, Dai Xianlong, declared that a quarter of all loans were nonperforming.[72] Given that the losses from these loans would potentially exceed the capital of the banks, China's banking system was effectively insolvent. The closed and controlled nature of the financial system, China's banks would not be forced to recognize their bad loans. Instead, what began was a major recapitalization of the entire banking sector. In 1998, the Ministry of Finance issued RMB 270 billion in bonds and then used the funds to recapitalize the four largest state-owned banks, Industrial and Commercial Bank of China, the Bank of China, the Agricultural Bank of China, and China Construction Bank. Regulators ordered the banks to undergo a massive restructuring to cut costs and improve efficiency. Tens of thousands of bank branches were closed and hundreds of thousands of employees were fired.

In 1999, the government set up four state-owned asset management companies. These entities were effectively "bad banks," designed to take the bad debts off the balance sheets of the state banks. In the first wave of bad loan disposal, the asset management companies purchased RMB 1.2 trillion in loans from the banks at full value. In a market-based system, distressed debt investors purchase troubled loans for a substantial discount to reflect the risks that funds may never be recovered. By selling their loans to the asset management companies at full price, the banks were able to avoid recognizing a loss. To fund their purchases of these overpriced loans, the asset management companies sold bonds to the banks. This created a conflicted structure whereby the state banks were financing the asset management companies in order for them to buy their bad loans at inflated prices. Given that these loans would never be recovered in full, the repayment of the bonds had to be extended multiple times to prevent the asset management companies from defaulting on their loans. An analysis from 2006 estimated that the banking cleanup process cost at least $500 billion, an amount greater than 20% of China's 2005 GDP.[73]

Concurrent with the banking cleanup was an effort to restructure the mechanisms of control over the financial system. In 1998, the Party established the Central Financial Work Commission which sought to centralize and reinforce its control over the banking, securities, and insurance industries.[74] The Commission served as the implementing body for the Party's policies, coordinating the financial regulatory agencies, conducting discipline inspections, performing investigations, and making personnel recommendations.[75] Final approval over key appointments at the largest state banks was made by the Party's Central Organization Department.[76] In 2002, the Party dissolved Central Financial Work Commission and transferred many of its functions to the newly created China Banking Regulatory Commission. Structured to be a modern banking regulator, the China Banking Regulatory Commission was fully separate from the central bank and focused on prudential regulation. In 2003, Central Huijin, a holding company for the government's ownership rights in the banks, was established. Huijin was initially set up by the People's Bank of China as a limited liability company, as opposed to a government agency. This was done in order run the new entity more efficiently, with the governance structures of a modern structure rather than a government bureaucracy.[77] Huijin was granted nearly $80 billion from China's foreign exchange reserves to recapitalize the banks.[78] In 2007, the Ministry of Finance stepped in to exert greater control over Huijin. It issued bonds that were used to purchase Huijin's equity which was then used to capitalize China Investment Corporation, China's new sovereign wealth fund.

Foreign Strategic Investments and Overseas Listings: The restructuring of SOEs and the state banks was helped put them on a path to solvency. To further consolidate these improvements, the Chinese government implemented a multi-year project to list many of the largest state enterprises and banks on the Hong Kong stock exchange. Public listing has two primary goals. The first was to provide a new source of funding for cash-strapped SOEs and boost capital levels for banks, making them more financially resilient. The second was to impose modern corporate governance structures on these companies, including public financial reporting, establishing a board of directors, and allowing shareholder votes on major corporate decisions.

To prepare for a public listing, foreign strategic investors were invited to make investments in the largest Chinese banks. Between 2004 and 2006, Chinese banks received over $20 billion in foreign investment.[79] Table 1 shows the strategic investments that were made in China's largest banks during this period. Echoing Deng's mantra of "capitalist tools in socialist hands," the foreign strategic investors were brought in to provide both new capital and technical assistance to the Chinese banks as they sought to implement modern risk management practices and develop new business lines, such as consumer lending. However, statements from Chinese regulators that the state should "maintain absolute control over large banks" made clear that while the foreign investors would be invited to help improve the banks, their influence would face limitations.[80] Most of the foreign strategic investors gradually wound down their investments a few years later, effectively marking the end of the experiment. While many foreign strategic investors had profited from these investments, their ability to reshape the Chinese banks was limited.

Chinese policymakers hoped that the combination of increased capital and better governance would put an end to the chronic problems that plagued the banks and SOEs, including low profitability, high debt levels, and reliance on government subsidies. Hong Kong was chosen as the

Table 1 Foreign strategic investments in China's largest banks (2004–2006)

Chinese bank	Foreign strategic investor	Ownership	Board seats
Bank of Communications	HSBC	19.9%	Two Board Seats
China Construction Bank	Bank of America	8.5%	One Board Seat
	Temasek	6%	One Board Seat
Bank of China	Royal Bank of Scotland	9.6%	One Board Seat
	UBS	1.6%	None
	Temasek	4.8%	None
Industrial and Commercial Bank of China	Goldman Sachs, Allianz, and American Express	8.5%	One Board Seat

Source International Monetary Fund[81]

listing venue for the SOEs. This was done to access an international investor base that was comfortable investing in the Hong Kong market but not in China's less well-regulated domestic exchanges. Additionally, China retained capital controls that prevented many foreign investors from investing directly in the A-share market.

Some of the SOEs that underwent this listing process were newly created specifically for this purpose. China Mobile, formerly known as China Telecom, was one such example. The company was cobbled together by combining provincial mobile network operators into one larger conglomerate. The company was among the vanguard of SOEs that were listed in the late 1990s, raising over $4 billion, and was the largest IPO by any Asian company outside of Japan.[82]

The process of publicly listing and introducing foreign shareholders did not represent the privatization of SOEs, nor did it signal the Party's willingness to gradually give up control over the companies that occupied the commanding heights of the Chinese economy. To maintain its influence over these firms, the Party kept four important levers of control. First, in many instances, only a portion of an SOE group's assets were listed. The holding company of the listed subsidiary remained fully state-owned and held the largest ownership share, thereby giving it control. Second, the Party retained control over the appointment of executives at listed SOEs through an internal personnel system. Heads of key SOEs were frequently rotated between stints at management positions at SOEs and roles in the government. The career progression of SOE executives was determined by the Party, with outside shareholders of the newly listed enterprises having little influence. Third, the Party established a parallel governance system through the creation of party committees within corporate structures. Party committees sit outside of the normal corporate governance structure of enterprises, where decisions are made by management and boards of directors. Yet party committees retain the ability to weigh in on major corporate decisions at their discretion. Fourth, the Party retained the ability to force compliance through a requirement that SOEs contribute to national policy objectives, as outlined in the Company Law and Banking Law. The combined effect of these different levers of control meant that even as banks became more marketized they remained firmly within the grasp of the Party.

A clear indication of these levers of control can be seen in the Hong Kong offering documents for ICBC, China's largest bank. Disclosures in the document state that the Ministry of Finance and Huijin, the holders of the government's ownership interest will control:

- The timing and amount of the distribution of dividends
- The issuance of new securities;
- The election of directors and supervisors;
- Business strategies and policies;
- Any plans relating to mergers, acquisitions, joint ventures, investments, or divestitures; and
- Amendments to articles of association.[83]

The document additionally states that the Ministry of Finance and Huijin have "strong interests" in implementing the economic and fiscal policies enacted by the State Council, which "may not be in the best interest" of either the company or its shareholders.

In summary, the public listing of SOEs did not represent a move toward privatization. Instead, it was a policy designed to recapitalize and revitalize the state sector. Chinese leaders believed public listing could increase market discipline on SOEs and help them become more efficient, ultimately making them viable over the long term. However, as will be discussed in later chapters, this goal would be undermined by the Party's efforts to direct the operations of SOEs toward supporting political goals.

Joining the Global Trading System: During the 1990s, deeper integration into the global trading system became a major policy objective for China's top leadership. Jiang Zemin and Zhu Rongji believed that trade had the potential to sustain China's rapid economic growth in the face of problems in the state sector and financial system. Membership in the World Trade Organization (WTO) would expand China's exports by reducing the trade barriers faced by Chinese firms in foreign markets. However, joining the WTO would require significant reforms to China's management of SOEs and tight control over many industries.

The belief that trade could drive forward the country's growth was constant throughout the reform period. A major motivation for establishing the special economic zones in the early 1980s was to boost growth through exports. While China's exports remained modest throughout the 1980s, Chinese firms had started to achieve considerable success by the 1990s. Between 1978 and 1998, China's exports grew by a factor of nineteen, and Chinese firms were becoming dominant in several industries such as textiles and apparel, furniture, consumer goods, and low-end electronics.[84]

The embrace of the capitalist trading system, embodied by the WTO, was complicated for China's leaders. Bill Clinton, among many other Western leaders at the time, believed that the reforms required of China to join the WTO would push the country toward greater openness and freedom.[85] However, Jiang, Zhu, and others in China's leadership were not pursuing WTO membership to liberalize China's economy and society. Instead, they believed that through intervention in the economy, the Party could manage globalization and use it to advance the country's national interests.[86] Moreover, China's leaders felt confident that they could combat foreign pressures that might seek to undermine the Party's control over the economy.

China faced a lengthy list of reforms necessary to join the WTO, including reducing tariffs, granting market access to foreign firms in industries like banking and insurance, reducing government support for SOEs, and strengthening its legal protections for intellectual property rights. While SOEs were larger exporters than private firms at the time, they were also less efficient and therefore more susceptible to foreign competition. Thus, China's reforms to gain WTO membership could have a significant negative impact on SOEs and by extension the Party's control over the economy. One contemporary observer described China's WTO entry negotiations as a debate over how much protection the Chinese government could retain for SOEs from foreign competition.[87]

China's leadership desired to use the WTO to boost growth and reform SOEs. However, reform was focused on making SOEs more efficient, not allowing them to be entirely displaced by foreign competition. In retrospect, there is a broad consensus that the reforms that China adopted for WTO membership were insufficient to address the problems associated with SOEs. The commitments made by the Chinese government regarding SOEs, such as forcing enterprises to operate on a commercial basis and reducing the influence of the Chinese government over SOE activity, proved to be highly subjective in their interpretation and therefore difficult for outside parties to enforce.[88]

Coopting the Private Sector: In 1997, the Party issued a new policy that upgraded the status of the private sector. Previously referred to as a "supplement to the state-owned economy," the private sector was now classified as an "important component of the social market economy."[89] The shift represented an acknowledgment that the private sector was now a much more significant force in the Chinese economy relative to the past and also one that needed to be controlled. In 2000, the Party announced that self-employed and privately owned businesses would be supported, encouraged, and guided.[90]

Jiang Zemin laid out his thinking about the balance between the state and private sectors during a speech to the National People's Congress.[91] According to Jiang, SOEs must be "in a dominant position in major industries and key areas that concern the life-blood of the national economy," "play a leading role in economic development," and manifest their "control power." In this context, even if the state sector began to account for a smaller proportion of the total economy, as many estimates put the private sector's share of the economy near 50% at the time, China could remain socialist. The dominance of SOEs across the commanding heights of the economy was the key guardrail that allowed Chinese leaders to become more comfortable with a more influential private sector.

However, strong SOEs were not enough to quell concerns about control. New mechanisms had to be created to co-opt the growing private sector and bring it firmly within the orbit of the Party. In early 2000, Jiang Zemin announced the "Three Represents," a policy designed to grapple with the increased importance of the private sector. The most important change embedded within the new policy was a declaration that the Party "must represent the development trend of China's advanced productive forces." This represented a significant ideological change for the Party as Jiang defined the private sector as one China's advanced productive forces. It was therefore incumbent upon the Party to represent the private sector. What "represent" would come to mean over time was establishing Party structures within companies and coopting businesspeople by bringing them into the Party.

After issuing the Three Represents in 2001, Jiang Zemin invited private entrepreneurs to become Party members.[92] Many would do so in the hopes that tighter connections with the Party could benefit their businesses. This new policy provoked a backlash from some conservative elements in the party.[93] Jiang Zemin subsequently moved to quash this opposition, closing down media outlets that had publicly opposed his policy.[94] The new relationship between the Party and the private sector would be made permanent in 2002 following an update to the Party's constitution.

4 The Rise of the Private Sector and the Global Financial Crisis (2000–2011)

The period following China's WTO accession saw dramatic changes in the Chinese economy. Despite efforts to strengthen the state sector in the late 1990s, the private sector continued to dramatically increase its share of the total economy throughout the 2000s. This led to countervailing efforts by the Party to reestablish control over an increasingly market-driven economy and preserve the power of SOEs. The rapid growth of the economy during this period also reduced the impetus toward further economic reforms. China's new leadership, Hu Jintao and Wen Jiabao, were increasingly focused on issues of economic redistribution rather than pursuing new market-oriented reforms. By the end of the decade, the global financial crisis severely weakened capitalist economies worldwide, reinforcing the Party's belief that tight control over the market was essential.

Expansion of the Private Sector: The restructuring of the state sector in the late 1990s and entry into the WTO in 2001 laid the groundwork for the rapid expansion of the private sector in China. Agriculture had been almost entirely privatized via the spread of household farming in the 1980s. However, the industrial and service sectors remained dominated by SOEs. Private firms faced legal and regulatory restrictions in many sectors and they struggled to compete against heavily subsidized SOEs that were able to operate with soft budget constraints. As mentioned above, the "Grasp the Large, Let go of the Small" Policy for SOEs implemented by Jiang Zemin and Zhu Rongji resulted in thousands of SOEs in non-strategic areas of the economy being downsized or shut down.

This opened space for private firms to enter many new areas of the economy. In the span of a few short years, SOEs were displaced by private firms in China's industrial production. One estimate shows by 2003, using a broad definition, private firms accounted for nearly 56% of China's industrial output.[95] By 2007, the share of private firms grew another 7%.[96] Private firms also grew rapidly in retail services and the production of consumer goods. SOEs maintained dominant roles in areas subject to legal and natural monopolies, such as tobacco, electric power, and oil and gas. However, in the areas where private companies were allowed to freely compete, SOEs were almost entirely displaced.

A similar but less dramatic transformation took place in the services industry. In certain sectors, such as wholesale and retail trade, the private sector made significant progress in displacing SOEs. By 2008, around 50% of wholesale and retail trade was by private firms.[97] In the catering industry, private firms were responsible for two-thirds of total revenue.[98] However, in other areas of the service sector, including financial services and telecommunications, state firms retained a large presence. As with the industrial sector, private firms displaced SOEs in sectors where they were allowed to freely compete and struggled to make inroads in sectors where state firms were protected by regulatory barriers.

Following admission to the WTO, Chinese firms faced lower tariffs in overseas markets. This set the stage for a dramatic expansion of China's exports. Between 2001 and 2011, China's exports grew sevenfold, reaching nearly $1.9 trillion per year.[99] State firms, however, were largely left out of this export bonanza. As shown in Fig. 3, the share of total exports from SOEs fell precipitously during the 2000s. SOEs were first replaced by foreign-funded enterprises, which set up manufacturing and assembly plants in China, and then subsequently by private firms that have now become China's largest exporters.

Exports were a major driver of China's growth during the 2000s. The country's trade surplus exceeded 7% of GDP in 2007, an extraordinarily high figure for a major economy.[101] As discussed above, this trade was being done by foreign and private firms, not SOEs. This outcome contrasted sharply with the desire of China's policymakers to use WTO members to make SOEs globally competitive firms and boost their growth through exports. As China became the world's factory during the 2000s, it was accomplished by non-state firms.

Opening Industries to Private Investment and Property Rights: During the Hu Jintao—Wen Jiabao Administration there were some efforts to promote the expansion of the private sector. In 2005, the State Council released the "Opinions on Encouraging, Supporting, and Guiding the Development Individual Businesses, Private Firms, and Other Parts of the Non-State Economy," which became commonly referred to as the 36 Articles. The 36 Articles call for simultaneously "consolidating and developing" the state-owned economy as the "mainstay" of the economy while also supporting and guiding the development of the private sector.[102] In addition, the 36 Articles establishes equal treatment, in theory, for SOEs and private firms in areas of the economy where

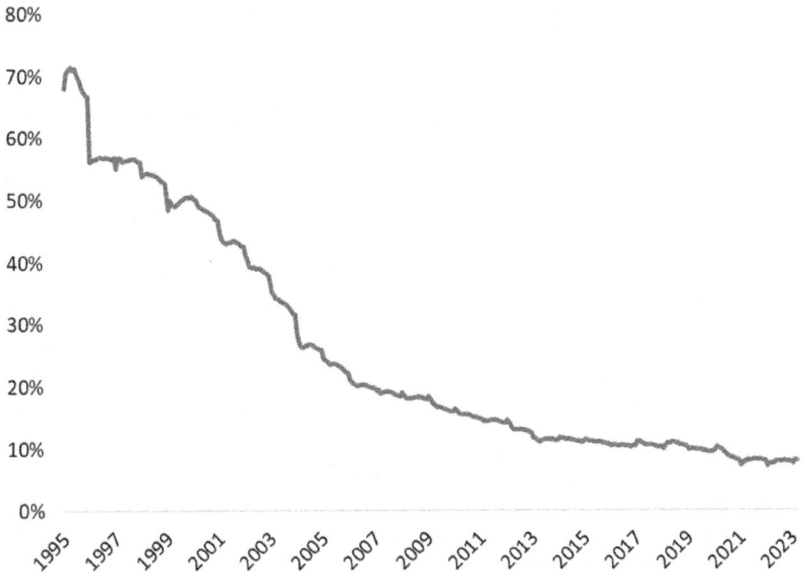

Fig. 3 SOE share of total exports (*Source* China General Administration of Customs)[100]

private firms are permitted to enter. Private capital would be permitted to invest in, but not necessarily compete with, state-controlled industries, such as electric power, electronic communications, rail, civil aviation, and petroleum. Other sectors were to be opened as well, including infrastructure, education, healthcare, and financial services to additional private investment. While the 36 Articles represented progress toward greater economic openness, it also highlighted the Party's continued efforts to influence the actions of private firms. The 36 Articles are replete with "guidance," "encouragement," and "support" for private firms to participate in government policy initiatives, like state-owned enterprise restructuring and developing China's western region. Private enterprises were also required to comply with the government's macroeconomic controls and improve their "quality" as defined by the Party.

Many of the reforms outlined in the 36 Articles made little progress after the policy was released. As a result, five years later, the State Council released a follow-up document, "Opinions on Encouraging and Guiding the Healthy Development of Private Investment," which became referred to as the New 36 Articles.[103] The document called for further refinement of government regulations for the private sector and called for full implementation of the original 36 Articles, an implicit acknowledgment that the original 36 Articles had not solved many of the logjams that prevented the private sector from entering industries dominated by SOEs.[104]

The 36 Articles and the New 36 Articles were evidence that Chinese leaders recognized that the private sector was more efficient, profitable, and innovative than the state sector. Private investment in inefficient state-controlled industries was necessary to drive forward economic growth. Yet there was a reluctance to allow private firms to directly compete with state firms in "lifeline" industries, which a term which could be interpreted broadly. Private firms also needed to "strictly follow" national industrial policies. The Party was happy to encourage private enterprises to invest in sectors like financial services, transportation infrastructure, defense industry, telecommunications, oil and gas, and other industries. But given that private firms would face a glass ceiling in these industries once they became sufficiently large and influential, private entrepreneurs were understandably reluctant to invest in many of these areas.

In 2004, the Chinese constitution was revised to provide further support to the private sector. The constitution was revised to state that the state "encourages, supports and guides the development" of the non-public sector and "in accordance with law, exercises supervision and control."[105] Private property was officially recognized via a statement that "citizens' lawful private property is inviolable." This was a major development as it was the first time that private property had been given legal recognition at such a high level.[106] However, this inclusion of greater support for private firms and private property generated backlash from some intellectuals as "mimicking Western capitalism" and out of step with China's socialist system, delaying the final approval of a Property Law until 2007.[107] The delay proved that defining the different types of ownership (state collective, and private) and providing protections to private property owners was a controversial undertaking.

Regulatory Consolidation and Overseas Expansion: The rapid displacement of the state sector by private firms in the late 1990s and early 2000s led the Party to enact new policies to support the state sector. Between 1995 and 2003, the number of SOEs had decreased by 84,000, and workers employed in the state sector decreased by 44 million people.[108] The increase in unemployment led to social discontent and protests, forcing SOEs and local governments to find ways to support the millions of newly jobless workers.[109] While the Party called for supporting and retraining for these workers, many were eventually forgotten or forced into early retirement on meager pensions. The real focus was on saving the enterprises themselves, not the workers, as China's top leaders continued to declare that SOEs were the "pillar of the national economy" and that enterprises operating in strategic industries must remain under the control of the state.[110] The goal of China's leaders was not to roll back economic reforms or restrict the growth of private enterprises, but rather to strengthen SOEs to avoid their wholesale replacement by the private sector. Even though the Party had taken steps to increase its influence over the private sector, there was no substitute for SOEs to maintain influence over the commanding heights of the economy. China also began to look to SOEs as instruments of foreign policy.

One major problem from the Party's perspective was that some of the levers of control over SOEs had been weakened during the reform of the late 1990s when Zhu Rongji abolished most of the industrial ministries and created the unsuccessful Asset Management Agency.[111] SOEs thus were able to operate with relatively little oversight, acting as independent fiefdoms, expanding into non-core businesses such as property, and reinvesting profits into wasteful projects rather than remitting funds back to the government. To strengthen the government's supervision over SOEs, the State-Owned Assets Supervision and Administration Commission (SASAC) was established underneath the State Council. Among the stated goals of the new organization was to "develop and expand the state-owned economy" and "preserve and grow" SOE assets.[112]

SASAC's effectiveness in the mission was decidedly mixed. SASAC was originally granted authority over 196 SOEs owned by the government. The organization set about reducing that number substantially through mergers of weaker SOEs into stronger ones. It also accelerated the process of SOE corporatization, reorganizing enterprises to have modern corporate governance structures.[113] However, SASAC faced limitations in its ability to exercise oversight over the SOEs it supervised. One problem was that SASAC's chairman was equal in rank within the government to the heads of many large SOEs, making it difficult to give them orders.[114] Another issue was that for strategically important

SOEs, the Party's organization department kept control over appointments, despite SASAC having legal authority to do so.[115] SASAC also faced resistance to exercising its authority over SOE budgets and business activities. SASAC struggled to force SOEs to increase the dividends they paid to the government and to exit side businesses such as real estate.[116]

There was a major push for SOEs to expand overseas during this period as well.[117] International expansion for SOEs was seen as a way to promote their competitiveness, forcing enterprises to compete outside of protected domestic industries. It was also a channel for expanding China's foreign policy interests. The "Going Out" policy sought to bolster the overseas presence of SOEs and increase China's outward foreign direct investment.[118] SOEs began to engage in foreign mergers and acquisitions to secure access to critical raw materials, resources, and energy.[119] The Party increasingly viewed SOEs as a key tool to promote China's economic and strategic interests abroad.

Reasserting State Control: In 2006, the State Council issued a policy that outlined the Chinese government's revised approach to managing the economy. The Guiding Opinions on Promoting the Adjustment of State-owned Capital and the Restructuring of State-owned Enterprises was a response to the erosion of state control that had occurred over the past several years.[120] The policy sets forth a basic principle of "consolidating and developing" the public sector in order to "enhance the control, influence and driving force" of the state-owned economy. Furthermore, the main objective of the new policy was to "further promote the concentration" of state-owned capital in important industries, key areas related to national security, and other important "lifelines" of the economy. According to the policy, the market can play a fundamental role in allocating resources, but one that must be subject to government guidance and regulation.

Through this document and subsequent comments by Chinese officials, the Party laid out new markers for the industries it expected SOEs to remain dominant.[121] Li Rongrong, the then-head of SASAC, identified three classifications of the industry (Table 2).

The government's intention to maintain state dominance in these sectors was not the same as achieving it. As some economists have pointed out, in many of these industries the state share of total assets declined in subsequent years despite being designated as a strategic sector.[123] This was due to the persistent underperformance of state firms relative to the private sector.

Promoting Strategic Industries: During this period, Chinese leaders undertook several initiatives to revitalize planning over economic sectors viewed as strategic. Chinese policymakers were intent on moving into

Table 2 Sectors targeted for state control

Classification	Level of control	Example sectors
National Security and Economic Lifelines	Absolute state control	Electric grid, petroleum and petrochemicals, coal, air transportation, shipping
Fundamental and Pillar Industries	Key companies in these industries should remain under absolute or relative state control	Automobiles, electronic information, construction, steel, non-ferrous metals, chemicals, survey and design, technological industries
Other Industries	The state maintains holdings in industry leaders	Transportation and logistics, investment, medicine, building materials, agriculture, geological survey

Source Xinhua[122]

higher value-added industries and developing capabilities for indigenous innovation. This motivated the creation of several major policy initiatives during the 2000s. One such effort was the establishment of the Medium to Long-Term Plan for the Development of Science and Technology (MLP) in 2006. China has had a long history of national science and technology plans, such as the 863 and 973 plans, formulated in 1986 and 1997, respectively, that promoted basic scientific research in a variety of different areas, such as biotechnology, informational technology, space, and energy.[124] However, the MLP was a significant development due to its scope and ambition. The MLP sought to promote seven different strategic industries and undertake 16 so-called "megaprojects." It also set forth the goal of achieving parity with the world's leading technological powers by 2020.[125] At the heart of the program was an effort to reduce reliance on foreign sources of technology. Chinese leaders believed foreign suppliers would withhold critical technologies in fields that impacted the "lifeblood" of the national economy and national security.[126] Therefore, the Chinese government needed to push domestic industries to develop these capabilities. These fears were confirmed a decade later as the United States took action to restrict technology exports to China during the course of the U.S.-China Trade War.

The focus on strategic industries was further reinforced in 2010 by the State Council promulgating the Decision on Accelerating the Development of Strategic Emerging Industries.[127] The document states that through a combination of "the market and guidance and promotion by the government" China will endeavor to make breakthroughs in key technologies in order to hold an advantageous position in future international competition.[128] These key emerging industries were identified as Energy Conservation and Environmental Protection, Next Generation Information Technology, Bioindustry, High-end Manufacturing, New Energy, New Materials, and New Energy Vehicles.

Redistribution over Reform: Policy priorities under Hu Jintao differed significantly compared to Jiang Zemin. Whereas Jiang acted with urgency to reform the state sector in order to save it and preserve China's growth, Hu reaped the dividends of hard reforms undertaken by his predecessor. China experienced rapid growth throughout the 2000s, driven by increased exports as a result of WTO accession, better performance in the state sector following the shutting down of many SOEs, and a private sector that was transforming large parts of the economy. This tailwind of growth provided Hu Jintao with the latitude to focus on other issues and less on economic reforms.

While some analysts have described the Hu Jintao Era as a "lost decade" for reform, these critiques overlook Hu's contributions in other areas, such as improving the social safety net and addressing rural concerns. No longer facing the severe economic challenges of the late 1990s, Hu was able to focus on more socialist economic policies, such as creating a "Harmonious Society" and building a "New Socialist Countryside" through economic policies based on the socialist conception of a "Scientific Outlook on Development." At the heart of these policies was a greater focus on economic redistribution, supporting farmers and migrants, reducing regional inequities, and increasing budgetary resources for pensions, health care, and education.[129] Hu believe that the growing rural–urban divide was a source of social instability in China needed to be addressed. With the economic crisis of the late 1990s resolved, Chinese leaders shifted their focus to addressing the destabilizing impacts of rapid economic growth.

Global Financial Crisis: The 2008 Global Financial Crisis played a pivotal role in strengthening the belief among China's leaders that failure to guide and control the market represented a major threat to China's economic growth and stability. Viewed from Beijing, the global financial crisis was a cautionary tale of market forces running wild. In a speech at the World Economic Forum Annual Meeting in 2009, Wen Jiabao attributed the crisis to inappropriate economic policies and unsustainable models of development in "some countries," a clear reference to the United States and other Western countries.[130] Wen also criticized excessive growth by financial institutions that were driven by pursuit of profit and a lack of action by financial regulators. For the Party, the meltdown of the U.S. financial system and the painful recession that followed were proof that market forces were too unstable to be left unmanaged. Moreover, for years U.S. officials had told their Chinese counterparts in the Chinese government that they should reduce the role of the government in the Chinese economy. However, these arguments now appeared hypocritical as the U.S. government bailed out the country's financial industry and automakers.

As the Global Financial Crisis overtook the U.S. economy, Chinese leaders expressed a sense of vindication of the Chinese economic model compared to U.S. capitalism. In a famous exchange, then Vice Premier Wang Qishan remarked to U.S. Treasury Secretary Hank Paulson that while previously he had looked to Paulson (and by implication the United States) as a teacher, he now wasn't sure that China should be learning from him anymore.[131] The humbling of the U.S. economic model during the 2008 economic meltdown was an enormous setback to those in China who had advocated greater market reforms. Whereas the pressures from the Asian Financial Crisis and the SOE sector in the late 1990s had motivated China to implement difficult economic reforms modeled off the capitalist world, the Global Financial Crisis inspired the opposite reaction.

The impact of the global financial crisis on China was immense. Faced with a sharp drop in demand from the U.S. and other overseas markets, China's export focused industries began to lay off workers by the millions. One study estimated that 49 million rural workers who had left the countryside to seek employment in factories and the cities lost their jobs between October 2008 and April 2009.[132] Faced with a major economic crisis, the Party leaned into its levers of control over the economy. In its rollout of economic stimulus in response to the crisis, China's leaders used their control over both the state banks and SOEs to stabilize the economy and implement government policy.[133] China launched an enormous stimulus package, the largest in proportion to its economy of any major country, to offset the projected collapse in export demand and avoid huge job losses. Much of the stimulus was focused on infrastructure investment. State-owned banks lent huge sums of money to local governments via their off-balance sheet financing vehicles. These financing vehicles, in turn, financed a nationwide surge in infrastructure projects. SOEs, the recipients of much of these funds, dramatically increased their investment levels, helping to stabilize growth. Figure 4 shows the massive increase in fixed asset investment by SOEs during the stimulus. SOEs also maintained stable employment levels during this period at a time when Chinese workers, particularly migrant workers, were being laid off by the millions.

Chinese leaders viewed the ability to direct SOEs to spend and invest and avoid laying off workers as a key component of maintaining economic stability during the global financial crisis. Giving voice to these ideas, in 2009 Li Rongrong, the head of SASAC, touted the important role played by central and local SOEs in implementing the Chinese government's directives to stabilize the economy and preserve growth.[134] One

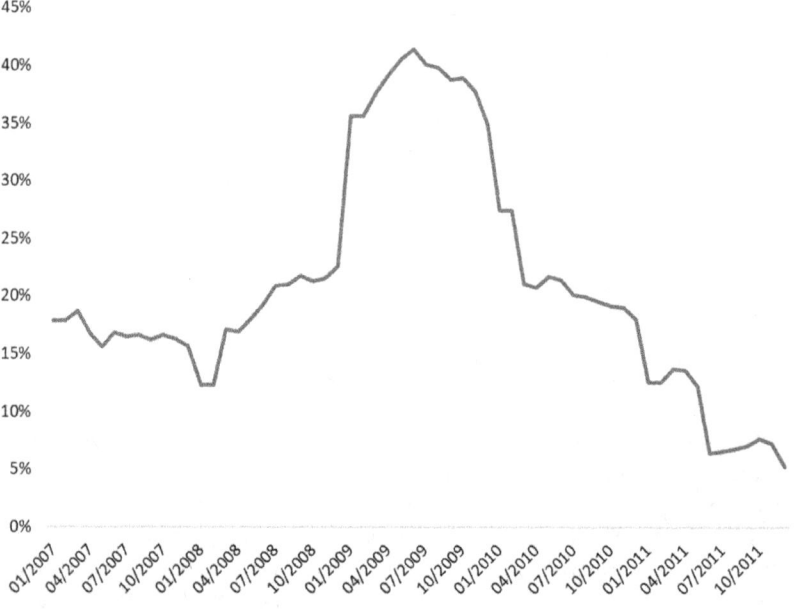

Fig. 4 SOE fixed asset investment growth (YoY, YTD) (*Source* China National Bureau of Statistics)

senior Chinese leader remarked on the striking contrast between the United States falling into its most serious economic crisis since the Great Depression while the Chinese economy continued to grow strongly.[135]

In retrospect, Chinese leaders assigned too much credit to the state sector for fueling the country's economic recovery. A careful analysis of the economic data during that period by economist Nicholas Lardy reveals the critical role played by the private sector in driving forward the economy.[136] The parts of the economy that grew rapidly after the financial crisis, including housing and exports, were closely linked to private companies. Individual and small-scale private businesses also expanded rapidly in the years following the crisis. In contrast, even in areas where state firms had been given ample support and access to credit, they tended to underperform. For example, as shown in Fig. 5, the revenue growth of state-owned industrial firms dramatically lagged behind that of private enterprises. Nonetheless, from the perspective of China's leadership, the value of having a strong state sector that could act as a stabilizer during periods of economic crisis was clear.

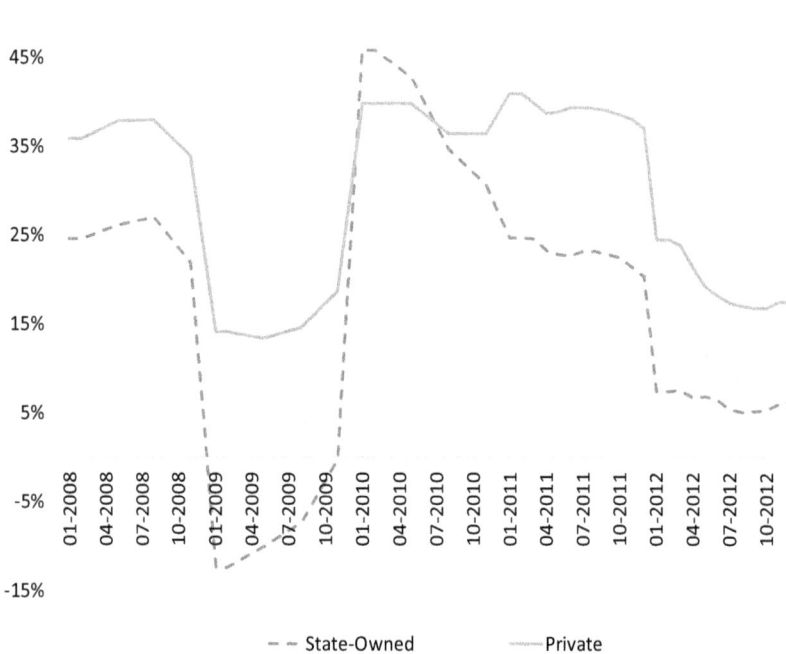

Fig. 5 Private vs. state industrial enterprises, growth of sales revenues (YoY, YTD.) (*Source* China National Bureau of Statistics)

5 Conclusion

The events outlined above reveal a much more complicated history of economic reform in China. The Reform and Opening Era that began in 1978 was a not clear break in ideology and goals for the Party. After a series of economic disasters, the Party abandoned the economic policies implemented by Mao. While the economic policies implemented by the Party changed dramatically compared to the Mao Era, the Party had not given up on its goal of using socialism to restore China to its prior wealth and power. The Party began to selectively use elements of markets and economic liberalization to restore the economy. Even as markets grew and gained influence in the 1980s, 1990s, and 2000s, the Party was careful to set limits and intervene when it felt its control over the economy was weakening. Returning to the metaphor of the bird and the cage, the cage gradually expanded during the first three decades of economic reform. By the end of the period, the Chinese economy had transformed into one largely driven by markets and private enterprise, but with a state sector that retained control over many key industries. The expansion of the private sector was uneven and sometimes perilous, with moments when the bird risked being crushed by the cage. While allowing more space for market to grow the economy, the Party also remained focused on maintaining control over China's economic development.

In 2012, more than 30 years after the start of reforms, Hu Jintao gave his final report as General Secretary. In the report, Hu declared that the underlying issue facing China's economic reforms was "to strike a balance between the role of the government and that of the market."[137] Hu called for the Party to enhance "the vitality of the state-owned sector" and "its capacity to leverage and influence the economy." At the same time, the Party would "unswervingly encourage, support and guide the development" of the private sector, albeit along lines approved by the Party. The balance between the market and government outlined by Hu was remarkably consistent with the approach of Deng Xiaoping so many years before. For three decades, the Party had sought to make use of market forces without giving up control over the economy.

Notes

1. Tony Saich, *From Rebel to Ruler: One Hundred Years of the Chinese Communist Party* (Harvard University Press, 2021).
2. Angus Maddison, "Chinese Economic Performance in the Long Run: Second Edition, Revised and Updated 960–2030 AD," *Development Centre of the Organisation for Economic Co-Operation and Development*, 2007, http://piketty.pse.ens.fr/files/Maddison07.pdf.
3. Dwight H. Perkins and Thomas G. Rawski, "Forecasting China's Economic Growth to 2025," Chapter In *China's Great Economic Transformation*, edited by Loren Brandt and Thomas G. Rawski, 829–86 (Cambridge: Cambridge University Press, 2008).
4. Based on a PPP calculation. Jutta Bolt and Jan Luiten van Zanden, "Maddison Style Estimates of the Evolution of the World Economy: A New 2023 Update," *Journal of Economic Surveys* (2024): 1–41, https://doi.org/10.1111/joes.12618.
5. Frederick C. Teiwes and Warren Sun, "China's New Economic Policy Under Hua Guofeng: Party Consensus and Party Myths," *The China Journal*, no. 66 (2011): 1–23, http://www.jstor.org/stable/41262805.
6. Guofeng Hua, "Hua Guofeng's Speech at the Opening Session of the CCP Central Work Conference," *The Wilson Center*, November 10, 1978, https://digitalarchive.wilsoncenter.org/document/hua-guofengs-speech-opening-session-ccp-central-work-conference.
7. Barry Naughton, "Deng Xiaoping: The Economist," *The China Quarterly*, no. 135 (1993): 491–514, http://www.jstor.org/stable/654099.
8. Xiaoping Deng, "Carry Out the Policy of Opening to the Outside World and Learn Advanced Science and Technology From Other Countries," *The Selected Works of Deng Xiaoping*, October 10, 1978, https://dengxiaopingworks.wordpress.com/2013/02/25/carry-out-the-policy-of-opening-to-the-outside-world-and-learn-advanced-science-and-technology-from-other-countries/.
9. Xiaoping Deng, "Speech at the Opening Ceremony of the National Conference on Science," *China.org.cn*, March 18, 1978, http://www.china.org.cn/english/features/dengxiaoping/103390.htm.

10. Ezra Vogel, *Deng Xiaoping and the Transformation of China*, Reprint (Belknap Press: An Imprint of Harvard University Press, 2013).
11. Frank Dikötter, *China After Mao: The Rise of a Superpower* (Bloomsbury Publishing, 2022).
12. Frank Dikötter, *China After Mao: The Rise of a Superpower* (Bloomsbury Publishing, 2022).
13. Ezra Vogel, *Deng Xiaoping and the Transformation of China*, Reprint (Belknap Press: An Imprint of Harvard University Press, 2013).
14. Ezra Vogel, *Deng Xiaoping and the Transformation of China*, Reprint (Belknap Press: An Imprint of Harvard University Press, 2013).
15. Nicholas Lardy, "The Changing Role of the Private Sector in China," In *Structural Change in China: Implications for Australia and the World*, edited by Iris Day and John Simon, RBA Annual Conference Volume, *Reserve Bank of Australia*, 2016, https://www.rba.gov.au/publications/confs/2016/pdf/rba-conference-volume-2016.pdf.
16. Ezra Vogel, *Deng Xiaoping and the Transformation of China*, Reprint (Belknap Press: An Imprint of Harvard University Press, 2013).
17. Sai-leung Ng, "Township and Village Enterprises and Rural Environment in China," *China Review* (2000): 529–51, http://www.jstor.org/stable/23453382.
18. Xiaoping Deng, "In Everything We Do We Must Proceed From the Realities of the Primary Stage of Socialism," *The Selected Works of Deng Xiaoping*, July 29, 1987, https://dengxiaopingworks.wordpress.com/2013/03/18/in-everything-we-do-we-must-proceed-from-the-realities-of-the-primary-stage-of-socialism/.
19. Yasheng Huang, "How Did China Take Off?," *Journal of Economic Perspectives* 26, no. 4 (2012), https://pubs.aeaweb.org/doi/pdfplus/10.1257/jep.26.4.147.
20. Yuen Yuen Ang, *How China Escaped the Poverty Trap* (Cornell University Press, 2016), https://doi.org/10.7591/9781501705854.

21. Ezra Vogel, *Deng Xiaoping and the Transformation of China*, Reprint (Belknap Press: An Imprint of Harvard University Press, 2013).
22. Ross Garnaut, Ligang Song, Yang Yao, and Xiaolu Wang, "Private Enterprise in China," *Australian National University E Press* (2012).
23. Ezra Vogel, *Deng Xiaoping and the Transformation of China*, Reprint (Belknap Press: An Imprint of Harvard University Press, 2013).
24. "Provisional Regulations on Private Enterprises," *Asian Legal Information Institute*, June 25, 1988, http://www.asianlii.org/cn/legis/cen/laws/prope517/.
25. Victor Nee and Sonja Opper, *Capitalism from Below: Markets and Institutional Change in China* (Harvard University Press, 2012).
26. Ligang Song, "State-Owned Enterprise Reform in China: Past, Present and Prospects," In *China's 40 Years of Reform and Development: 1978–2018*, edited by Ross Garnaut, Ligang Song, and Cai Fang (ANU Press, 2018), https://press-files.anu.edu.au/downloads/press/n4267/html/ch19.xhtml.
27. Karen Jingrong Lin, Xiaoyan Lu, Junsheng Zhang, and Ying Zheng, "State-Owned Enterprises in China: A Review of 40 Years of Research and Practice," *China Journal of Accounting Research* 13, no. 1 (March 1, 2020): 31–55, https://doi.org/10.1016/j.cjar.2019.12.001.
28. Ligang Song, "State-Owned Enterprise Reform in China: Past, Present and Prospects," In *China's 40 Years of Reform and Development: 1978–2018*, edited by Ross Garnaut, Ligang Song, and Cai Fang (ANU Press, 2018), https://press-files.anu.edu.au/downloads/press/n4267/html/ch19.xhtml.
29. Xiaoping Deng, "On The Reform of Enterprises and of the Banking System," *The Selected Works of Deng Xiaoping*, December 19, 1986, https://dengxiaopingworks.wordpress.com/2013/03/18/on-the-reform-of-enterprises-and-of-the-banking-system/.
30. Xiaoping Deng, "Reform Is the Only Way For China to Developed Its Productive Forces," *The Selected Works of Deng Xiaoping*, August 28, 1985, https://dengxiaopingworks.wordpress.com/2013/03/18/on-the-reform-of-enterprises-and-of-the-banking-system/.

31. Julian Gewirtz, *Never Turn Back: China and the Forbidden History of the 1980s* (Belknap Press of Harvard University Press, 2022).
32. Mette Thuno, "Reaching Out and Incorporating Chinese Overseas: The Trans-territorial Scope of the PRC by the End of the 20th Century," *The China Quarterly*, February 15, 2002, https://library.fes.de/libalt/journals/swetsfulltext/12919248.pdf.
33. Peiqing Bao, *Y.K. Pao, My Father* (Hong Kong University Press eBooks, 2013), https://ci.nii.ac.jp/ncid/BB17649705.
34. Ann Fenwick, "Evaluating China's Special Economic Zones," *International Tax & Business Law* 2 (1984): 376, https://heinonline.org/hol-cgi-bin/get_pdf.cgi?handle=hein.journals/berkjintlw2&section=24.
35. Yue-man Yeung, Joanna Lee, and Gordon Kee, "China's Special Economic Zones at 30," *Eurasian Geography and Economics* 50, no. 2 (2009): 222–240, https://www.tandfonline.com/doi/abs/10.2747/1539-7216.50.2.222.
36. Eztra Vogel, *Deng Xiaoping and the Transformation of China*, Reprint (Belknap Press: An Imprint of Harvard University Press, 2013).
37. Steven Mufson, "China Loses One of Its 8 Immortals," *Washington Post*, April 12, 1995, https://www.washingtonpost.com/archive/politics/1995/04/12/china-loses-one-of-its-8-immortals/1da5d352-ba3b-480e-8d74-7aa002facb44/.
38. Douglas Zhi Hua Zeng, "How Do Special Economic Zones and Industrial Clusters Drive China's Rapid Development?," In *Building Engines for Growth and Competitiveness in China Experience with Special Economic Zones and Industrial Clusters* (The World Bank, 2010), 10, https://documents1.worldbank.org/curated/pt/294021468213279589/pdf/564470PUB0bui110Box349496B01PUBLIC1.pdf.
39. Ezra Vogel, *Deng Xiaoping and the Transformation of China*, Reprint (Belknap Press: An Imprint of Harvard University Press, 2013).
40. Xiaoping Deng, "Address to Officers at the Rank of General and Above in Command of the Troops Enforcing Martial Law In Beijing," *The Selected Works of Deng Xiaoping*, June 9, 1989, https://dengxiaopingworks.wordpress.com/2013/03/18/on-the-reform-of-enterprises-and-of-the-banking-system/.

41. Ezra Vogel, *Deng Xiaoping and the Transformation of China*, Reprint (Belknap Press: An Imprint of Harvard University Press, 2013).
42. Barry Naughton, "The Impact of the Tiananmen Crisis on China's Economic Transition," *China Perspectives* 78 (2009): 63–78, https://www.taylorfrancis.com/chapters/edit/10.4324/9780203842607-16/impact-tiananmen-crisis-china-economic-transition-barry-naughton.
43. Julian Gewirtz, *Never Turn Back: China and the Forbidden History of the 1980s* (Belknap Press of Harvard University Press, 2022).
44. Bruce J. Dickson, "Integrating Wealth and Power in China: The Communist Party's Embrace of the Private Sector," *The China Quarterly*, no. 192 (2007): 827–54, http://www.jstor.org/stable/20192850.
45. Ezra Vogel, *Deng Xiaoping and the Transformation of China*, Reprint (Belknap Press: An Imprint of Harvard University Press, 2013).
46. Xiaoping Deng, "With Stable Policies of Reform and Opening To the Outside World, China Can Have Great Hopes For the Future," *The Selected Works of Deng Xiaoping*, September 4, 1989, https://dengxiaopingworks.wordpress.com/2013/03/18/with-stable-policies-of-reform-and-opening-to-the-outside-world-china-can-have-great-hopes-for-the-future/.
47. Suisheng Zhao, "Deng Xiaoping's Southern Tour: Elite Politics in Post-Tiananmen China," *Asian Survey* 33, no. 8 (1993): 739–56, https://doi.org/10.2307/2645086.
48. Ezra Vogel, *Deng Xiaoping and the Transformation of China*, Reprint (Belknap Press: An Imprint of Harvard University Press, 2013).
49. Ezra Vogel, *Deng Xiaoping and the Transformation of China*, Reprint (Belknap Press: An Imprint of Harvard University Press, 2013).
50. Barry Naughton, "China: Economic Transformation Before and After 1989," Paper Presented at the Conference "1989: Twenty Years After," University of California, Irvine, November 6–7, 2009.

51. Zemin Jiang, "Establish a Socialist Market Economy," *Selected Works of Jiang Zemin* (Foreign Languages Press, 2010), https://ebook.theorychina.org.cn/ebook/upload/storage/files/2022/07/22/d5c57cbba2077d855c3974821884236512478/mobile/index.html.
52. Nicholas Lardy, *Markets Over Mao: The Rise of Private Business in China*. Peterson Institute for International Economics, 2014.
53. "Company Law of the People's Republic of China," *The National People's Congress of the People's Republic of China*, July 1, 1994, http://www.npc.gov.cn/zgrdw/englishnpc/Law/2007-12/12/content_1383787.htm.
54. Jude Blanchette, "Against Atrophy: Party Organisations in Private Firms," *Made in China Journal*, April, 2019, https://madeinchinajournal.com/2019/04/18/against-atrophy-party-organisations-in-private-firms/.
55. "Company Law of the People's Republic of China," *The National People's Congress of the People's Republic of China*, July 1, 1994, http://www.npc.gov.cn/zgrdw/englishnpc/Law/2007-12/12/content_1383787.htm.
56. Nicholas Lardy, "Private Sector Development," In *China's 40 Years of Reform and Development: 1978–2018*, edited by Ross Garnaut, Ligang Song, and Cai Fang (ANU Press, 2018), https://press-files.anu.edu.au/downloads/press/n4267/html/ch19.xhtml.
57. Nicholas Lardy, Markets over Mao: The Rise of Private Business in China. Peterson Institute for International Economics, 2014.
58. Yan Sun, *Corruption and Market in Contemporary China* (Cornell University Press, 2004), https://doi.org/10.7591/9781501729980.
59. Seth Faison, "China's Paragon of Corruption; Meet Mr. Chu, a Hero to Some, an Embezzler to Others," *The New York Times*, March 6, 1998, https://www.nytimes.com/1998/03/06/business/china-s-paragon-of-corruption-meet-mr-chu-a-hero-to-some-an-embezzler-to-others.html.
60. Nicholas Lardy, "The Challenge of Bank Restructuring in China," Strengthening the Banking System in China: Issues and Experience, *Bank for International Settlements*, October 31, 1999, https://www.bis.org/publ/plcy07.htm.

61. See two speeches made by Zhu Rongji after the Asian Financial Crisis: "Deepen Financial Reforms and Guard against Financial Risks" and "Truly Learn the Lessons of the Asian Financial Crisis." English versions of these speeches are available in Zhu Rongji, June Y. Mei, Henry A. Kissinger, and Helmut Schmidt, *Zhu Rongji on the Record: The Road to Reform: 1991–1997* (Brookings Institution Press, 2013).
62. The Economist, "China Adopts the Chaebol," *The Economist*, June 5, 1997, https://www.economist.com/business/1997/06/05/china-adopts-the-chaebol.
63. Zemin Jiang, "Jiang Zemin's Report to the 15th National Congress of the Communist Party of China (江泽民在中国共产党第十五次全国代表大会上的报告)," The Central People's Government of the People's Republic of China (中华人民共和国中央人民政府), September 12, 1997, https://www.gov.cn/test/2008-07/11/content_1042080_3.htm.
64. "The Decision of the Central Committee of The Communist Party of China on Major Issues Concerning the Reform and Development of State-Owned Enterprises," *China Law Info*, September 22, 1999, http://www.lawinfochina.com/Display.aspx?lib=law&Cgid=23496.
65. Wendy Leutert, and Sarah Elaine Eaton, "Deepening Not Departure: Xi Jinping's Governance of China's State-Owned Economy," *The China Quarterly* 248 (S1) (2021): 200–21, https://doi.org/10.1017/s0305741021000795.
66. Chang-Tai Hsieh and Zheng Michael Song, "Grasp the Large, Let Go of the Small: The Transformation of the State Sector in China," *Brookings Papers on Economic Activity* (2015): 295–346, http://www.jstor.org/stable/43684105.
67. Chen Li, "Holding 'China Inc.' Together: The CCP and The Rise of China's 'Yangqi,'" *The China Quarterly*, no. 228 (2016): 927–49, http://www.jstor.org/stable/26291583.
68. Yingyi Qian and Wu Jinglian, "China's Transition to a Market Economy: How Far Across the River," *Stanford Center for International Development*, August 2000, https://kingcenter.stanford.edu/sites/g/files/sbiybj16611/files/media/file/69wp_0.pdf.

69. Yingyi Qian and Wu Jinglian, "China's Transition to a Market Economy: How Far Across the River," *Stanford Center for International Development*, August 2000, https://kingcenter.stanford.edu/sites/g/files/sbiybj16611/files/media/file/69wp_0.pdf.
70. "Commercial Bank Law of the People's Republic of China," *Asian Legal Information Institute*, May 10, 1995, http://www.asianlii.org/cn/legis/cen/laws/cblotproc396/.
71. Zhu Rongji, June Y. Mei, Henry A. Kissinger, and Helmut Schmidt, "Deepen Financial Reforms and Guard against Financial Risks: November 18, 1997," In *Zhu Rongji on the Record: The Road to Reform: 1991–1997*, 418–36 (Brookings Institution Press, 2013), http://www.jstor.org/stable/10.7864/j.ctt4cg7hn.60.
72. Nicholas Lardy, China's Unfinished Economic Revolution (Brookings Institution Press, 1998).
73. Guonan Ma, "Sharing China's Bank Restructuring Bill," *China & World Economy* 14, no. 3 (March 2006): 19–37, https://www.bis.org/repofficepubl/apresearch0605ma.pdf.
74. Sebastian Heilmann, "Regulatory Innovation by Leninist Means: Communist Party Supervision in China's Financial Industry," *The China Quarterly*, no. 181 (2005): 1–21, http://www.jstor.org/stable/20192441.
75. Heilmann, "Regulatory Innovation," 2005.
76. Chen Li, "Holding 'China Inc.' Together: The CCP and The Rise of China's 'Yangqi,'" *The China Quarterly*, no. 228 (2016): 927–49, http://www.jstor.org/stable/26291583.
77. Carl W. Walter, and Fraser J. T. Howie, *Red Capitalism: The Fragile Financial Foundation of China's Extraordinary Rise* (Wiley, 2011), https://ci.nii.ac.jp/ncid/BB04996874.
78. Jie Gao, "China's Bank Reform and the Roles of Sovereign Wealth Fund," *Universität Potsdam*, November 2013, https://publishup.uni-potsdam.de/opus4-ubp/frontdoor/deliver/index/docId/6644/file/EFC_Jie_Gao_73_84.pdf.
79. Lamin Leigh and Podpiera Richard, "The Rise of Foreign Investment in China's Banks—Taking Stock," *The International Monetary Fund*, December 2006, https://www.imf.org/external/pubs/ft/wp/2006/wp06292.pdf.

80. "Introducing Qualified Strategic Investors to Promote Mutual Benefits for Chinese and Foreign Banks (引进合格战略投资者,促进中外资银行双赢)," *The Central People's Government of the People's Republic of China* (中央人民共和国中央人民政府), November 11, 2005, https://www.gov.cn/ztzl/2005-11/03/content_90094.htm.
81. Lamin Leigh and Podpiera Richard, "The Rise of Foreign Investment in China's Banks—Taking Stock," *The International Monetary Fund*, December 2006, https://www.imf.org/external/pubs/ft/wp/2006/wp06292.pdf.
82. Goldman Sachs, "Goldman Sachs Commemorates 150 Year History—China Telecom Privatization Shines through the Shadow of the Asian Financial Crisis," 2019, https://www.goldmansachs.com/our-firm/history/moments/1997-china-telecom-privatization.html.
83. "Industrial and Commercial Bank of China Limited—Global Offering," *Hong Kong Exchange*, October 16, 2006, https://www1.hkexnews.hk/listedco/listconews/sehk/2006/1016/ltn20061016000.htm.
84. CEIC Data, accessed April 21, 2023.
85. Julian Gewirtz, *Never Turn Back: China and the Forbidden History of the 1980s* (Belknap Press of Harvard University Press, 2022).
86. Hui Feng, *The Politics of China's Accession to the World Trade Organization: The Dragon Goes Global* (Routledge, 2005).
87. David Wall, "China and the WTO: The Role of the Private Sector," *The Journal of East Asian Affairs* 15, no. 1 (Spring/Summer 2001), https://www.jstor.org/stable/23255899.
88. Philip Levy, "The Treatment of Chinese SOEs in China's WTO Protocol of Accession," *Robert Schuman Centre for Advanced Studies*, April 2017, https://papers.ssrn.com/sol3/papers.cfm?abstract_id=2947668.
89. Zuijin Zhao, "Private Sector Development in the People's Republic of China," *Asian Development Bank Institute*, September 2004, https://www.adb.org/sites/default/files/publication/159390/adbi-private-sector-development-people-republic-china.pdf.

90. Bruce J. Dickson, "Integrating Wealth and Power in China: The Communist Party's Embrace of the Private Sector," *The China Quarterly*, no. 192 (2007): 827–54, http://www.jstor.org/stable/20192850.
91. Jiang Zemin, "Hold High the Banner of Deng Xiaoping Theory for an All-Around Advancement of the Cause of Building Socialism with Chinese Characteristics in the 21st Century," *The Beijing Review*, 1997, http://www.bjreview.com.cn/document/txt/2011-03/25/content_363499_5.htm.
92. Bruce J. Dickson, "Integrating Wealth and Power in China: The Communist Party's Embrace of the Private Sector," *The China Quarterly* 192, no. 12 (2007): 827–54, http://proxy.alumni.jhu.edu/login?url=https://www.proquest.com/scholarly-journals/integrating-wealth-power-china-communist-partys/docview/229494940/se-2.
93. Joseph Fewsmith, "Rethinking the Role of the CCP: Explicating Jiang Zemin's Party Anniversary Speech," *China Leadership Monitor* (December 2001), https://www.hoover.org/sites/default/files/uploads/documents/clm2_JF.pdf.
94. Barry Naughton, "A Perspective on Chinese Economics: What Have We Learned? What Did We Fail to Anticipate?" Edited by Anne Thurston, *Engaging China: Fifty Years of Sino-American Relations* (Columbia University Press, 2021).
95. The broad definition of private includes firms with foreign investment, firms with less than 5 million RMB in revenue, and firms that have mixed ownership but the dominant shareholder is designated as private. Nicholas Lardy, *Markets Over Mao: The Rise of Private Business in China* (Peterson Institute for International Economics, 2014).
96. Nicholas Lardy, *Markets Over Mao: The Rise of Private Business in China* (Peterson Institute for International Economics, 2014).
97. Lardy, *Markets Over Mao*, 2014.
98. Lardy, *Markets Over Mao*, 2014.
99. CEIC Data, accessed April 27, 2023.
100. CEIC Data, accessed April 25, 2023.
101. CEIC Data, accessed December 26, 2024.

102. State Council of the People's Republic of China, "Opinions on Encouraging, Supporting and Guiding the Development of Individual, Private, and Other Sectors of the Non-Public Economy (国务院关于鼓励支持和引导个体私营等非公有制经济发展的若干意见)," *The Central People's Government of the Peoples Republic of China* (中华人民共和国中央人民政府), August 12, 2005, http://www.gov.cn/zwgk/2005-08/12/content_21691.htm.
103. State Council of the People's Republic of China, "Opinions on Encouraging and Guiding the Healthy Development of Private Investment," *The Central People's Government of the People's Republic of China* (中华人民共和国中央人民政府), May 7, 2010, http://www.gov.cn/zhengce/content/2010-05/13/content_3569.htm.
104. Nicholas Lardy, *Markets Over Mao: The Rise of Private Business in China* (Peterson Institute for International Economics, 2014).
105. "National People's Congress, 2004 Amendments to the PRC Constitution," *USC US-China Institute*, March 14, 2004, https://china.usc.edu/national-peoples-congress-2004-amendments-prc-constitution.
106. Mo Zhang, "From Public to Private: The Newly Enacted Chinese Property Law and the Protection of Property Rights in China," *Berkeley Business Law Journal* 5 (2008): 317, https://heinonline.org/hol-cgi-bin/get_pdf.cgi?handle=hein.journals/berkbusj5&section=12.
107. Bruce J. Dickson, "Integrating Wealth and Power in China: The Communist Party's Embrace of the Private Sector," *The China Quarterly* 192 (12): 827–854, http://proxy.alumni.jhu.edu/login?url=https://www.proquest.com/scholarly-journals/integrating-wealth-power-china-communist-partys/docview/229494940/se-2.
108. Ligang Song, "State-Owned Enterprise Reform in China: Past, Present and Prospects," In *China's 40 Years of Reform and Development: 1978–2018*, edited by Ross Garnaut, Ligang Song, and Cai Fang (ANU Press, 2018), https://press-files.anu.edu.au/downloads/press/n4267/html/ch19.xhtml.

109. Hong Yung Lee, "Xiagang, the Chinese Style of Laying Off Workers," *Asian Survey* 40, no. 6 (2000): 914–37, https://doi.org/10.2307/3021195.
110. Zemin Jiang, "Full Text of Jiang Zemin's Report at the 16th Party Congress," *China.org*, November 2002, http://www.china.org.cn/english/2002/Nov/49107.htm.
111. Barry Naughton, "Top-Down Control: SASAC and the Persistence of State Ownership in China," *University of Nottingham*, June 23, 2006, https://www.nottingham.ac.uk/gep/documents/conferences/2006/june2006conf/naughton-june2006.pdf.
112. "Interim Regulations on the Supervision and Administration of Enterprise State-Owned Assets (企业国有资产监督管理暂行条例)," *The Central People's Government of the People's Republic of China* (中华人民共和国中央人民政府). May 2003, http://www.gov.cn/zwgk/2005-05/23/content_152.htm.
113. Barry Naughton, "The Transformation of the State Sector: SASAC, the Market Economy, and the New National Champions," Chapter In *State Capitalism, Institutional Adaptation, and the Chinese Miracle*, edited by Barry Naughton and Kellee S. Tsai, Comparative Perspectives in Business History (Cambridge University Press, 2015), 46–72, https://doi.org/10.1017/CBO9781139962858.003.
114. Mikael Mattlin, "Whose Money? The Tug-of-War over Chinese State Enterprise Profits," *The Finnish Institute of International Affairs*, April 2011, https://www.files.ethz.ch/isn/128535/UPI_Briefing_Paper_79.pdf.
115. Barry Naughton, "Top-Down Control: SASAC and the Persistence of State Ownership in China," *University of Nottingham*, June 23, 2006, https://www.nottingham.ac.uk/gep/documents/conferences/2006/june2006conf/naughton-june2006.pdf.
116. Wendy Leutert and Sarah Elaine Eaton, "Deepening Not Departure: Xi Jinping's Governance of China's State-Owned Economy," *The China Quarterly* 248 (S1): 200–21, https://doi.org/10.1017/s0305741021000795.
117. Wendy Leutert and Sarah Elaine Eaton, "Deepening Not Departure: Xi Jinping's Governance of China's State-Owned Economy," *The China Quarterly* 248 (S1): 200–21, https://doi.org/10.1017/s0305741021000795.

118. Meg Rithmire, "Going Out or Opting Out? Capital, Political Vulnerability, and the State in China's Outward Investment," *Harvard Business School*, April 2021, https://www.hbs.edu/ris/Publication%20Files/20-009_664c9264-f0ee-4e43-acbd-d5da9f08caf1.pdf.
119. Ligang Song, "State-Owned Enterprise Reform in China: Past, Present and Prospects," In *China's 40 Years of Reform and Development: 1978–2018*, edited by Ligang Song, Ross Garnaut, and Cai Fang, 345–74 (ANU Press, 2018), http://www.jstor.org/stable/j.ctv5cgbnk.27.
120. State Council of the People's Republic of China, "Guiding Opinion on Advancing the Adjustment of State-Owned Capital and Restructuring State-Owned Enterprises (关于推进国有资本调整和国有企业重组的指导意见)," *The Central People's Government of the People's Republic of China* (中华人民共和国中央人民政府, December 5, 2006, http://www.gov.cn/gongbao/content/2007/content_503385.htm.
121. Mikael Mattlin, "The Chinese Government's New Approach to Ownership and Financial Control of Strategic State-Owned Enterprises," BOFIT Discussion Paper No. 10/2007, April 13, 2007, https://ssrn.com/abstract=1001617.
122. The State-owned Assets Supervision and Administration Commission of the State Council, "The State-Owned Economy Should Maintain Absolute Control Over Seven Industries (国有经济应保持对七个行业的绝对控制力)," *The Central People's Government of the People's Republic of China* (中华人民共和国中央人民政府), December 18, 2006, http://www.gov.cn/jrzg/2006-12/18/content_472256.htm.
123. Nicholas Lardy, "Private Sector Development," In *China's 40 Years of Reform and Development: 1978–2018*, edited by Ross Garnaut, Ligang Song, and Cai Fang (ANU Press, 2018), https://press-files.anu.edu.au/downloads/press/n4267/html/ch19.xhtml.
124. Nicholas Borst, "China's Tech Rush: How the Country's Strategic Technology Campaign Is Shaping Markets," *Seafarer Capital Partners*, September 2018, https://www.seafarerfunds.com/commentary/chinas-tech-rush/.

125. Tai Ming Cheung, Thomas Mahnken, Deborah Seligsohn, Kevin Pollpeter, Eric Anderson, and Fan Yang, "Planning for Innovation: Understanding China's Plans for Technological, Energy, Industrial, and Defense Development," *University of California Institute on Global Conflict and Cooperation*, July 28, 2016, https://www.uscc.gov/sites/default/files/Research/Planning%20for%20Innovation%20-%20Understanding%20China%27s%20Plans%20for%20Tech%20Energy%20Industrial%20and%20Defense%20Development072816.pdf.
126. Adam Segal, "Innovation, Espionage, and Chinese Technology Policy," *The Council on Foreign Relations*, April 11, 2011, https://cdn.cfr.org/sites/default/files/pdf/2011/04/Segal%20HFA%20testimony.pdf.
127. The US-China Business Council, "China's Strategic Emerging Industries: Policy, Implementation, Challenges, & Recommendations," March 2013, https://www.uschina.org/sites/default/files/sei-report.pdf.
128. "Decision on Accelerating the Cultivation and Development of Strategic Emerging Industries (国务院关于加快培育和发展战略性新兴产业的决定)," *The Central People's Government of the Peoples Republic of China* (中华人民共和国中央人民政府), October 18, 2010, http://www.gov.cn/zwgk/2010-10/18/content_1724848.htm.
129. Barry Naughton, "A Political Economy of China's Economic Transition," Chapter In *China's Great Economic Transformation*, edited by Loren Brandt and Thomas G. Rawski, 91–135 (Cambridge University Press, 2008), https://doi.org/10.1017/CBO9780511754234.005.
130. "Wen Jiabao Delivers a Special Message at the World Economic Forum Annual Meeting 2009," *The Ministry of Foreign Affairs of the People's Republic of China*, January 29, 2009, https://www.fmprc.gov.cn/mfa_eng/xw/zyjh/202405/t20240530_11340045.html.
131. Hank Paulson, *Dealing with China: An Insider Unmasks the New Economic Superpower* (Twelve, 2015).

132. Jikun Huang, Huayong Zhi, Zhurong Huang, Scott Rozelle, and John Giles, "The Impact of the Global Financial Crisis on Off-farm Employment and Earnings in Rural China," *The World Bank—Policy Research Working Paper*, October 2010, https://documents1.worldbank.org/curated/en/416571468167981075/pdf/WPS5439.pdf.
133. Nicholas Borst, "SOE Reform in China—Implications for Policymakers and Investors," *Seafarer Capital Partners*, March 2021, https://www.seafarerfunds.com/prevailing-winds/soe-reform-in-china-implications-for-policymakers-and-investors/.
134. Rongrong Li, "Speech at the National Conference on Supervision and Administration of State-owned Assets (李荣融在全国国有资产监督管理工作会议上的讲话)," *State-owned Assets Supervision and Administration Commission of the State Council*, December 24, 2009, http://www.sasac.gov.cn/n2588020/n2588072/n2591482/n2591484/c3734752/content.html.
135. Rush Doshi, *The Long Game* (Oxford University Press EBooks, 2021), https://doi.org/10.1093/oso/9780197527917.001.0001.
136. Nicholas Lardy, *Markets Over Mao: The Rise of Private Business in China* (Peterson Institute for International Economics, 2014).
137. Center for Strategic and International Studies, "Firmly March on the Path of Socialism With Chinese Characteristics and Strive to Complete the Building of a Moderately Prosperous Society in All Respects—Report to the Eighteenth National Congress of the Communist Party of China," November 8, 2012, https://interpret.csis.org/translations/firmly-march-on-the-path-of-socialism-with-chinese-characteristics-and-strive-to-complete-the-building-of-a-moderately-prosperous-society-in-all-respects-report-to-the-eighteenth-national-cong/.

CHAPTER 3

Xi Jinping's New Era for the Economy

The prevailing narrative about Xi Jinping is that he has steered the Chinese economy in a profoundly different and more state-driven direction. This change in trajectory has created a sense of whiplash as many foreign observers expected Xi Jinping to be a strong economic reformer based on his background. Some of the hopes placed upon Xi were a reaction to the disappointment of the Hu Jintao era, where new reforms seemed to slow to a crawl. The belief that Xi would be a strong reformer was further strengthened when many analysts interpreted his first major set of economic policies as a breakthrough for market forces. Hopes began to fade around 2015 as many of those reforms failed to be implemented and support for the state sector grew stronger. Many observers now feel a sense of jilted disappointment as Xi has shifted China toward greater state control and away from the market-driven reforms they had anticipated.

This chapter will argue that the reality of the situation is more complicated. Xi's policies began largely as a continuation of his predecessors but evolved into a significant departure that has put China on a new economic trajectory. To explore this evolution, this chapter will focus on four main assertions. The first argument is that Xi Jinping's view on the correct balance between the state and market forces shares a common ideological throughline with Deng Xiaoping, Chen Yun, Jiang Zemin, and Hu Jintao. Like his predecessors, Xi believes that while market forces were essential to China's development, the Party should guide the economy and that SOEs should continue to be large and influential.

The second argument is that Xi's early policy agenda was misinterpreted by many observers as a strong embrace of market-oriented economic reform. Key among the misconceptions was that the Third Plenum, which called for a "decisive" role for the market, signaled a more liberal shift in the Party's approach to managing the economy. In fact, Xi's early economic policies continued to stake out a strong role for both SOEs and state intervention in the economy.

The third argument is that Xi's reassertion of state control was done as a response to a series of high-profile financial risks that buffeted the economy between 2015–2018. Faced with economic challenges, Xi adjusted policies to restrict markets and private firms. These policies were damaging and disruptive to the private sector, but not without precedent. Xi's actions echoed prior periods where the Party undertook efforts to put the bird back in the cage.

Finally, this chapter will argue that Xi's economic policies have now departed from the historical cycle of restriction and relaxation that characterized China's Reform Era. The reason behind this is less about ideological change by Xi or within the Party, but rather a sharp deterioration in U.S.-China relations. Xi has embraced a more interventionist role in the economy as a geostrategic imperative given the threats he believes China faces. Xi believes the Party must guide the economy toward supporting national security goals for China to prevail in its strategic competition with the United States.

This chapter is interspersed with case studies of individual companies, both state-owned and private, that Xi's policies have impacted. These case studies are instructive because they provide a lens to understand how the Party intervenes in the economy to achieve its goals.

1   Xi's Rise to Power

A review of Xi's background and upbringing provides clues regarding his approach to governance and managing the economy. Xi was born as a princeling, an elite group of the children of high-ranking communist officials. His father, Xi Zhongxun, joined the Communist Party in 1928 and was a revolutionary in the 1930s and 1940s. After the Party took control of China, he served in various high-ranking Party and government posts. However, the Xi family's role in the upper echelons of power came to an abrupt end when the elder Xi was purged from office in 1962 when Xi Jinping was only ten years old. A few years later, Xi Zhongxun was further abused during the purges of officials in the Cultural Revolution. Xi Jinping and his family members were targeted because of their father, subjected to denunciation, jailing, and threats of violence. The turmoil of the Cultural Revolution split apart Xi's family and he was sent down to the countryside along with millions of youths in China to labor as agricultural workers. It was a dramatic upheaval for a youth born into power and privilege.

Accounts of his life indicate that these years were formative, creating a profound aversion to chaos and disorder.[1] Xi survived the turmoil of his youth by becoming "redder than red" and embracing a view that the Party must be powerful and unified to ensure social stability and national strength.[2] While many of his princeling peers eschewed politics in favor of business, Xi sought to join the Party despite his father's continuing political difficulties. Xi's application for Party membership was rejected nine times before being accepted.[3]

After the death of Mao, Xi's father was among the many fallen officials who were restored to power by the 1978 Third Plenum. The elder Xi became one of China's leading economic reformers during the late 1970s and 1980s. Deng Xiaoping chose him as the head of Guangdong province, and in that role, Xi Zhongxun was responsible for establishing Shenzhen as China's first special economic zone (SEZ). Though he embraced economic reform, Xi Zhongxun was similar to Deng Xiaoping and China's other reformers in his view that despite its failings and missteps, the Party was essential in restoring China's national greatness.[4]

After his seven-year stint in the countryside during the Cultural Revolution, Xi Jinping was admitted to China's prestigious Tsinghua University. He then secured an appointment as an aide to a high-ranking PLA official. After several years of building connections in the PLA, he sought an appointment as a local official in the provinces to establish his political credentials. Over the next two decades, Xi served in various provincial postings, including Fujian, Zhejiang, and Shanghai. During his early career, he garnered a reputation for avoiding controversy and not making enemies.[5] His governance record was as unremarkable and cautious.[6] When scandals did emerge under his watch, such as a large-scale smuggling scandal in Fujian while he was a high-ranking local official, Xi managed to avoid being implicated in any wrongdoing.[7]

Early in his career, Xi generally avoided public statements about his personal views. In occasional contributions to written publications, Xi did express his perspective on the market and socialism. Xi rejected both a dogmatic approach to socialism and a wholesale embrace of liberal economic reform. According to Xi, China should use the market to expand the economy's productive capacity and advance socialism while resisting the negative aspects of capitalism.[8] Furthermore, Xi emphasized the role of the proper balance between the government and market forces and the necessity to avoid corrupt entanglements between Party officials and entrepreneurs.[9] Despite these concerns, while serving as Party Secretary of Zhejiang, Xi reportedly supported the growth and development of the province's large private sector firms.[10]

Xi entered the upper echelons of Chinese power in 2007 when he was appointed to the Politburo Standing Committee. For years, there had been an unspoken competition between Xi and Li Keqiang, another rapidly rising party official, over who would get the top spot.[11] Both men represented different factions within the Party and were appointed to the Standing Committee that year. As stated above, Xi was a member of the princeling faction while Li rose to power through the Communist Youth League. Xi's higher ranking within the group, sixth in rank as opposed to seventh for Li, put him ahead of Li in the race to succeed Hu Jintao as the next General Secretary.[12] The following year, he was appointed vice president.

As heir apparent, Xi was cautious about expressing his personal views, absent an uncharacteristic outburst in Mexico about foreigners criticizing China.[13] However, there were two significant developments underway during those years that appear to have shaped Xi's thinking, as evidenced by his later policy priorities. First was a pervasive sense among both intellectuals and Chinese society at large that the government had become undisciplined and mired in corruption.[14] Disorder and corruption in the Party significantly undermined its ability to implement policies. Officials in local governments could not be trusted to reliably follow the central government's directives because they were instead pursuing their own personal business interests. Land transactions were a major source of corruption for officials and firms connected to the family members.[15] This corruption seeped into the highest levels of Chinese politics. In 2014, Zhou Bin, the son of Politburo Standing Committee member Zhou Yongkang, was arrested for acquiring billions of dollars of land and coal mines from the government at below market prices.[16]

This situation at SOEs was similarly problematic. Instead of reforming their enterprises to become more efficient and reliable contributors to national policy, SOE managers used their positions to enrich themselves. Inextricably linked to these problems was a growing cohort of politically connected private entrepreneurs, often the children of high-ranking Party members, who used personal connections with government officials to build wealth. By the time Xi took power, it was an open secret that many children and grandchildren of senior Party members were extremely wealthy, almost certainly due to their families' political connections.[17] Xi believed China needed strong centralized leadership to combat the disorder and corruption.[18]

The second development that appears to have shaped Xi's views during this period were changing perceptions toward the United States among China's leaders. As the global financial crisis engulfed the U.S. economy in 2007 and 2008, there was a consensus in the Party that the balance of power was shifting in China's favor.[19] As outlined in the prior chapter, China's leaders were stunned to see the U.S. financial system brought to the brink of collapse. The American economy looked like it depended on debt-fueled consumption and risky financial engineering. The wrenching domestic political fights in the United States over the response to the crisis further reinforced the view that America's fractious political system was incapable of meeting the challenges it faced. In contrast, the Chinese government responded to the financial crisis with a massive fiscal stimulus, swiftly returning to rapid growth in 2009. The readout from the December 2009 Central Economic Work Conference triumphantly stated that despite the global financial crisis and a worldwide recession, the Party and Government had led the economy to recovery and demonstrated the advantages of the socialist system.[20]

Xi's public statements about foreign policy and the United States were generally quite circumspect. However, one internal Party report, never officially released to the public but subsequently leaked, provides another window into Xi's thinking at the outset of his tenure. The infamous Document 9, issued by the Central Party Office in April 2013, is a broad-ranging screed against Western influence in China and its alleged threats to the Party and socialism. The report lashes out against neoliberals who seek to loosen macroeconomic controls and privatize SOEs to "weaken the government's control of the economy."[21] Furthermore, the document denounces both critics who say China's reforms have gone too far and deviated from socialism and those who say China should reform according to Western standards. It finishes by calling for an across the board increase in ideological control over public opinion and the media. The document, which could not have been published without the approval of Xi, showed the Party's underlying fears about an economic slowdown, Western ideological competition, and public dissatisfaction from corruption.[22]

2 Xi's Early Economic Agenda

The triumphal mood in Beijing about the superiority of China's economic model would not persist for long. By the time Xi assumed power in 2012, the hangover effects of China's massive stimulus in 2008 were weighing heavily on the economy. When the global economy entered a recession at the end of 2008, demand from China's main export markets, the United States and Europe, declined steeply. By the beginning of 2009, the global slowdown was having a significant impact on employment in China, with an estimated 20 million migrant workers losing their jobs and returning to the countryside.[23]

In response to the global financial stimulus, the Chinese government acted aggressively, announcing a RMB 4 trillion stimulus package and giving banks the green light to expand lending greatly. Between 2008 and 2011, the amount of outstanding credit doubled.[24] The impact of this stimulus and lending helped the Chinese economy rapidly recover but also led to fears among policymakers and economists about overheating and inflation. Nevertheless, the swift recovery of the Chinese economy stood in stark contrast to the United States, which was mired in a deep recession.

Stimulus Hangover: By 2012, China's economic picture began to change. The economy was slowing, and there were growing concerns that excessive credit growth had created significant financial risks. In an environment of loose credit conditions, a vast and extensive shadow banking system had emerged. Shadow banking is a term to describe the growth of borrowing and lending activities outside of the traditional banking system. Shadow banking is risky because it often occurs in areas of the market that are not well-regulated. Chinese banks, bound by prudential restrictions for on-balance-sheet lending, began finding new ways to extend credit off-balance sheet. As shown in Fig. 1, shadow banking, defined as credit growth outside of traditional, well-regulated channels, proliferated after the global financial crisis. Shadow banking created a web of murky liabilities within the financial system and made it difficult to determine how exposed banks were to financial risks. One high-level official at a Chinese bank described the growth of one type of popular shadow banking products, wealth management products, as "fundamentally a Ponzi scheme."[25]

The rapid credit expansion had been necessary to buoy the Chinese economy amid falling external demand. Between 2009 and 2014, China's net exports were either flat or negative. Household consumption in China was low as a share of GDP and, therefore, struggled to be a significant driver of growth. Thus, to keep the economy growing rapidly, China dramatically increased domestic investment in infrastructure and real estate.

The increase in investment successfully maintained growth, but it came at a cost. To finance high investment rates, local governments borrowed heavily through off-balance sheet vehicles. The debt of these

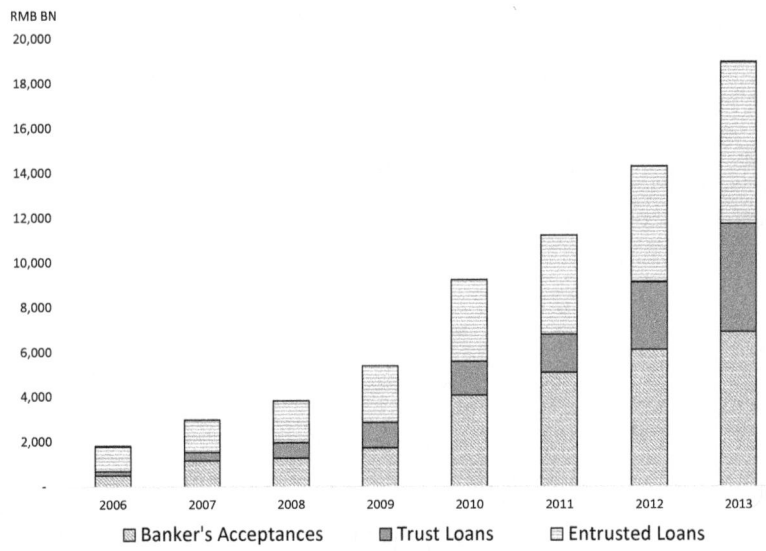

Fig. 1 Growth of shadow banking products in China, 2006–2013 (*Source* People's Bank of China)

local government financing vehicles (LGFVs) rapidly spiraled upwards. To get a handle on the situation, the central government's National Audit Office twice launched nationwide audits of local government debts. By the middle of 2013, local government had incurred debts equal to a third of GDP despite legal restrictions prohibiting them from borrowing.[26]

The imbalances in the Chinese economy—too much investment and insufficient consumption—were exacerbated by the economic stimulus. As shown in Fig. 2, the investment share of gross domestic product (GDP), already at high levels, grew even further relative to household consumption. Thus, as Xi took power at the end of 2012, he inherited a difficult economic situation. According to Xi's own recounting, the economy faced a "shift in growth rate, a painful structural adjustment, and a need to absorb the fallout from previous stimulus policies."[27] The economy was facing both short-term financial risks and worsening long-term structural imbalances.

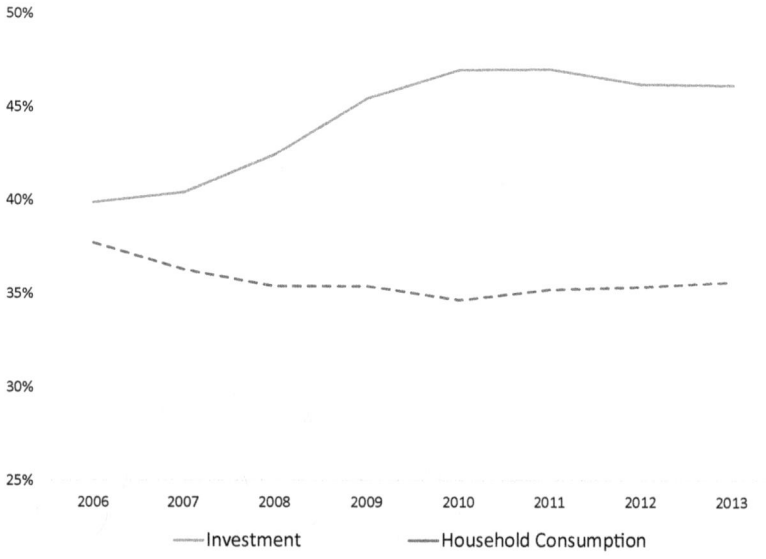

Fig. 2 Investment and household consumption share of GDP, 2006–2013 (*Source* China National Bureau of Statistics)

The Third Plenum: The major unveiling of Xi's economic priorities occurred in November 2013 during the Third Plenum of the 18th Party Congress. The third plenum refers to the third meeting of the central committee for each five-year Party Congress. Third plenums have had a special significance since Deng Xiaoping launched reform and opening in 1978 at the Third Plenum of the 11th Party Congress. Subsequent third plenums in 1984 and 1992 also contained critical economic reforms.[28]

Xi was named General Secretary at the conclusion of the 18th Party Congress in 2012. By November 2013, Xi had a year to formulate his economic plans. A document called a communiqué is released in conjunction with the meeting and summarizes many of the decisions made. The communiqué issued after the 2013 Third Plenum was notable for the new language is contained about the role of the market in the economy. The role of the market had been upgraded to playing a "decisive role" in allocation of resources in the economy.

> The underlying issue is how to strike a balance between the role of the government and that of the market, and let the market play the decisive role in allocating resources and let the government play its functions better.[29]

Expectations that Xi would guide policymaking in the direction of more economic reforms were further bolstered by a major policy document released after the plenum—the Decision of the Central Committee of the Communist Party of China on Some Major Issues Concerning Comprehensively Deepening the Reform[30] An implementation-focused report issued after the Communiqué, detailed a long list of new market-based policies and reforms. The Decisions document provided further details on what it meant to let the market play a decisive role in the economy and adjust the role of the government.

> It is a general rule of the market economy that the market decides the allocation of resources. We have to follow this rule when we improve the socialist market economy. We should work hard to address the problems of market imperfection, too much government interference, and poor oversight.
> The main responsibility and role of the government is to maintain the stability of the macro-economy, strengthen and improve public services, safeguard fair competition, strengthen oversight of the market, maintain

market order, promote sustainable development and common prosperity, and intervene in situations where market failure occurs.[31]

Many observers, including the author, viewed the new language about the role of the market and the list of proposed reforms as significant, signaling a greater emphasis on the role of the market and less government interference in the economy.[32]

However, in retrospect, it has become clear that the Third Plenum represented less of a change than was hoped at the time. The themes of control and guidance of the economy by the Party are prevalent throughout the Communiqué and Decision documents, as is an emphasis on the important role of SOEs. For example, the Communiqué for the plenum leaves no doubt about the Party's goals of maintaining its approach toward controlling the economy:

> What is the most important is to uphold the leadership of the Party, adhere to the Party's basic line, reject both the old and rigid closed-door policy and any attempt to abandon socialism and take an erroneous path, firmly take the socialist road and ensure that our reform is in the right direction.[33]

The Party's basic line, mentioned above, is to focus on economic development, persist in reform and opening, and maintain the Four Cardinal Principles outlined by Deng Xiaoping in 1979. The Four Cardinal Principles, as discussed in the prior chapter, was a statement by Deng of the red lines that could not be crossed or challenged as China pursued modernization, including the absolute rule of the Communist Party and a commitment to socialism.

The Plenum Communiqué also emphasizes that while the Party was seeking to carve out more space for the private sector, and SOEs would continue to play a dominant role:

> We must unswervingly consolidate and develop the public economy, persist in the dominant position of public ownership, give full play to the leading role of the state-owned sector, and continuously increase its vitality, controlling force and influence. We must unwaveringly encourage, support, and guide the development of the non-public sector, and stimulate its dynamism and creativity.[34]

Included in the Decisions document was a long series of significant economic and legal reforms relating to state firms. SOEs were to be reformed into more market-oriented entities, called state-owned capital investment operations, but their ultimate role was still to support national policy initiatives.

> State-owned capital investment operations must serve the strategic goals of the state, invest more in key industries and areas that are vital to national security and are the lifeblood of the economy, focusing on offering public services, developing important and forward-looking strategic industries, protecting the ecological environment, supporting scientific and technological progress, and guaranteeing national security.[35]

Further shedding light on Xi's thinking, the Decisions document was accompanied by a lengthy explanatory note under Xi's personal authorship.[36] In the note, Xi laid out his views on the economy in great detail. He wrote that economic reform was necessary to achieve China's goals of national rejuvenation and that the economy was threatened by "unbalanced, uncoordinated and unsustainable development."

In the Explanatory Note, Xi acknowledged the importance of the market and the need to adjust the role of the government when it conflicted with economic development.

> Both theory and practice have proved that the allocation of resources by the market is the most effective means to this end. It is a general rule of the market economy that the market decides the allocation of resources, and a market economy in essence is one in which the market determines resource allocation. We have to follow this rule when we improve the socialist market economy. We should work harder to address the problems of market imperfection, too much government interference, and lack of oversight.[37]

However, Xi also indicated that he thought there were limits to this approach.

> Our market economy is of a socialist nature, of course. We need to give leverage to the superiority of our socialist system, and let the Party and government perform their positive functions. The market plays a decisive role in allocating resources, but is not the sole actor in this regard.[38]

Xi also emphasized his view that SOEs should continue to play an influential role in the economy:

> It is emphasized in the Decision that we must unswervingly consolidate and develop the public economy, persist in the dominant position of public ownership, give full play to the leading role of the state-owned economy, and incessantly increase its vitality, control, and influence.[39]

Foreshadowing his future crackdown on the tech sector, Xi also gave a hint of his discomfort with China's freewheeling internet sector:

> With fast growth in the users of micro-blogs, WeChat and other social network services and instant communication tools, which spread information quickly and can mobilize large numbers of users, how to strengthen oversight within a legal framework and guide public opinion, and how to ensure the orderly dissemination of online information, while at the same time safeguarding national security and social stability have become pressing problems for us.[40]

From the three documents, the Communiqué, the Decisions document, and the Explanatory Note from Xi himself, it is possible to discern Xi's views on the market at the outset of his rule. Xi recognized that the pattern of economic development over the past decade had created severe imbalances in the economy. To address these imbalances, it was necessary to give the market greater play within the economy, allowing it to play a decisive role. However, in his Explanatory Note, Xi indicates that there will be limits on the extent to which the market will determine outcomes, and the Party should continue to play a critical role in overall leadership in the economy.

Additionally, there is no indication that Xi would deviate from his predecessors in seeking to preserve and strengthen SOEs. It is clear from the documents that Xi and the Party continued to believe that SOEs were a critical part of the Chinese economy and that they should be used to advance the Party's policy priorities.

Xi's economic policy agenda, as outlined during the Third Plenum, offered new economic reforms and a greater role for the market in determining prices within the economy. However, his agenda also maintained a high degree of ideological continuity with the core policies advocated by the Party for decades—an economy guided by the Party and a bulwark of SOEs that would implement the Party's policy priorities.

3 Grey Rhinos and Black Swans

Beginning in 2013, China experienced a series of major financial and economic disruptions. These disruptions shook the confidence of Xi and many in the Party regarding the stability of the domestic economy and financial system. They also cast doubt on the reliability of the private sector in delivering stable and predictable growth. As a result, many of the economic reforms outlined by the Third Plenum were later abandoned.

While Xi entered office calling for a more significant role for the market, after a few years both his and the Party's rhetoric about the economy shifted dramatically. Party and government officials began discussing economic issues increasingly in terms of risk. Official media started to refer to two distinct types of risk facing the Chinese economy.[41] The first were "Grey Rhinos," known threats that China was unprepared for. The second were "Black Swans," unpredictable crises for which no preparation is possible. The change in rhetoric reflected the Party's defensive reaction to economic volatility and a souring on further economic liberalization. It also set the stage for a dramatic crackdown on private enterprises and a resurgence of government control over the economy in 2016 and 2017.

Interbank Financing Crunch: The first financial disruption occurred before the Third Plenum reform agenda was finalized. In June 2013, rates in the Chinese interbank bond market suddenly soared. As credit expanded rapidly following the 2008 stimulus, interbank lending increased substantially. Banks, usually smaller and regional banks, borrowed heavily in the interbank market to lend more than what their deposit bases could support. The availability of cheap and plentiful capital in the interbank market soon became a dependency for many banks. The People's Bank of China precipitated the crunch. The central bank sought to clamp down on excessive credit growth by withholding its typical liquidity injections into the market.[42] However, this caused liquidity conditions to deteriorate and interest rates to skyrocket (Fig. 3). The stock market fell precipitously, and rumors swirled that several banks were facing severe financing problems. After a prolonged silence, the PBOC again injected liquidity into the system to prevent widespread defaults. The interbank market turmoil exposed that many Chinese banks were vulnerable to a funding crisis.

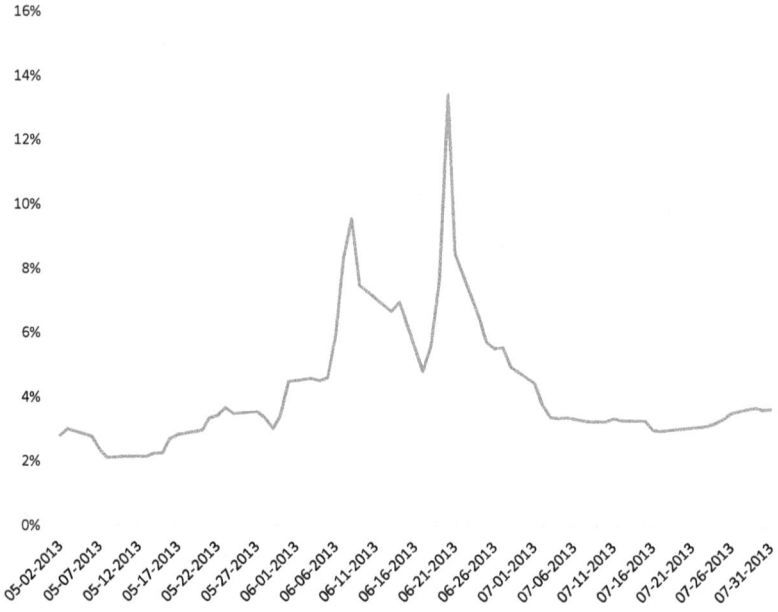

Fig. 3 SHIBOR overnight rate, May 15–July 16, 2013 (*Source* China National Interbank Funding Center)

The Housing Market Downturn: In 2014, China's housing market began to slow abruptly. By 2015, the slowdown had turned into a sharp correction. As shown in Fig. 4, the construction of new residential housing collapsed, showing negative year-on-year growth in 2015. After many years of rapid growth, China faced a significant housing glut. Property developers had built far more apartments than were required by the population. The excess apartments were either sitting empty or purchased by speculators. As demand slowed, prices began to fall. Some analysts speculated that China faced an unprecedented housing bubble that could lead to a financial crisis. Beyond the financial risks, weakness in the real estate market threatened the overall economy. Real estate played a central role as both a driver of GDP growth and a source of revenue for local governments. As discussed in Chapter 2, the central government implemented a major fiscal reform in the early 1990s that directed more tax revenues toward Beijing at the expense of the provinces. This led to growing financial problems for local governments as they attempted to fund growing demands for infrastructure and social spending amid a smaller share of total tax revenues. To manage their growing revenue shortfall, local governments turned to land sales as one of the tools available to increase their tax revenues. In 2012, land sale revenue and land-related tax revenue were equal to more than a third of total local government income.[43] Thus, the property slowdown not only put pressure on property developers and industries linked to the real estate market, but also undermined the finances of local governments.

To arrest the property market decline, Chinese authorities increased lending and began to implement spending programs. The central bank took action by cutting mortgage rates. In August 2014, the Chinese government announced a large expansion of the shantytown redevelopment program for the next three years.[44] The program, which targeted rundown housing in low-income areas, sought to build 18 million new homes between 2015 and 2017.[45] To finance the program, the China

Fig. 4 Growth residential floor space under construction, 2012–2017(YoY, YTD) (*Source* China National Bureau of Statistics)

Development Bank, People's Bank of China, and state-owned commercial banks funded property developers.[46] The program was a significant injection of demand into the market, either through cash payments to residents or by providing a new home. By 2017, the property market had recovered, and high levels of speculative activity resumed. Government intervention to boost demand had successfully revived housing activity, but it had not resolved the underlying problem of the property bubble. The Chinese government would continue to see housing as a market that needed to be tightly managed and guided by the government and not one where the market would play a decisive role.

Stock Market and Currency Turmoil: The turmoil in the interbank market and the housing market downturn would soon be overshadowed by even larger problems. 2015 and 2016 would prove to be a turning point for Xi's economic policies as significant volatility in the stock market and exchange rate threatened China's financial stability. Left unchecked, these problems would undermine China's economic and social stability. A precipitous decline in financial markets might destroy the wealth of households and shake confidence in the economy. If a severe financial crisis were to occur, it could derail the entire economy and lead to large-scale unemployment. While not abandoning his rhetoric around reform and the decisive role of the market, Xi also emphasized that in response to turmoil in the financial market, the state must assert its role as a "visible hand" to guide the market back toward "self-correction and adjustment."[47]

In mid-2014, China's domestic stock market experienced a surge, fueled in part by a sharp rise in margin lending.[48] By 2015, the stock market mania reached a crescendo. As shown in Fig. 5, the stock market index increased by more than 50% from the start of the year through mid-June, with an even steeper growth in margin lending. State media fueled the speculation, arguing that stocks could rise even further.[49] The stock market boom was cheered on by government officials, including the head of the Securities Regulatory Commission.[50]

The stock market mania came to an abrupt end during the summer of 2015. Prices peaked in June and then tumbled due to overstretched valuations and new draft regulations from the CSRC that sought to restrict margin lending. In July, Chinese regulators announced new steps to restrict the flow of shadow banking funds into the stock market, putting further pressure on the market.[51] Around 1,500 companies, with market capitalization representing about half of the total market, suspended trading their stocks.[52]

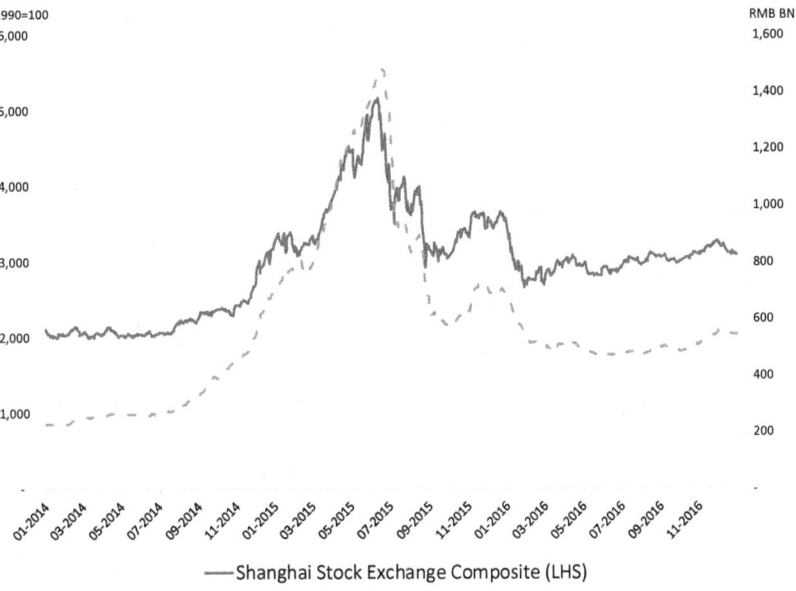

Fig. 5 Shanghai stock exchange composite index and margin lending outstanding, 2014–2016 (*Source* Shanghai Stock Exchange)

While the Chinese stock market had always been volatile, the market turmoil in 2015 was unprecedented in terms of the overall financial losses. Chinese authorities implemented a draconian series of market restrictions in response to market pressures. A group of Chinese state-owned financial institutions, the so-called "national team," purchased the shares of thousands of companies, spending RMB 1.6 trillion to support the market.[53] Chinese regulators also imposed restrictions on selling for large shareholders, limited net selling by brokerage firms, suspended new IPOs, and restricted short selling to support share prices.[54] Perhaps most disturbingly, the Chinese government began to arrest individuals it viewed as contributing to market volatility, accusing them of illegal trading, stock price manipulation, and spreading false market information.[55] Xu Xiang, one of China's most prominent investors, was arrested for insider trading in dramatic fashion after police sealed off the 22-mile Hangzhou Bay Bridge to capture him.[56] The Party severely restricted negative media coverage of the stock market rout. The efforts of the national team did little to staunch the decline in equity prices, with many of its members soon coming under investigation for insider trading related to their purchases.[57]

Seemingly unaware of the potential impact of its actions, the central bank made matters worse in the midst of the crisis. On August 11, the central bank announced a change to the exchange rate mechanism for the yuan that led to additional market volatility.[58] The central parity rate, also known as the fixing rate, is a set exchange rate versus the dollar around which limited fluctuations were allowed to occur. The change to the central parity rate was intended to make the exchange rate more responsive to market forces, pushing the currency toward more flexibility. However, given the ongoing financial stresses in the economy, the move rattled markets and led traders to speculate that the Chinese government was trying to devalue the currency. The depreciation led to another sharp fall in equity prices and more pressure on the exchange rate. As shown in Fig. 6, the currency depreciated sharply over the next year and a half.

Like with the equity market, the response to capital outflows was severe. The central bank introduced a "counter-cyclical factor" which would guide it toward greater intervention in the currency market, undermining previous reforms to let the currency move more freely. As shown in Fig. 7, starting in July 2015 through the end of 2016, China experienced a massive upsurge in financial outflows. China would use nearly 1 trillion USD of its foreign exchange reserves to prevent the currency from collapsing further. To combat outflows, Chinese authorities implemented a slew of new capital account restrictions, including heightened scrutiny of outbound investment and slow approval of the repatriation of funds by foreign companies operating in China.[59]

New types of financial risks also proliferated during this period. One new area of risk was the thousands of peer-to-peer (P2P) lending platforms that had been established over the past few years. These platforms allowed users to make small-scale loans to small businesses and individual borrowers. P2P lending platforms addressed a gap in the Chinese financial system by giving small borrowers, often overlooked by banks, access to credit. However, P2P lending platforms also did little to prevent malicious borrowers from overloading on debt they never intended to repay. P2P lending platforms soon had tens of billions in outstanding loans. In late 2015, one of the most prominent and largest platforms, Ezubao, imploded. Ezubao had raised over 9 billion USD-equivalent

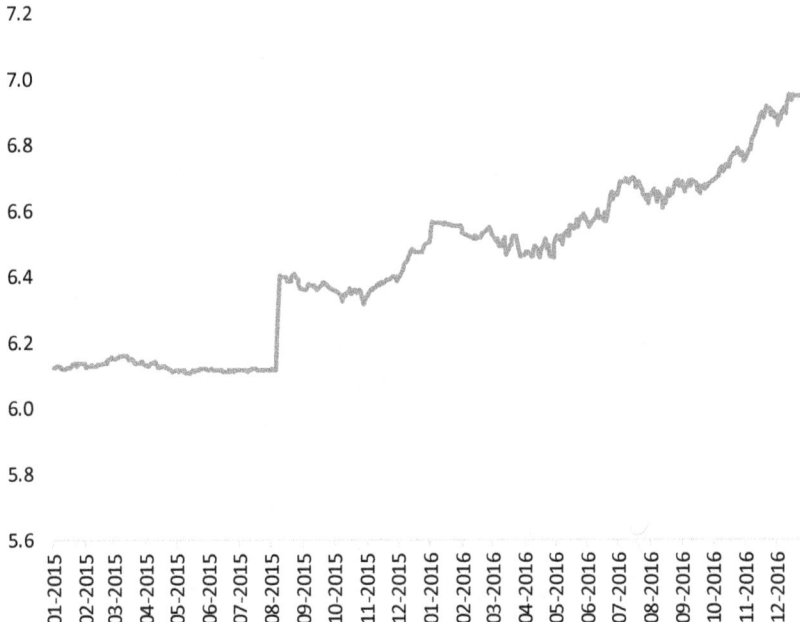

Fig. 6 RMB/USD Central parity rate (*Source* China Foreign Exchange Trading Center)

from Chinese retail investors. The company sought to increase its credibility by advertising in state-controlled media and courting government officials.[60] Chinese authorities began investigating the company after rumors of it being a Ponzi scheme emerged. Soon after, Ezubao froze investors' accounts and ceased operation. Some of Ezubao's 900,000 individual investors began protesting in cities across China, demanding that the government take action to return their funds. The founder of Ezubao, along with his brother, received life sentences for their roles in the scheme. In the following years, most P2P platforms would shut down due to bankruptcy and regulatory pressure.

The turmoil that had occurred in the financial markets and the currency reportedly soured Xi Jinping on pursuing additional economic reforms.[61] Xi viewed the economic volatility as a political fiasco, and it reinforced his view that stability was paramount.[62] The economic reforms outlined in the Third Plenum began to recede from view. The focus of

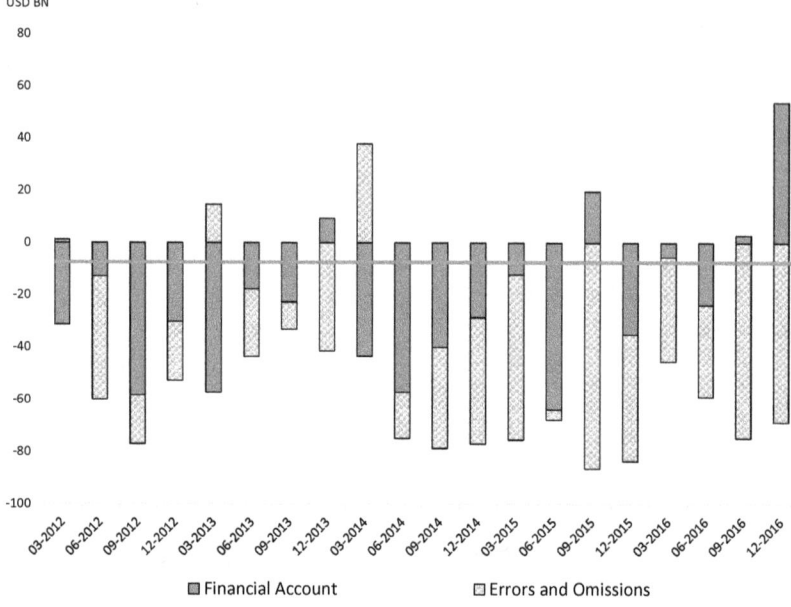

Fig. 7 China capital outlfows, 2012–2016 (*Source* China State Administration of Foreign Exchange)

policymaking began to decisively shift toward risk reduction and greater government control over the economy.

The Regulatory Windstorm: Four years into his rule, Xi Jinping's perception of growing financial risks prompted him to take dramatic action. In December 2016, China's Central Economic Work Conference, chaired by Xi, emphasized that the country faced accumulating financial risks, called for reducing corporate debt, and denounced speculation in the housing market.[63] China's financial minister from 2013–2016 would later describe the capital markets during this period as "severely chaotic."[64] In February 2017, Guo Shuqing was appointed head of the China Banking Regulatory Commission and launched a large number of new financial regulations that would be referred to as the "Regulatory Windstorm."

Highlighting the urgency, in April 2017, Xi chaired a special meeting on financial risks for the politburo that included the Governor of the

People's Bank of China and the heads of all the financial regulatory agencies. During the meeting, he declared that controlling financial risks was a matter of national security.[65] The meeting represented Xi's official backing for a regulatory crackdown, imbuing China's regulators with much-needed authority to tackle financial risks.

In July 2017, China created a new government body, the Financial Stability and Development Committee, to combat financial risks and coordinate the work of financial regulators. In his speech to the new body, Xi again compared financial and national security risks, and called for strengthening the Party's leadership over the financial system and enhancing party committees within companies.[66] In December 2017, China's government declared that combatting financial risks was one of the "three critical battles" to be fought over the next three years.[67]

The financial crackdown that unfolded over the next several years profoundly impacted the Chinese economy. Chinese regulators issued a flurry of new regulations for the banking, insurance, and asset management industries. The banking regulator announced a special campaign against "financial risks," "chaos," and "lawbreaking," targeted at banks and asset management companies.[68] The insurance industry was subject to a regulatory clampdown on selling insurance products that regulators viewed as vehicles for financial speculation rather than insuring risk.[69] Regulators forced the asset management industry to adopt strict new rules to reduce risks in wealth management products and other new financial products.[70] The rapid and draconian reshaping of industries in response to a perceived threat would foreshadow the technology crackdown that occurred in 2020 and 2021.

Private Sector Financing Crunch: The financial crackdown was paradoxical because while regulators sought to reduce risks in the financial system, they ended up creating new ones. The root of the problem was that China's formal banking system remained skewed toward large borrowers and SOEs. While shadow banking is risky, it had grown rapidly to meet the demands of borrowers underserved by the banking system. It served as a lifeline for many small and medium enterprises, charging high rates but offering credit when many state-owned financial institutions would not. The financial crackdown led to a collapse of peer-to-peer lending platforms, bankers' acceptances, and loans from non-bank financial institutions, all critical sources of financing for private firms. As shadow banking activity declined, a financing crunch emerged for private firms, as the formal financial system continued to overlook them. Consequently, financial risks increased as these firms struggled to secure access to credit.

By late 2018, it was clear that the financial crackdown was significantly impacting growth. The Shanghai and Shenzhen Stock Markets fell by nearly 25% in 2018. Official statistics showed that while the economy was slowing, full-year growth for the year was the lowest recorded in 28 years. Unofficial efforts to estimate China's growth show several economic activity indicators falling sharply into negative territory in the second half of 2018.[71]

The financial crackdown exposed deep structural distortions within the Chinese economy. The Party's push for greater control over the perceived "chaos" in the financial sector unintentionally damaged the private sector, which had been the main engine of economic growth. Faced with mounting economic pressures, policymakers began emphasizing the need to support access to credit for private companies and seeking to restore confidence in markets. In response, the People's Bank of China (PBOC) implemented several measures to support the private sector. These included cutting the required reserve ratio four times, with some of the released funds earmarked for small and medium-sized enterprise (SME) financing. Additionally, the PBOC issued two rounds of RMB 150 billion in relending and rediscount quotas to further boost SME lending, while also offering a tax exemption on interest income for small borrowers.

To tackle financing challenges in the capital markets, policymakers simplified the bond registration system and created a guarantee fund to support private companies' debt issuance. Restrictions on private share placements, a vital funding source for many private firms, were eased to reinvigorate the market. In several regions, including Shenzhen, local authorities pooled funds to prevent the forced liquidation of pledged share loans. At the national level, the Securities Association of China established a similar fund. Regulators also issued guidance to banks, encouraging them to increase lending to private enterprises without raising interest rates for SMEs. China's chief banking regulator, Guo Shuqing, went further by advocating specific lending quotas for the private sector: one-third of loans at large banks, two-thirds at medium-sized banks, and 50% of all corporate loans within three years.

Xi and other top leaders walked a fine line between trying to reassure the private sector while not deviating from the approach of stamping out financial risks and promoting economic stability. In October 2018, Liu

He, the Vice Premier in charge of economic policy, issued an unusual public statement reaffirming the government's "unwavering support" for the private sector.[72] Shortly after, in early November, Xi convened a meeting with private entrepreneurs to discuss issues affecting private firms.[73] In a speech that reads defensively, Xi reassured the entrepreneurs that the Party's support for the private sector had not changed and denied that the Party sought to control private companies through Party committees. Xi acknowledged that the private sector was responsible for most of China's gross domestic product (GDP), employment, and technological innovation.

However, Xi also made sure to declare in the speech that SOEs were the "mainstay" of the economy and the Party remained committed to consolidating and developing the state sector. At the same time, the Party sought to "support and guide" the private sector and that the process of supporting both the state and private sectors should be "complementary and mutually reinforcing" rather than "exclusive and offsetting." He announced several support measures for private firms, including lowering taxes, increasing access to finance, leveling the playing field between private firms and SOEs, and protecting property rights. He urged Party officials to listen to the legitimate concerns of private businesses but also called on entrepreneurs to "ardently love the motherland, ardently love the People, and ardently love the Party." He further encouraged them to "practice core socialist values" and "be models of patriotism and self-dedication."

The Conglomerate Crackdown: The actions taken during the "Regulatory Windstorm" coincided with a significant crackdown on several large conglomerates. Over the preceding decade, several politically connected private entrepreneurs had established large and powerful conglomerates, such as Anbang Insurance Group, Tomorrow Holding Group, Baoneng, HNA Group, Dalian Wanda, Fosun, and CEFC China Energy, a group known as the Grey Rhinos.[74] These conglomerates borrowed heavily from state banks and the shadow banking system to expand their empires and acquire overseas assets. Many of these conglomerates partnered with SOEs and local governments to secure access to financing and win lucrative contracts. The Grey Rhinos represented what Xi had long railed against—corrupt government and private sector ties.

The crackdown against these companies was driven by concerns about financial risk and a desire to eliminate the ability of the private conglomerates to challenge the power of the Party and SOEs.[75] These conglomerates' size and systemic interconnectedness began to be viewed as a threat to financial stability. Moreover, regulator and officials in the Party believed that these private firms were "looting" the public by borrowing vast amounts from Chinese savers and engaging in risky financial transactions.[76] In a few years, many of these private conglomerates would find their businesses cut off from financing, the scope of business curtailed, under investigation by the authorities, and in some cases, effectively nationalized.

One incident during this crackdown, the attempted hostile acquisition of Vanke, represented a clear example of the Party's discomfort with large, influential, and politically connected private firms. Several private conglomerates tried to wrest control of one of the crown jewels of corporate China from an SOE. The company in contention was Vanke, a real estate developer established in 1984 in Guangdong province by entrepreneur Wang Shi. Like many companies of this era, Vanke was initially a subsidiary of a state-owned enterprise that became partially privatized over time and publicly listed.[77] Under Wang's leadership, Vanke became China's largest real estate developer. Control over Vanke was valuable due to its scale, profitability, and control over prized land developments.

Although Vanke was a publicly listed company, its largest shareholder since 2000 had been China Resources Group, a major state-owned enterprise (SOE) also based in Guangdong. Despite being under state control via China Resources, Vanke reportedly enjoyed a significant degree of operational autonomy.[78] For Vanke, close connections to the government helped the company access credit and valuable land plots for development. Meanwhile, for the local government in Guangdong, maintaining control over Vanke offered both influence and the ability to direct the company's resources toward supporting local economic development projects.

This cozy relationship came under threat in 2015 as Baoneng Group, a relatively unknown private property conglomerate, sought to take control of Vanke. To finance the acquisition, Baoneng used its two insurance subsidiaries to raise funds from the public by selling high-yielding asset management plans.[79] These funds were used as part of a leveraged buyout of Vanke's stock. By August 2015, Baoneng had become the largest shareholder of China's largest property developer.[80]

The battle to take control of Vanke would soon become a free-for-all. In December 2015, another private conglomerate, announced it had taken a 6.2% stake in the company. Together, the two private conglomerates controlled a stake more than double that of China Resources, effectively challenging its control over the country. Vanke's founder, Wang Shi, was strongly opposed to the takeover attempt by Baoneng. In response, Vanke's management suspended trading of its shares in December 2015 as it worked on restructuring plans to fend off the acquisition. China's financial regulators began to take notice, stating that any transaction would be reviewed to ensure that the interests of all shareholders would be protected.[81] In March 2016, Vanke announced a deal whereby it would issue up to $9.3 billion in shares and give them to state-owned Shenzhen Metro in exchange for the acquisition of several real estate projects. The deal was emblematic of the tight connection between Vanke and the government.

In August 2016, yet another private conglomerate, Evergrande Group, began aggressively acquiring shares of Vanke. Using resources from its insurance subsidiary, Evergrande became Vanke's third-largest shareholder, potentially challenging Baoneng, Anbang, and China Resources for control of Vanke. In December 2016, China's chief securities regulator denounced "barbarians and bandits" engaged in hostile takeovers, clearly referring to the battle for Vanke.[82] Figure 8 illustrates the changing nature of Vanke's leading shareholders from 2014 to 2020.

In early 2017, the Chinese government moved decisively to assert its control over Vanke and terminate the private takeover attempts. Baoneng's insurance arms were suspended from selling high-yield investment products, and its Chairman, Yao Zhenhua, was banned from the insurance industry for ten years.[83] Executives from Evergrande's insurance arm also faced multi-year industry bans, and the company was restricted from making investments for one year. Soon after the crackdown, one of Baoneng's insurance subsidiaries announced that it would be forming a Party committee to "improve its corporate development capabilities."[84] The head of the China Insurance Regulatory Commission, Xiang Junbo, was arrested in April 2017 for "serious violations of regulations."

In January 2017, China Resources Group sold its stake to Shenzhen Metro Group. Around the same time, Evergrande Group gave up on its effort to capture Vanke, publicly declaring its intention not to seek

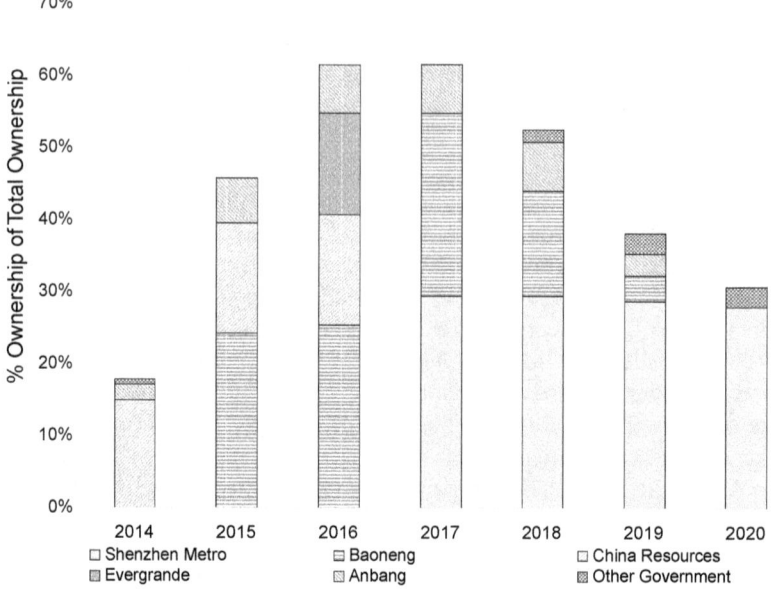

Fig. 8 Changes in Vanke's major shareholders, 2014–2020 (*Source* Vanke Annual Reports, Author's Calculations)

control of the company. In March 2017, Evergrande transferred its voting rights in Vanke to Shenzhen Metro as part of a proxy deal.[85] In June 2017, Evergrande sold its shares to Shenzhen Metro at a nearly $1 billion loss. Meanwhile, Baoneng quietly began divesting its stake in Vanke over the following year. As a result, Shenzhen Metro Group emerged as the largest shareholder of Vanke, a position it continues to hold today. Vanke's would-be acquirers tested the Party's willingness to relinquish control over key state companies and found that the cage limits the private economy was still very much in place.

4 Strengthening SOEs and Guiding the Market

Starting early in his tenure, Xi would undertake a series of policy campaigns designed to reform the state sector, enact large-scale industrial policy, expand China's global economic influence, and exert greater control over private companies. To achieve these goals, Xi and the Party sought to guide SOEs and private companies toward supporting state policies. These efforts produced mixed results, with numerous examples of failure and resource misallocation. The campaigns would, however, reinforce to Xi and the Party the importance of maintaining state control over key parts of the economy.

SOE Consolidation: Soon after coming to power, Xi moved to strengthen and consolidate the position of SOEs within the economy. Xi has long believed that SOEs are essential in advancing his goals of strengthening the Party and achieving national rejuvenation. As early as 2009, when he was Vice President, Xi signaled his stance by stating that SOEs are "an important foundation of Communist Party rule."[86] In Xi's view, SOEs play a special role in the economy, providing public services, stabilizing the economy during periods of volatility, supporting government industrial policy, implementing the policy goals of the Party, and helping China expand its international footprint.[87] Unlike the private sector, SOEs are viewed as more reliable, controllable, and less likely to become political threats. The stock market turmoil was instrumental in reinforcing views by Xi and other top leaders that large and centrally controlled SOEs were essential tools for managing the economy and mitigating financial risk.[88]

After the Third Plenum in 2013, Xi Jinping established the Central Leading Small Group for Comprehensively Deeping Reform, naming himself Chairman. Within that body, Xi's closest economic advisor, Liu He, led an effort on SOE reform. In 2015, the "Guiding Opinion on Deepening the Reform of SOEs" was announced.[89] The 2015 Reform was framed as a plan to make SOEs "stronger, better, and larger" and strengthen the control of the Party over SOEs. The reform plan called for improving the governance of SOEs through greater oversight and restructuring to allow market discipline. Like earlier efforts to reform the state sector, such as the "Grasp the Large, Let Go of the Small Policy" in the late 1990s, the focus was on revitalizing the state sector to preserve its ability to influence the economy.

One key component of the 2015 Reform was notable for categorizing SOEs according to the degree to which they would be subjected to market forces.[90] The three different categories of state-owned enterprises were (Table 1).

According to the 2015 Reform, SOEs in the first two categories, Public Service SOEs and Commercial SOEs in Strategic Sectors, should become

Table 1 Categorization of state-owned enterprises

Public Service SOEs	Provide public goods and services, such as utilities, in areas fully controlled by the government
Commercial SOEs in Strategic Sectors	Operate in sectors of the economy that are strategically important or natural monopolies
Commercial SOEs in Fully Competitive Sectors	Operate in sectors where there is significant competition from private and foreign firms

Source State Council[91]

more efficient through corporate governance reform and tighter government oversight. However, these SOEs were not to become primarily market-oriented. The 2015 Reform specified that Public Service SOEs should focus on serving society and providing public goods, while Commercial SOEs in Strategic Sectors should promote national policy, strategic projects, and guide the state-owned economy.[92] It was only for the final category, "Commercial SOEs in Fully Competitive Sectors," that reforms were truly market-focused. In theory, these SOEs were free to raise capital from the private sector, reduce the overall share of state ownership, hire outside managers, and go bankrupt if they failed commercially. Given these changes, these SOEs might start to function much more like private firms and be less subject to state influence. Chinese leaders at the highest levels, including Premier Li Keqiang, also publicly committed to the competitive neutrality between SOEs and private firms in fully competitive sectors.[93]

Key to achieving these transformations was developing what the document referred to as the "Mixed Ownership Economy." Endorsed in the 2013 Third Plenum and then reaffirmed in the 2015 Reform, mixed ownership entailed SOEs opening themselves up to non-state capital through capital contributions, equity acquisitions, convertible bonds, and equity swaps. Revealingly, the 2015 Reform also called for increased state investment in private companies, focusing on public services, high-tech industries, environmental protection, and strategic industries. The Mixed Ownership Economy was a vision of a deeply intertwined private and SOE sector, acting in concert to develop the economy according to the Party's guidance.

However, this reform has largely failed to materialize. A key roadblock has been that the central government has not made public the results of that exercise. The categorization effort was delayed for years, presumably due to resistance from vested interests at SOEs that sought to avoid a commercial classification.[94] As of the end of 2020, SASAC reported that it had completed the process for the central SOEs, but it has yet to share the result with the public.[95] In contrast, some localities, notably Shanghai and Guangzhou, have released their lists.

Among the SOEs that could reasonably be assumed to fall into the commercial category, there is little evidence of a shift toward greater market orientation. One notable instance of private sector investment into an SOE, that of China Unicom, has demonstrated the ineffectiveness of this approach. In 2017, China Unicom announced that it would engage in mixed ownership reform. This transaction was the highest-profile test case of this new approach. China Unicom is the smallest of China's three national telecom companies and has historically been viewed as over-staffed and inefficient.

To "improve the company's corporate governance" and "improve market incentives," it would reduce the "proportion of state-owned equity" and invite new state and private investors.[96] China Unicom raised 11.7 billion USD in capital from a group of outside investors, including many of the largest private sector tech companies such as Alibaba, Tencent, Didi Chuxing, Suning, JD.Com, and Baidu.[97] For their investment, the investors gained three board seats and a 35% stake in China Unicom's Shanghai unit. The parent SOE, China Unicom Group, reduced its stake from 62.7% to 37.7%.[98] Figure 9 shows the change in ownership in China Unicom due to the transaction.

The newly raised funds were to be used for building out China Unicom's 4G and 5G networks, and the private sector investors were to act as strategic partners in helping the company expand into new business lines, such as the Internet of Things (IoT) and the Industrial Internet.[99] The company announced technology partnerships for cloud computing and big data with its new strategic investors that would become a "driving force for innovative business development."[100] Many investors appeared to believe that a transformation of the company was imminent.

Judging from the performance of the share price and other financial indicators, the new investors have yet to succeed in significantly improving the company's operations. The share prices rallied initially after the announcement but fell precipitously for most of the next five years.

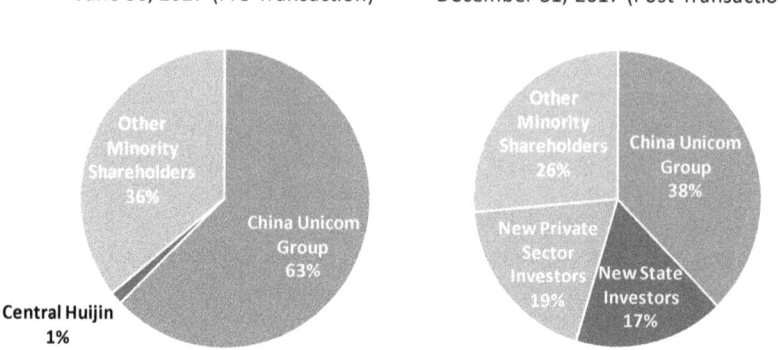

Fig. 9 China Unicom change shareholder structure (*Source* Wind Information)

Shares once again rallied when Tencent announced another partnership with the company but now remain well below their pre-2017 transaction levels. State ownership of the company, as measured by China Unicom Group's holdings and those of the other state investors, remains above 50%. It continues to have a lower return on assets and equity than its larger state-owned competitors, China Mobile and China Telecom.[101] Despite the hype surrounding the announcement of the deal, it's now clear in retrospect that the Party never intended to give up control over China Unicom. Instead, it tapped private sector investors to help recapitalize the company and pay for the expensive buildout of its new wireless networks.

While the effort to make some SOEs market-orientated and promote mixed ownership reform raised expectations, by and large these policies were disappointments. The Party was not interested in exposing unproductive SOEs to true market-based competition or allowing private firms to by controlling stakes. In fact, the total assets of centrally owned SOEs continued to grow even while the productivity of these firms stagnated.[102]

The 2015 Reform was notable for unleashing a series of large-scale SOE mergers across a variety of industries, including energy, infrastructure, food and beverage, and manufacturing. One of the key mega-mergers of SOEs during the Xi administration was between Shenhua Group and China Guodian in 2017 to strengthen state control over the coal industry.[103] The transaction was emblematic of Xi's approach to SOE reform.

During the mid-2010s, China's coal industry was plagued by problems. Local governments invested heavily in coal plants as way to boost GDP in their provinces and supply power to China's rapidly growing manufacturing sector.[104] State-owned coal miners, following directives from the local governments that controlled them, expanded production to the point of creating massive overcapacity. Coal production exceeded energy demand, leading to many coal power plants sitting idle much of the time.[105] Compounding the industry's challenges, a series of high-profile mining disasters occurred, resulting in numerous fatalities among coal miners due to unsafe working conditions.

In 2016, the State Council announced significant capacity reductions for the coal industry.[106] The plan included halting approvals for new coal mine projects, shutting down unsafe mines and those located in environmentally sensitive areas, and encouraging consolidation within the sector.

A mega merger between two of China's largest energy SOEs emerged from this policy. Shenhua Group was China's largest coal producer, with a listed subsidiary in Hong Kong (China Shenhua Energy). China Guodian was a large power producer with a listed subsidiary in Hong Kong (Guodian Technology and Environment Group). Shenhua, the more profitable entity, acquired Guodian to create a new conglomerate, China Energy Investment Corporation, with nearly $300 billion in total assets. The goal was to stabilize the coal market and improve profitability and efficiency by coordinating coal mining with electrical production.[107] The new company was estimated to be the largest power producer in the world by installed capacity and had over 300,000 employees.[108]

However, the new conglomerate has made little progress in becoming more efficient and market-oriented. The company reports little about its financial condition other than annual assets and net profit. Using this information, the group's return on assets in 2023 was a meager 3.37%. On its website, China Energy Investment Corporation claims to be "guided by Xi Jinping Thought on Socialism with Chinese Characteristics for a New Era" and committed to "thoroughly implement the guiding principles of the 19th CPC National Congress and the decisions and plans made by the CPC Central Committee and the State Council."[109] Further reinforcing the state orientation of this entity, China Energy

Investment Corporate's publicly listed subsidiaries extensively reference Party guidance and policy in their annual reports to investors.

Another SOE policy document released in 2016, Guiding Opinions of the General Office of the State Council on Promoting the Structural Adjustment and Reorganization of Central Enterprises, clarified the core principles of SOE reform. Inherent in the document is the underlying tension between market and state objectives. The policy calls on SOEs to serve national development goals, implement national development strategies, and implement national industrial policies.[110] At the same time, it calls on SOEs to respect the laws of the market and implement modern enterprise reforms. The policy sets for goal that by 2020, central SOEs would become stronger and more efficient and serve as better implementers of the Party's policies in the areas of national security, strategic industries, and emerging technologies. It expresses a vision SOEs improving their efficiency and strategic importance, without ceding ground to the private sector.

Early in Xi's tenure, there was hope that the Party might embrace an approach in which SASAC maintained its ownership in SOEs but became less involved in their operations. State press published articles about China adopting the "Temasek Model," referencing Singapore's state holding firm for the country's SOEs.[111] Temasek has long been cited globally for its comparative ability to manage the Singapore's SOEs professionally and efficiently. If SASAC followed in Temasek's footsteps, it would entail reducing its interference in the day-to-day activities of SOEs and personnel appointments, and instead manage its ownership of the company from a capital ownership framework.

SASAC has taken small steps in this direction. In 2018, SASAC launched a pilot program to convert several central SOEs into State-owned Capital Investment Companies (SOCIC), with 21 companies having undergone this conversion so far.[112] In theory, these entities will be permitted to implement management and structural reforms, such as allowing its subsidiaries to raise private capital and partner with outside firms. Becoming a SOCIC involves the devolution of operational management authority from SASAC to the company itself. However, the restructuring does not remove the requirement for the enterprises to promote the Party's policy goals. In fact, one of the cited motivations of the plan is to increase the effectiveness of SOEs in strategic sectors.[113] Moreover, rather than engage in privatization, many of these entities have used their access to financial resources to invest in private companies, sometimes taking a controlling stake.[114]

Over the past decade, Xi has failed to follow through on policies that might reduce the Party's control over SOEs, such as mixed ownership and market-based competition. Instead, Xi has overseen greater centralization and reinforcement of weaker SOEs in an effort to solidify the Party's grip on the state sector.

Industrial Policy and Made in China 2025: Industrial policy has been a significant focus of Xi and the Party as a method to guide the economy toward supporting policy goals. Key among these goals is technological self-sufficiency. While the Chinese government has long engaged in industrial policy, Xi has accelerated those efforts due to concerns that foreign countries would restrict China's access to critical technology. For Xi, industrial policy is a tool to drive domestic innovation and break these restrictions. Soon after taking power in 2012, Xi Jinping began emphasizing the importance of mastering "core technologies" so that China would reduce its dependence on foreign technology.[115] As will be discussed later in the chapter, Xi's focus on this issue would only increase over time as it became clear how vulnerable China was to U.S. restrictions on semiconductors and other key technology areas.

Under Xi's direction, the Chinese government began developing ambitious industrial policies to break China's reliance on foreign technology. In contrast to prior industrial policy efforts, these efforts would recruit both state and private firms to support national initiatives. In 2013, the State Council released a document that identified steps for strengthening the role of enterprises in promoting innovation through increasing investment, establishing research and development (R&D) centers, supporting the commercialization of research, and promoting partnerships between research institutions, companies, and industry alliances.[116]

In 2014, Xi ordered the National Development and Reform Commission (NDRC) and the central government's Financial and Economic Affairs Group to craft a detailed innovation-driven development strategy for the economy.[117] A formal plan, the National Innovation-Driven Development Strategy Outline (National Innovation Strategy), was jointly released in 2016 by both the Communist Party and the State Council. The Outline was notable for setting an explicit target for China to be an international leader in innovation by 2030 and a global "powerhouse" of scientific and technological innovation by 2050.

Many of China's efforts to develop domestic sources of technology have centered around manufacturing. In 2013, the Chinese Academy of Engineering and the Ministry of Industry and Information Technology convened a group of over 150 scholars and technical experts to create a report addressing how China could become a manufacturing superpower.[118] The report ultimately coalesced into the "Made in China 2025" plan adopted by the State Council in 2015. The Plan drew upon and updated the 2006 Medium to Long-Term Plan for the Development of Science and Technology issued during Hu Jintao's administration.[119] The Plan declares that while China's manufacturing sector is large, it lags behind in terms of efficiency, quality, and level of technology. In Xi's vision, turning China into a high-tech manufacturing power, especially one less reliant on foreign technology, is essential.[120]

Made in China 2025 was ambitious in its goals for China's manufacturing sector. The plan sets forth the following timeline:

- By 2020, consolidate China's status as a great manufacturing power and achieve the integration of the country's manufacturing sector with information technology.
- By 2025, greatly enhance the overall level of quality and innovation across the manufacturing sector and create new internationally competitive multinational corporations and industrial clusters.
- By 2035, China's manufacturing sector will enter the ranks of the world's manufacturing powers, having achieved breakthroughs in critical industries and global leadership innovation leadership across several sectors.

The Plan is explicit in its push for seeking technology breakthroughs in critical areas and reducing reliance on foreign suppliers. The Plan sets targets for reducing the dependence on foreign suppliers for essential spare parts and key materials to less than 30% by 2025. Furthermore, it targets ten strategic industries, as shown in Table 2, for industrial policy and support.[121] These industries represented the commanding heights of the new economy and areas where China was reliant on foreign technology. Made in China 2025 clearly reflects a sense of vulnerability by the Party to potential foreign economic pressure.

Like many of Xi's policies, Made in China 2025 reflected the tensions between the Party's desire to guide the economy and the necessity

Table 2 Made in China 2025 priority sectors

- New generation IT, including integrated circuits, communication equipment, and industrial software
- High-end digitally controlled machine tools and robots
- Aerospace and aeronautic equipment
- Ocean engineering equipment and advanced shipping
- Advanced rail transportation equipment
- Energy-efficient and new energy vehicles
- Electrical power equipment
- High-end agricultural equipment
- Advanced new materials
- Biomedicine and advanced medical equipment

Source State Council[122]

of using market forces to achieve the desired results. While The Plan declares that it will "let the market lead with government guidance,"[123] in practice, the Party expects companies to support the goals set out in Made in China 2025 by aligning investments with the targets outlined in the plan.[124] To support these efforts, the Plan pledges government support for major strategic projects, research, industrial technology upgrading, mergers and acquisitions, and cross-border expansion. In China's domestic economy, SOEs dominate many of the critical industries targeted by Made in China 2025.[125] This presented a conundrum because while SOEs are generally willing implementers of government policy, they often lack the competitiveness to compete globally, casting doubt on whether an SOE-driven push could accomplish the Plan's goals.

The Party has increasingly made use of a new tool, government guidance funds, to help ensure that the country's industrial policy goals are successful. Government agencies have established government guidance funds at the central, provincial, county, and city levels to promote the development of a specific industry, encourage innovation more broadly, or finance the restructuring of existing enterprises. Table 3 lists several of the significant government guidance funds.

Government guidance funds are seeded with initial capital from the government and staffed by professional managers to oversee the investments. In contrast to the government directly making investments itself, guidance funds represent an attempt to use market-based methods to further policy goals. Professional managers of the fund are tasked with supporting the development of a specific sector but given operational

Table 3 Select national state-guided investment funds

- The National Integrated Circuit Fund
- The Advanced Manufacturing Industry Investment Fund
- The National Strategic Emerging Industries Investment Guiding Fund
- The Made in China 2025 Strategic Cooperation Fund
- The Internet Investment Fund
- The National Fund for Technology Transfer and Commercialization
- The China Reform Holdings Fund

autonomy to choose the best investments. The hope is that this structure might be more effective and lead to less waste than putting government bureaucrats directly in charge of the investments. However, guidance funds have thus far failed to achieve this balance of policy and inefficiency.

An example of how government guidance funds and state-owned enterprises (SOEs) can go awry in pursuing industrial policy goals is the case of the Integrated Circuit Fund and Tsinghua Unigroup. The Integrated Circuit Fund was established in 2014 to promote the development of China's domestic semiconductor industry and was endowed with an estimated $20 billion in capital.[126] The funding came primarily from the Chinese government, SOEs, and state institutions, including the Ministry of Finance, China Development Bank, China National Tobacco Corp, and Beijing E- Town.[127] The Integrated Circuit Fund was a key tool in advancing the Made in China 2025 Plan, which set a goal for China to produce 70% of the semiconductors it uses domestically, a significant leap from its then level of 20%.[128]

Tsinghua Unigroup was founded in 1988 as a spinoff of Tsinghua Holdings, an SOE affiliated with Tsinghua University, often referred to as China's MIT. In 2009, Zhao Weiguo, a former employee of Tsinghua Unigroup, purchased a 49% stake in the company.[129] At that point, the firm remained quasi-state-owned, with Tsinghua University retaining a 51% stake. Starting around 2014, the company went on an ambitious deal spree that aligned with the Made in China 2025 Plan and other government initiatives related to semiconductors. Tsinghua Unigroup acquired two Chinese chipmakers, Speadtrum Communications and RDA Microelectronics. Tsinghua Unigroup then convinced Intel Ito make a $1.5 billion investment in the companies and for the companies to produce chips based on Intel's technology. At the time, Zhao stated that "it has become a national priority for China to grow its semiconductor industry" and that the deal "represented Intel's confidence" in the Chinese market.[130]

In 2015, despite its relatively small scale, Tsinghua Unigroup made an audacious $23 billion bid to buy Micron, an American company that is one of the largest memory producers in the world.[131] However, the deal was scuttled due to concerns that U.S. regulators would reject it over national security concerns.[132] Similarly, Tsinghua Unigroup's $3.78 billion investment in Western Digital, a major computer drive manufacturer, was also blocked over security concerns.[133] Through its subsidiary, Hua Capital Management, the company successfully acquired Omnivision, an American firm specializing in advanced image sensors. Hua Capital Management also made an unsuccessful attempt to acquire Fairchild Semiconductor, a company that had played a pivotal role in the creation of the semiconductor industry in the 1960s and 1970s. Additionally, Tsinghua Unigroup acquired a small stake in Lattice Semiconductor.

Tsinghua Unigroup also sought to make significant investments outside the United States to gain access to key semiconductor technology. In 2015, it made a substantial investment in Powertech Technology, a Taiwanese semiconductor testing and assembly company, but the deal was terminated after failing to secure approval from Taiwanese regulators.[134] Zhao, Tsinghua Unigroup's chairman, also publicly expressed interest in acquiring Mediatek, a major Taiwanese chip design firm, and investing in TSMC, the world's leading semiconductor foundry.[135] In 2018, Tsinghua successfully acquired the French smart chip component maker Linxens for 2.2 billion euros.[136] The company reportedly also attempted to purchase a 20% stake in the Korean memory company SK Hynix but was rejected.[137]

Tsinghua Unigroup also invested a tremendous amount of capital in China's domestic semiconductor industry. Along with its affiliates, the company invested in China's leading foundry, Semiconductor Manufacturing International Corporation (SMIC). In partnership with the Hubei provincial government and the Integrated Circuit Fund, it founded Yangtze Memory, with a total investment of $24 billion. In 2017, the company received $16 billion from the China Development Bank and $7 billion from the Integrated Circuit Fund.[138] That same year, Tsinghua Unigroup invested RMB 200 billion in an "international circuit town" in Chengdu and RMB 260 billion in a semiconductor base in Nanjing.[139]

Tsinghua Unigroup crashed in 2020 after its debts grew too large to manage. By 2021, the company was in bankruptcy proceedings and was ultimately purchased and restructured by a state-owned firm called JAC Capital.[140] In 2022, Zhao Wei Guo was detained and later pled guilty to corruption charges.[141] Chinese authorities later detained and investigated several of the managers in charge of the National Integrated Circuit Fund.[142] The failure of Tsinghua Unigroup was a stunning example of how the Party's efforts to fuse state and private capital and direct it toward policy goals could go very wrong.

Made in China 2025 proved to be highly controversial. Many of China's trading partners criticized the Plan, complaining that it was an effort to push their companies out of the Chinese market and create Chinese competitors to challenge them internationally. Due to international backlash, China began to deemphasize references to Made in China 2025 in public announcements.[143] However, the spirit of the campaign remains alive through subsequent industrial policies and calls by Xi and the Party to break through foreign chokepoints of strategic technology.

The Belt and Road Initiative: Xi's efforts to shape economic affairs were not limited solely to China's domestic economy. In 2013, Xi announced his signature foreign policy campaign, the Belt and Road Initiative (BRI). The BRI represented Xi's vision of China increasing its overseas economic influence. The Belt and Roads was presented as China providing financing and know-how to build roads, power plants, ports, railways, and other infrastructure with developing countries. Chinese state-controlled financial institutions would provide much of the financing necessary to support this wave of infrastructure development. In turn, Chinese firms, particularly SOEs, would be well placed to win BRI contracts, given their close connections to these state banks. The BRI drew upon the "Going Out" strategy of the mid-2000s under Hu Jintao, but also represented a significant expansion in scope and ambition. Some analysts christened the BRI as "China's Marshall Plan" a magnanimous effort to share China's expertise and capital with the developing work. Other, more skeptical observers, labeled the BRI as an effort to establish a Chinese sphere of influence and entrap less developed countries with debt. As a testament to Xi's power over the Party, the BRI initiative was written into the Party's charter in 2017.[144]

The BRI once again represented an effort to mobilize market forces on behalf of Party policy initiatives. Xi's designation of the BRI as a major policy initiative unleashed a flood of money and state assistance for projects linked to the effort. The early years of the BRI were chaotic, as companies rushed to brand projects as part of the BRI and the government exercised little oversight. Driven by both financial incentives and political direction, SOEs have been major participants in the BRI, undertaking thousands of projects.[145] The political goals embedded within the BRI have been illuminated by a series of overseas projects by SOEs that appear to be primarily driven by geostrategic, rather than economic, considerations.

Among the most notable examples were the China Merchants Group and the Hambantota Port in Sri Lanka. In 2017, China Merchants Group Port Holdings, a subsidiary of China Merchant Group, paid $1.1 billion to secure a 99-year lease on Hambantota Port.[146] In turn, the Sri Lankan government pledged to use the funds to pay back debt owed to China and other international creditors. On its website, China Merchant Port portrays Hambantota Port as a strategic asset close to international shipping lanes.[147] In 2023, the company announced another $392 million investment to build a logistics center at the port.[148]

Whether these investments make economic sense for China Merchants Port is highly questionable. At the time, the Hambantota Port was remote and had little cargo business.[149] Several years later, the Hambantota Port was still not ranked among the top 100 global ports measured by cargo shipments.[150] China Merchant Port took on substantial debt as part of the transaction, liabilities grew by 43% the year of the Hambantota transaction, and the company shareholders seemed skeptical of the deal, with the share price initially rallying before falling sharply throughout 2018.[151] As of late 2024, the company's stock remains substantially below the level when the deal was signed.

Private firms have generally been more reluctant to embrace the BRI compared to SOEs.[152] This is likely due to a fear that many politically driven BRI projects may prove to be unprofitable. However, that has not prevented some private firms, particularly those with close ties to the state, from trying to co-opt the BRI to support their projects. One such politically connected private company is Country Garden, one of China's largest real estate developers. In 2013, Country Garden began a project called Forest City in a joint venture with the Sultan of Johor. The project is strategically located on a small island across the Straits of Johor from Singapore. The project initially encountered several construction challenges and was criticized by Singapore's government for its environmental impact.[153] The project, developed in cooperation with a Malaysian state-owned firm, is massive in scope, with a planned $100 billion investment to construct high-rise apartment buildings, hotels, and golf courses across 30 square kilometers. The scope of the project was to house 700,000 people across four reclaimed islands.[154]

In 2016, Country Garden rebranded its Forest City project as part of the BRI. The project was feted in People's Daily as a national "key project" for the Belt and Road that would serve as a bridgehead for Chinese companies to expand overseas and establish international production capacity.[155] The Party likely viewed the project as strategically beneficial as it created tight financial links with the Malaysian government and sought to establish a large community of Chinese nationals in a strategic location. A perceived alignment with the state appears to have helped the company access easy financing. Country Garden's liabilities increased massively from $42 billion in 2015 to $212 billion in 2018.

The Forest City project, however, has not progressed smoothly. Country Garden has only invested a fraction of the money it claimed it would, and much of the project remains unoccupied.[156] Moreover, after a change in leadership in Malaysia, close connections to the Chinese government became a liability for the project as the new leadership took an anti-China stance. In 2018, the new Malaysian Prime Minister announced that no foreigners would be allowed to live at the project.[157] As of late 2024, Country Garden was mired in financial distress and no longer able to service its massive debts.

As of the writing of this book, many Belt and Road projects have been scaled back due to problems such as those outlined above. Directing economic activity abroad has proved to be a complicated and costly affair. One clear indicator of this is China's emergency lending to developing nations. This lending reached more than $185 billion between 2016 and 2021, with almost all of the lending going to Belt and Road countries with significant outstanding debts to Chinese banks.[158] Absent this lending, it is likely that a high number of Belt and Road projects would now be in default.

Corporate Control: Beginning early in his tenure, Xi undertook a concerted effort to increase the Party's control over companies, both state-owned and private. One primary tool has been expanding and strengthening party committees within companies.[159] Party committees are distinct organizations within a company that are composed of employees who are also members of the Party. Often, but not always, the leadership of the party committees is the same as the company's management.

While the Party already owns SOEs and appoints their senior management, party committees are seen as another important tool of control. While party committees are ubiquitous at SOEs, China's leaders have often worried that they there were disorganized and ineffective. For example, President Jiang Zemin decried that many party committees operating in SOEs were "lax and powerless" and vowed to address the problem.[160]

Increasing the influence of party committees within SOEs has been a significant priority for Xi. Since 2013, the Party has issued a series of new policies to strengthen party committees in SOEs.[161] For example, in 2015, the "Regulations on the Work of Party Groups of the Communist Party of China - Trial Implementation" emphasized the need to establish Party committees in companies and social organizations.[162] Also, in 2015, Xi Jinping's signature SOE reform plan, the "Guiding Opinion on Deepening the Reform of State-owned Enterprises," called for strengthening the CCP's leadership over these companies.[163]

The CCP Constitution outlines specific powers for party committees within companies. It calls for party committees to be formed in any company with three or more party members. For SOEs, party committees should "participate in making decisions on major questions in the enterprises."[164] In a 2017 revision of the CCP constitution, the role of party committees in SOEs was further strengthened. For SOEs with a Leading Party members' group,[165] The Party committee shall "play a leadership role" and "discuss and decide on major issues of their enterprise in accordance with regulations"[166] (Table 4).

Due to investor disclosure requirements, the Party's efforts to strengthen Party committees in listed companies are well known. The Party has been focused on having SOEs formally revise their corporate charters to empower party committees. Such actions must be disclosed to other shareholders and are subject to a shareholder vote. In 2018, this requirement was officially incorporated into the China Securities Regulatory Commission's Code of Corporate Governance for Listed Companies.[167]

Two studies have analyzed the adoption of charter revisions by SOEs in the years immediately following the new requirement.[168] The results show significant variations in compliance. Some SOEs have only complied

Table 4 Excerpts from the Constitution of the Communist Party of China related to party committee in state-owned enterprises

- The leading Party members groups or Party committees shall play a leadership role, set the right direction, keep in mind the big picture, ensure the implementation of Party policies and principles, and discuss and decide on major issues of their enterprise in accordance with regulations
- Primary-level Party organizations in state-owned or collective enterprises should focus their work on the operations of their enterprise
- Guarantee and oversee the implementation of the principles and policies of the Party and the state within their own enterprise and shall support the board of shareholders, board of directors, board of supervisors, and manager (or factory director) in exercising their functions and powers in accordance with the law
- Wholeheartedly rely on the workers and office staff and support the work of workers'
- representative congresses, and they shall participate in making decisions on major issues in the enterprise
- Strengthen their own organizational development and lead work on political thinking, efforts toward cultural-ethical progress, and work on trade unions, Communist Youth League organizations, and other people's group organizations

Source Constitution of the Communist Party of China

in a perfunctory manner, adopting symbolic provisions that acknowledge the importance and leadership of the CCP. Other SOEs have gone further and required the board of directors to consult with the party committees before important strategic decisions. Finally, the more zealous SOEs have gone as far as declaring that the management of a company should consult with the party committees on important operational decisions and that the chairperson of the board also serves as the head of the party committees.

While Party membership became common for many private entrepreneurs in the 2000s, the situation at private companies was different. For many decades, most private companies did not have a party committee. This has changed in recent years. Figure 10 shows the prevalence of Party organizations in private companies during that period (2002) compared to the most recent data (2018). The prevalence in large private companies is much higher, with 92% of the top 500 private firms having a party committee.

The requirements for party committees in private enterprises, as outlined in the CCP constitution, are less stringent than those for SOEs. Party committees in private companies should "implement the Party's principles and policies," "guide and oversee their enterprises' observance

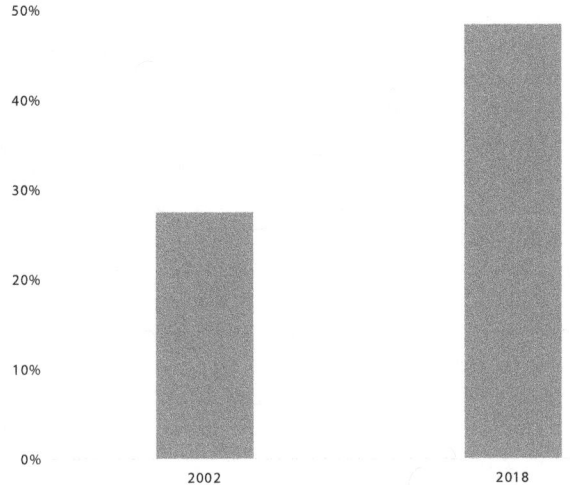

Fig. 10 Share of private companies in China with Communist Party Committees (*Source* All-China Federation of Industry and Commerce[169])

of state laws," and "promote unity and cohesion among workers and office staff, safeguard the legitimate rights and interests of all parties, and promote the healthy development of their enterprises."[170] As such, there is no formal requirement for Party committees in private companies to be consulted on corporate operational decisions. China's Company Law states that private and state-owned companies shall permit party committees to be established and provided the necessary conditions to operate.[171] Beyond that, there is no formal legal requirement that party committees be given operational influence within a company.

There has been a flurry of activity by the Party to promote the establishment of party committees in private companies. In a speech in 2016, Xi Jinping declared, "China's non-publicly owned economy has grown from small to large and from weak to strong under the guidance of the guidelines and policies of the Party and the State."[172] Xi called on entrepreneurs to love the Party, be patriotic, and practice core socialist values. Furthermore, he declared that "We should pay attention to the education and cultivation of the younger generation of people in the non-publicly owned economy, and guide them to inherit and carry forward the entrepreneurial spirit of the older generation of entrepreneurs and the glorious tradition of listening to the Party and following the Party."[173] In 2019, the Central Committee of the CCP and the Chinese State Council encouraged private companies to strengthen their efforts in establishing party committees.[174] In 2020, the Vice Chairman of the All-China Federation of Industry and Commerce called for a renewed push to establish party committees in private enterprises, describing private entrepreneurs as the "helmsmen of a ship" and party committees as the "compass" that guides the ship's direction.[175]

While private companies were not required to incorporate party committees into their charters, some have undertaken these changes voluntarily. Private firms with Party members on their management team or board of directors were more likely to incorporate the charter changes.[176] However, private companies have been reluctant to adopt provisions that grant party committees operational control relative to SOEs and generally favor only symbolic changes.

Xiaomi makes an interesting case study for the role of Party committees in private companies. In 2015, Xiaomi announced the establishment of a Party committee within the company at an event attended by Xiaomi's founder and CEO and representatives of the Beijing municipal government.[177] Given the influential role played by many tech companies, the Party has made it a priority to establish a presence within private companies operating in the sector. People's Daily praised Xiaomi, calling it a positive development for the integration of the private sector with the national political system, and it stated that Party committees helped private companies in "ideological construction, organizational coordination, entrepreneurial spirit, and corporate culture."[178]

While the announcement garnered positive attention from state media, it generated backlash on Chinese social media and in the overseas press due to concerns that other private companies in China would face pressure to do the same. At the time, it was unusual for a private technology company to publicize its links to the Party due to fear that it would generate a negative reaction from investors. At the time, Xiaomi tried to allay concerns that its business was becoming politicized, with a representative from Xiaomi stating that the Party committee would not be involved in business matters but rather that the company would give "full play to the leadership role of the party committee in publicity, education, and cultural leadership."[179]

Despite its apparent embrace of the Party, Xiaomi has subsequently provided few details on the activities of its Party committee. When Xiaomi pursued a Hong Kong listing in 2018, its prospectus did not provide information about the role or scope of the Party committee. Since going public, the company's annual report and other shareholder documents contain almost no references to the Party committee. In 2021, the Trump Administration targeted Xiaomi and other Chinese companies with the Communist Chinese Military Companies Executive Order. The order banned U.S. investors from investing in companies with ties to China's People's Liberation Army or China's military-industrial complex. Xiaomi took the U.S. government to court over the designation. As revealed in subsequent court filings, the evidence linking Xiaomi to China's defense establishment was sparse, and the company won an injunction against the designation.[180] While Xiaomi successfully refuted its connection to the Chinese military, it has not publicly explained the full extent of its relationship to the Party.

The push to establish party committees in companies has generated an intense backlash from foreign companies operating in China. The European Chamber of Commerce has been vocal about its opposition to an expansive role for party committees within European joint ventures with local SOEs.[181] At present, there are only scattered reports of foreign companies in China facing pressure to establish party committees or give existing ones more influence.[182] However, it is difficult to gauge the influence of party committees because many foreign businesses may be reluctant to complain for fear of damaging their relationship with the Chinese government.

In addition to party committees, golden shares are another tool of influence over private companies. A golden share, or a "special management share," is a small stake in a private or listed company that grants the holder significant influence over a company's activities. The idea of these special shares was included in the Third Plenum Decisions document:

> We will experiment in carrying out a system of special management shares in important state-owned media enterprises that have been transformed according to regulations.[183]

The experiment being described was to allow state-owned media companies to restructure into market-orientated businesses, while maintaining a special shareholding structure. The government would hold special management shares to retain control and oversight over these restructured entities. From the Party's perspective, this was necessary for companies operating in a sensitive sector, such as the media.

However, starting around 2016, the focus of special management shares shifted toward privately owned companies in the tech and media sectors.[184] These shares would allow the Party to exert more significant influence over private companies that were increasingly important in the flow of information and formation of public opinion in China. The shares are believed to include a seat on the board of directors and voting power to veto corporate decisions. Since then, the Party has taken small stakes in a variety of influential technology companies or their subsidiaries (Table 5).

Additionally, the China Internet Investment Fund, an investment fund controlled by the Cyberspace Administration of China, has reportedly taken small investment stakes in 40 Chinese tech companies, although these investments may not be full special management shares.[187] On the Fund's public website, it describes itself as having been created to implement the policies of the Party's Central Committee and the State Council for the internet sector.[188] As such, these investments in private internet companies are likely a way for the Party to guide the action of these companies toward supporting its policies.

Whether through party committees, golden shares, or direct investments in companies, the Party's efforts to establish greater influence over private companies have accelerated as these companies have become more important in the Chinese economy.

Table 5 Known golden share stakes held by the Chinese government

- Sina Weibo
- 36kr
- Kuaishou
- Bytedance
- Guangzhou Lujiao (Alibaba)
- Qutoutiao
- Full Truck Alliance
- Wangtou Zicheng (Tencent)

Sources Wall Street Journal,[185] Reuters[186]

5 Trade and Technology Conflict with the United States

During the first five years of his rule, Xi Jinping's desire to direct the economy toward geopolitical goals had already been revealed through campaigns such as the Belt and Road Initiative and Made in China 2025. Using carrots and sticks, Xi encouraged SOEs and private companies to participate in these campaigns and invest their resources. These efforts were increased significantly in response to the sharp deterioration in U.S.-China relations in 2017 and 2018. Having failed to avert a trade war, Xi redoubled his efforts to reshape the economy to support a protracted geopolitical struggle with the United States. This would ultimately lead to a substantial tightening of state control over many industries.

Outbreak of the Trade War: Relations between the United States and China have always been volatile. However, following the election of Donald Trump, the two countries entered an extended period of tension and mutual distrust not seen since diplomatic relations were reestablished in 1979. The Trump campaigned on the notion that China's economic rise had come at the expense of the United States and dramatic action was necessary to restructure an unfair trading relationship. While Trump's election may have been the catalyst for conflict, economic tensions between China and the United States had been growing for years. Many in the United States were frustrated that China had not fully liberalized its economy and that the state retained so much influence in economic affairs. Xi's reassertion of state control over the economy after the financial turmoil of 2015 and 2016 only added fuel to the fire.

Shortly after taking office in 2017, the Trump Administration sought to negotiate with China on a litany of trade complaints. This effort, known as the 100 Days Plan, failed to address the scope of American concerns about the trade relationship. Afterward, negotiations deteriorated into a full-blown trade war. The United States Trade Representative announced a wide-ranging Section 301 investigation in August 2017, targeted at determining "whether acts, policies, and practices of the Government of China related to technology transfer, intellectual property, and innovation are unreasonable or discriminatory and burden or restrict U.S. commerce."[189] By March 2018, the Section 301 report had been completed, documenting a long list of China's alleged unfair and discriminatory trade practices.¹⁹⁰ Upon the report's publication, President Trump threatened tariffs on a large swathe of Chinese goods.¹⁹¹ As shown in Fig. 11, by September 2019, two-thirds of Chinese exports to the United States would be subject to tariffs.

Technology Conflict and Sanctions: From China's perspective, growing conflict over technology and sanctions was more concerning than the tariffs. In 2018, the fear that China would be cut off from key foreign technologies, a recurring concern voiced by Xi since early in his rule, became a reality. The first instance was with ZTE Corporation, a prominent Chinese telecommunications company. The company had been found guilty of violating U.S. sanctions in 2017 for selling telecommunications equipment with U.S. components to Iran and North Korea. ZTE paid a hefty fine to the U.S. government and agreed to a seven-year denial of export privileges, meaning that further violations could revoke its ability to purchase critical technology from U.S. suppliers.¹⁹³ In April 2018, the U.S. government invoked that denial of export privileges once it was discovered that ZTE had failed to discipline the employees involved

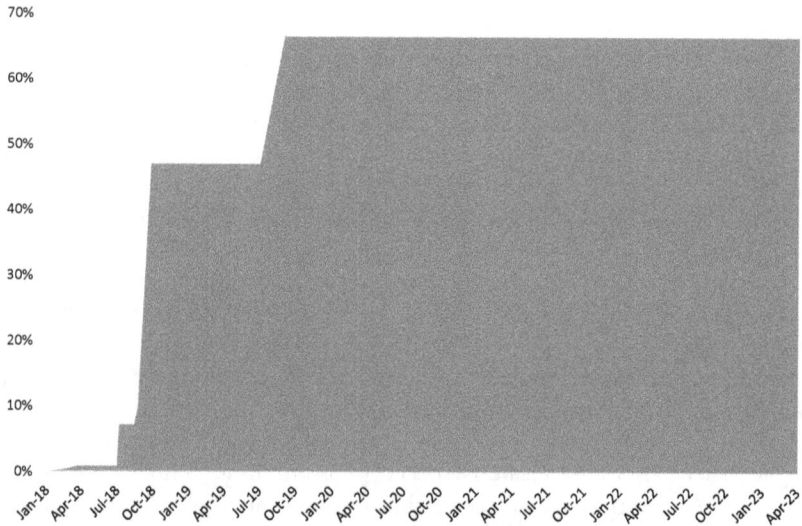

Fig. 11 Share of Chinese exports to the U.S. subject to tariffs (*Source* The Peterson Institute for International Economics¹⁹²)

in sanctions evasion.[194] The ban on purchasing American technology was a potential death sentence for the company as it relied on U.S. components for many of its products. Given the uncertainty around its fate, the company suspended its stock for an extended period.[195] ZTE was only granted a reprieve from sanctions following a direct phone call between Xi and Trump, where Xi reportedly requested that the company be spared due to concerns about job losses if the company were shutdown.[196]

Tensions over technology escalated further in an incident involving Huawei Technologies. Even more than ZTE, Huawei represented one of China's leading domestic technology companies. The company was a major domestic telecommunications infrastructure and mobile phone maker and was making considerable inroads internationally, particularly in the developing world. Additionally, through its HiSilicon subsidiary, Huawei was becoming increasingly skilled at chip design, a key component of China's overall semiconductor push. For many in China, Huawei represented a homegrown technology champion that could break the country's reliance on foreign technology.

In December 2018, Huawei became the central focus of U.S.-China competition with the arrest of Meng Wanzhou in Canada. Meng, the Chief Financial Officer of Huawei and the daughter of the company's founder was detained by Canadian authorities at the request of the United States. Meng was accused of lying to conceal Huawei's sales to Iran in violation of U.S. sanctions. The allegations set off a multi-year extradition fight between Meng and the U.S. government.

Following the arrest of Meng, the U.S. government began to take concerted action against Huawei. The company was added to the Commerce Department's Entity List in May 2019. Huawei and its affiliates were added to the Entity List because they "pose a significant risk of involvement in activities contrary to the national security or foreign policy interests" of the United States.[197] The Entity List subjects a company or person to additional licensing requirements before accessing U.S. technology. For these licenses, there is a "presumption of denial," meaning that most license requests will be rejected unless they can prove no negative impact on U.S. national security. In practical terms, this meant that Huawei was largely cut off from purchasing U.S. products and software, as well as products from other countries containing at least 25% in components from U.S. companies. The restrictions on Huawei were further tightened in 2020, with U.S. Senator Ben Sasse stating that the

United States should seek to "strangle" Huawei.[198] Huawei was effectively excluded from the global semiconductor industry, forcing it to halt product lines and severely constraining its international expansion.[199]

ZTE and Huawei were the opening shots fired by the United States in what would become a larger sanctions campaign against a broad swathe of Chinese companies. According to one analysis, the U.S. government has sanctioned hundreds of Chinese entities in sectors related to aviation, space, aerospace, artificial intelligence, semiconductors, and quantum computing.[200] Some of these sanctions have been quite damaging such as the export controls preventing the sale of advanced semiconductor technology to China that were enacted in 2022. The controls, which have subsequently been tightened further, threaten to keep China's semiconductor industry at a perpetual lag behind the cutting edge.

Further adding to China's fears was the ever-present threat of American financial sanctions. Because so much international trade and finance occurs in dollars, the U.S. government can wield unparalleled influence over the global financial system. American financial sanctions must be adhered to by other countries, or they risk being cut off from global finance. For example, a foreign bank that willfully violated U.S. sanctions would be banned from the U.S. banking system. Because most international dollar transactions ultimately clear through banks located in the United States, not having access to the U.S. banking system would cripple any bank with global operations. Prior to the trade war, two Chinese banks, Banco Delta Asia and Bank of Kunlun, were the target of U.S. sanctions. The threat expanded in 2020 when the United States began sanctioning Hong Kong officials involved in suppressing student protestors. Banks operating in Hong Kong were subject to these sanctions if they provided services to these officials.[201]

The U.S. government also took action to limit Chinese companies' access to American capital markets. In December 2020, the Trump Administration issued an executive order that banned nearly 60 Chinese companies from accessing U.S. capital markets and receiving investments from U.S. citizens. The purpose of the ban was to target "Communist Chinese Military Companies" that allow China to "directly threaten the United States homeland and United States forces overseas."[202] Under the Biden Administration, additional Chinese companies would be added to the list and a new rule for outbound investment were announced to discourage American investors from investing in Chinese technology companies.

The National Security Economy: The sharp deterioration in the U.S.-China relationship, combined with the severe disruptions brought about by the outbreak of COVID-19, was a tremendous shock to Xi and the Party's view on the risks and challenges faced by China. In many respects, Xi's earlier fears about foreign economic pressure has come to pass. China was facing large-scale trade and investment restrictions, bans on transfer of key technologies, and efforts to hobble leading Chinese companies.

Since 2017, the United States has curtailed China's access to American markets, capital, and technology and floated the idea of crippling sanctions. The trade restrictions were painful but manageable risks to the Chinese economy. Despite the rapid tariff escalation, China continued to grow its trade surpluses by shifting exports to other markets. The capital market restrictions were also damaging but not insurmountable. Given China's domestic savings surplus, Chinese companies were not dependent on access to U.S. capital.

However, American technology restrictions on China and the threat of further sanctions were much more damaging. Two of China's leading technology firms, ZTE and Huawei, had been severely hobbled by American restrictions. The ability of Chinese technology firms to surmount these challenges was viewed as a matter of national survival.[203] Further restrictions in the works by U.S. policymakers threatened to derail China's efforts to develop domestic sources of advanced technology, notably semiconductors. China was at risk of being shut out of the more advanced segments of the global value chain and remaining dependent on its chief geopolitical rival for access to critical technologies. Given the dual-purpose nature of many of these technologies, this threatened to put China at a perpetual military disadvantage. Finally, Chinese policymakers were fearful of the ability of the United States to exclude China from the international financial system, seize its overseas assets, and disrupt its access to critical resources through sanctions.

In response, Xi would accelerate his long-standing efforts to guide China toward greater economic self-sufficiency. In doing so, the Party would further expand its role in guiding the economy and move away from reliance on market forces to guide the allocation of resources. The growing focus on international threats and the need to prepare economy is evident in a series of speeches and policy documents produced by the Party starting in 2020.

One of the most explicit markers of prioritization of national security issues in economic policymaking was the 14th Five-Year Plan. Drafted in October 2020, the Plan set out the main development goals for China over the 2021–2025 period. The Plan prominently features the concept of "An Integrated Approach to Security and Development." This approach calls for implementing national security concerns into all aspects of economic development and defines security threats as anything that hinders China's modernization:

> A holistic approach to national security calls for the integration of national security imperatives into every aspect of national development, so as to be better able to implement our national security strategy, safeguard national security, respond effectively to both traditional and non-traditional threats, and forestall any challenges to China's modernization.[204]

Further elaborating upon this concept, the Plan establishes a definition of security that encompasses all aspects of Chinese society:

> As part of the effort to protect our national interests, strengthening national security requires a holistic look at a full spectrum of security issues, ranging from political security, which is of overarching importance, the security of the people, which is the ultimate concern, and economic security, which underpins all other considerations, to military, scientific and technological, cultural, and social perspectives, which reinforce efforts in other areas.[205]

Xi's own rhetoric about the economy began to shift sharply in the direction of threats and security. In January 2021, Xi laid out his updated vision for the economy. It represented a dramatic shift from the approach that had guided China through much of the prior forty years of reform. Previously, China's leaders believed that the country faced a relatively benign international environment, allowing the Party to prioritize economic growth, raising living standards, and integration into the global economy. However, according to Xi, China now faced a world full of threats and challenges:

> The world today is undergoing profound changes unseen in a century. Recently, the world situation could be best described by the word "chaos," and it appears that this trend will continue for quite some time.[206]

Xi further elaborates on this grim view of the international environment and the risks that China faces, stating:

> As the principal contradiction in Chinese society has changed and the global balance of power is steadily shifting, China will have to contend with more internal and external risks in development than before. We must be more aware of potential dangers, keep in mind worst-case scenarios, and be prepared for more complex and graver situations.[207]

While the rest of the world was in chaos, Xi was more convinced than ever of the superiority of China's system relative to the rest of the world:

> The response to the Covid-19 pandemic has highlighted the leadership capacities and strengths of the social systems of all countries. The fact that time and momentum are on our side gives us self-assurance, resolve, and confidence.[208]

Given the growing tensions with the United States, Xi states that increasing domestic innovation and reducing foreign technological dependence must be understood "as being vital to the survival and development of our nation."[209]

In the speech, Xi outlined a new policy framework called the New Development Philosophy (NDP).[210] First introduced in 2015, after 2020, the NDP began to coalesce into a new framework for managing China's economic development. The NDP states that after nearly 45 years of rapid growth, China's economy is massive but riven with distortions, inequality, and environmental degradation. These issues have produced domestic economic risks and social divisions that threaten China's social stability—and, by extension, the Party's unchallenged grip on power. The NDP declares that China will deprioritize rapid growth in favor of more balanced and sustainable economic development and "common prosperity." One of the core components of the NDP is giving more weight to security and political concerns in economic decision-making.[211]

The NDP takes pains to declare that China will not close its economy or enact new trade and investment restrictions. However, it also places the most importance on reducing China's technological dependency on Western countries. China has invested billions of dollars to develop domestic sources of crucial "chokepoint" technologies that it currently imports. The NDP seeks to leverage China's large domestic market against foreign economic pressure. As China's economy has grown, its domestic market has developed its own gravitational force for foreign companies and investors. China can use access to its domestic market to force concessions from trading partners and derail U.S. attempts to build economic coalitions against China.

A subsequent article attributed to China's National Development and Reform Commission, published in highly influential party publication Qiushi, describes the New Development Philosophy as a "magic formula" for dealing with domestic and international risks and challenges.

> Given the current instability and uncertainty in the international environment, relying on the advantages of our enormous domestic market, tapping the full potential of domestic demand, and ensuring smooth domestic and international economic flows will help to ameliorate external shocks and changes to the external environment as well as lead to new advantages in international cooperation and competition.[212]

Further cementing the shift toward national security, the Party published a rare historical resolution in November 2021. The ability to enact a new historical resolution was a testament to Xi's control over the Party. These resolutions are meant to codify the Party's official view on historical events, Mao and Deng issued historical resolutions in 1949 and 1981, respectively, to consolidate their control over the Party. Xi's historical resolution yet again makes clear the multitude of risks and challenges faced by China and the need for an expansive view of security:

> We must always be prepared for worst-case scenarios and mindful of potential dangers. We must uphold the primacy of our national interests and take the people's security as our ultimate goal, political security as our fundamental task, economic security as our foundation, military, technological, cultural, and social security as means of guarantee, and international security as the support. We must find a balance between development and security, between opening up and security, between traditional and non-traditional security, between China's domestic security and the common security of the world, and between safeguarding national security and creating conditions conducive to it.[213]

If there were any doubt about Xi's intentions, the historical resolution makes it clear.

> Comrade Xi Jinping has stressed that our Party should make national security its top priority. He has put forward a holistic approach to national security, which covers political, military, homeland security, economic,

cultural, social, technological, cyberspace, ecological, resource, nuclear, overseas interests, outer space, deep sea, polar, and biological security issues, among others.

The implications for the economy as a result of this shift were profound. The Party must shift China away from its old development model, which resulted in "imbalanced, uncoordinated, and unsustainable" growth. In its place, the New Development Philosophy would shift China toward an economic growth model more focused on sustainability, equality, and resiliency to foreign pressure.

While repeating the Party's commitment to "encourage, support, and guide" the private sector, the Resolution applauded the Party's efforts to strengthen the state sector and increase its influence:

> It has prompted state capital and state-owned enterprises to grow stronger, better, and larger, established a modern enterprise system with Chinese characteristics, and worked to make the public sector more competitive, innovative, risk-resilient, and capable of exerting a greater level of influence and control over the economy.[214]

The Resolution also reaffirms the country's commitment to technological self-reliance, prioritizing the effort as essential to China's economic development, and calling for mobilizing the economy to support it:

> The Party has been committed to the innovation-driven development strategy. It has made self-reliance in science and technology the strategic pillar for the country's development and developed a new system for mobilizing the resources nationwide for this purpose.[215]

Finally, as if to leave no question about Xi and the Party's intentions, the Resolution states that China seeks to prevail in an ongoing contest between socialism and capitalism:

> Our continued success in adapting Marxism to the Chinese context and the needs of our times has enabled Marxism to take on a fresh face in the eyes of the world, and significantly shifted the worldwide historical evolution of and contest between the two different ideologies and social systems of socialism and capitalism in a way that favors socialism.[216]

In summary, Xi undertook a significant reorientation of China's economic development framework in reaction to perceived domestic and international threats. Driven by an expansive definition of security, China would seek to create an economy that was more resilient and less exposed to foreign threats. SOEs would be strengthened so that they could serve as implementers of national policy and direct resources toward the Party's goals. There was still room for the private sector in this new vision, but it would need to develop in ways that support national objectives. Companies that failed to support the Party's goals or created economic risks would soon find themselves the targets of draconian regulatory crackdowns.

6 Putting the Bird Back in the Cage

Xi and the Party's focus on national security would translate to domestic economic policy that was intolerant of risk, volatility, and challenges to the state control. Starting in late 2020, the Party initiated a wide-ranging crackdown on numerous industries dominated by private firms. By the time the crackdown was over, the Party would force many of these firms to restructure their companies, sell off parts of their businesses, and comply with strict new regulations that limited their activities. The crackdown echoed the 2017–2018 pursuit of "grey rhino" private conglomerates but was broader in nature, more ideologically driven, and had the effect of hobbling many of China's leading private firms. It was a manifestation of Xi's new policymaking approach that emphasized combatting risks and guiding the economy toward the strategic goals promulgated by the Party.

The Tech Crackdown: The crackdown began with arguably the most famous company in China, Alibaba, and its outspoken founder, Jack Ma. Throughout the 2010s, Alibaba Group had grown in size and influence. The company has helped reshape retail in China through pioneering efforts to expand e-commerce. In the financial realm, Alibaba's subsidiary, Ant Group, created a hugely popular consumer payments and lending network. Alipay, Ant's payments network, processed trillions of dollars of retail payments yearly on its proprietary network, which competed with the state-owned UnionPay network. Ant also offered loans to customers making purchases on Alibaba's e-commerce site, Taobao, and small business loans to many small vendors operating on the platform. China's large state banks have historically overlooked small businesses and consumers. Ant had a new and flexible business models that allowed it to profitably serve these borrowers ignored by the larger banks. Ant's rapid takeover of this segment of the market raised alarm bells that left unfettered the company might further displace the state banks within the financial system.

Ant was coming under increased scrutiny due to its increasing prominence in an otherwise state-controlled financial system. As early as 2018, there was unease that a non-bank private financial firm was growing "too big to manage."[217] There were both legitimate concerns about whether Ant was sufficiently regulated and concerns that its growing influence threatened to weaken the Party's control over the financial system.[218] Jack Ma himself may have also been in Beijing's crosshairs. Chinese officials were reportedly unhappy that Ma had made a high-profile visit to Donald Trump in 2017, soon after his election.[219] In the meeting, Ma adopted an unusually high-profile role for a Chinese entrepreneur, appearing to play diplomat between the two countries and promising to create 1 million new American jobs. Ma also provoked criticism from the public for his comments extolling the virtues of long workdays for tech workers.[220] Ma's comments appeared crass given growing social discontent around conditions for workers at tech firms, particularly for low-level workers such as delivery workers.

Even as regulatory pressures began to build on Ant, the company raced toward an IPO in Hong Kong that was expected to be the largest in history. A few days before the IPO was set to occur, Ma gave a now infamous speech at the Shanghai Bund Summit. In the speech, Ma railed at financial regulators, which he described as an "old person's club," and used quotes from Xi to argue against further regulation of Ant.[221] The speech, viewed as defiant of government authority, generated significant backlash among officials, and according to reports, Xi Jinping himself ordered the cancellation of Ant's IPO.[222]

Both Alibaba and Ant soon faced a blistering regulatory onslaught. In early November 2020, Jack Ma and other Alibaba executives were called before the China Securities Regulatory Commission for a "regulatory interview."[223] Then, in December, Chinese regulators announced an anti-monopoly investigation into Alibaba.[224] In December 2020, the government called Ant Group for its own "regulatory interview" with the People's Bank of China, the China Banking Regulatory Commission, the China Securities Regulatory Commission, and the State Administration of Foreign Exchange. A statement subsequently released by the central bank stated that the purpose of the interview was to "urge and guide Ant Group to deeply implement the relevant spirit" of the Central Committee and State Council and rectify its business activities.[225] Ant group "must consciously abide by national laws and regulations," "integrate its corporate development into the overall situation of national development," and "effectively undertake corporate social responsibility."[226] These innocuous-sounding phrases were code for a massive corporate restructuring. Over the next two years, Ant would be forced to split up and spin off key parts of its business, create walls between its operations and Alibaba, subject itself to greater regulatory supervision, and share its trove of data with regulators. By the time Ant completed its rectification program in 2023, it had lost three-quarters of its pre-IPO valuation.[227]

Stretching from 2021 until mid-2023, Ant, Alibaba, and their subsidiaries would face an onslaught of fines and investigations. In April 2021, Alibaba was ordered to pay a record $2.8 billion fine for anti-trust violations and ordered to implement a "comprehensive rectification plan" to address its anti-competitive and anti-consumer behavior.[228] That same month, Ant was ordered to restructure as a financial holding company and cut links between its payment and lending services.[229] In May 2021, Alibaba food delivery service Eleme was fined for illegal business practices.[230] In September 2021, Ant's consumer credit scoring business was spun off, with several large state-owned investors taking stakes.[231] In July 2022, Alibaba was fined for disclosure violations for five prior acquisitions.[232] That same month, Alibaba and Ant terminated their data-sharing agreement and preferential Alipay terms for Alibaba.[233] In January 2023, Jack Ma announced he would give up control of Ant, going from 50.5% voting rights to 6%.[234] Throughout this period, Jack Ma largely disappeared from public view and was reportedly living in Japan. He finally returned to China in March 2023 to oversee an announcement from Alibaba that it was breaking up into six different units.[235] In July 2023, Ant was subjected to a $985 million fine for inappropriate business practices. The penalty was seen by many analysts as signaling an end to the "regulatory crackdown" on the firm.[236]

Alibaba and Ant were the first firms targeted in the crackdown, but it soon expanded to encompass many of China's other leading private firms. In April 2021, 34 companies were summoned by the State Administration and Regulation and ordered to conduct "self-inspections" or face "severe punishment" for violating rules.[237] In November that year, China's market regulator issued a flurry of fines on private firms, including Tencent, Baidu, JD.Com, Geely, and others for failing to seek approval for prior mergers and acquisitions.[238] Chinese regulators dramatically reduced their approval of new movies, tv shows, and video games, crippling the activities of many private media and entertainment companies. The private education industry, companies that offered after-school tutoring and test preparation services, was decimated by rules that effectively prohibited paid tutoring in the name of social equity. Chinese regulators banned cryptocurrency transactions, forcing Chinese crypto companies to shut down or depart the country.[239]

Didi Chuxing, China's dominant ride-hailing firm, was punished severely for publicly listing in the United States. Chinese regulators were reportedly unhappy that the firm, which had extensive information on its users and their travel patterns, had proceeded with an IPO in June of 2021 and was now de facto controlled by foreign investors. The company was forced to hastily delist from the New York Stock Exchange, and regulators prohibited new users from signing up for the service for 18 months.[240] Earlier that month, China had passed an expansive data security law that set strict new rules for corporate data management in the name of national security. Didi was ultimately forced to restructure its business, pay a hefty fine, and adhere to China's strict new data laws.

The Chinese real estate developer industry, dominated by private firms, was also crippled by new regulations. In 2020, the Chinese government introduced the Three Red Lines, a set of balance sheet constraints for property developers intended to force deleveraging.[241] There were ample reasons to reform the real estate industry. For years, economists had warned about the potential dangers of a real estate bubble. The share of the Chinese economy connected to real estate was extraordinarily high, and price levels in China's coastal cities had increased well beyond what could be supported by the income of a typical Chinese household. Moreover, many property developers expanded their businesses recklessly, borrowing heavily to fund an aggressive accumulation of land holdings and using pre-sales from one project to fund another. However, the new policies had a disparate impact on private real estate developers. Private developers saw their access to credit collapse, and many state-owned developers used the opportunity to buy properties from private developers cheaply. As shown in Fig. 12, property sales of private developers, both distressed and non-distressed, declined much more sharply than those of state-owned developers.

In addition to the actions against private companies, a shift in policy was articulated through official speeches, state media, and other pronouncements. In December 2020, not long after the cancellation of the Ant IPO, Xi chaired a meeting by the Politburo focused on economic policy. One of the policies called for in the meetings readout was strengthening the fight against monopolies and the "disorderly expansion of capital."[242] As might be expected, the monopolies most concerning to the Party were those of private enterprises, not entrenched SOEs.

An article in state media later that month clarified that the disorderly expansion of capital referred to the "platform economy," a concept that encompassed the social media apps and online marketplaces created by China's leading technology firms, including Alibaba, Tencent, Baidu, Didi Chuxing, and others. The companies had engaged in "market monopolization, disorderly expansion, and barbaric growth."[243] According to experts quoted in the article, these companies were engaging in practices

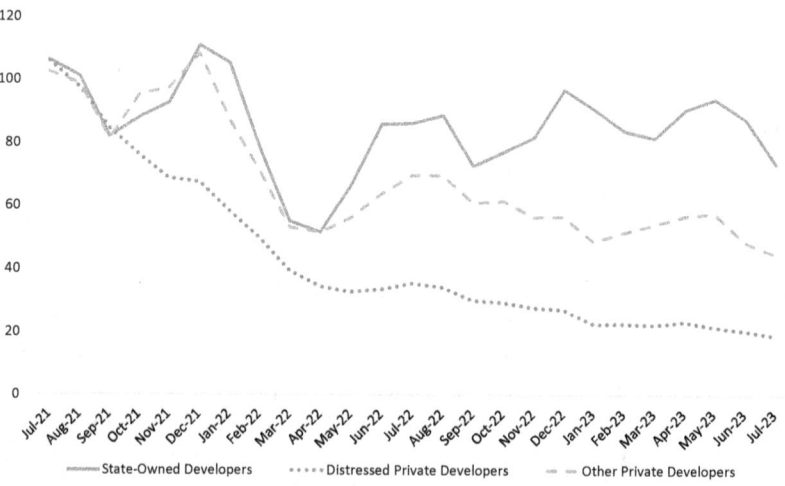

Fig. 12 Sales volume of property developers (*Source* International Monetary Fund, author's calculations)

not beneficial to China's technological progress and long-term development and needed to focus their efforts on helping China break through key foreign technology bottlenecks.[244]

An article published in the People's Daily in September 2021 outlined the Party's evolving approach to the private sector.[245] It acknowledged the broad scope of recent regulatory actions and praised them as "powerful measures" to enhance China's socialist market economy. Drawing on Xi's New Development Philosophy, the article argued that amid raging waves and turbulent seas, economic policies must prioritize strengthening China's survivability, competitiveness, development, and sustainability. It emphasized that economic policy must be tightly integrated with security considerations. While claiming that the Party's support for the private sector remained unchanged, the article also declares that the regulation should be used to "guide and urge companies to obey the Party's leadership, support national social and economic development, compete internationally, and contribute to scientific breakthroughs."

The message was clear: the Party expected private firms to abandon activities it deemed to be socially harmful, risk-inducing, or merely unproductive. Instead, private firms were to align their efforts with the Party's goals, particularly those goals related to bolstering China's domestic technology capabilities and reducing its reliance on foreign countries.

7   Conclusion

In a 2022 speech to the Politburo, Xi Jinping shared revealing insights into his views on the economy. He reflected on the Party's shift in 1979, when it broke free from a "restrictive mindset on ownership" and recognized that various forms of capital—including private and foreign—could be used "to promote economic and social development."[246] According to Xi, this realization was key to China's economic success over the past 40 years. However, he also warned that "capital is profit-driven by nature, and if unregulated and unconstrained, will cause immeasurable damage to the economy and society." He emphasized that "capital must always serve the interests of the people and the country" and contribute to "comprehensive socialist modernization and national rejuvenation."

Xi's words encapsulate the "bird and the cage" framework through which the Party views the economy. China leveraged the private sector and foreign investment to drive its economic transformation. The rapid growth of the past four decades would not have been possible otherwise.

Yet Xi and the Party retained a deep skepticism about the role of capital and market forces. They were useful but could also be dangerous. The Party, Xi asserted, must remain vigilant to ensure that capital always serves the national interest as defined by the Party.

As mentioned at the outset of this chapter, Xi's approach to the economy has bewildered many foreign observers. Many initially placed great hopes in Xi at the start of his tenure, believing he might steer the economy toward greater liberalization. However, these hopes were misplaced, as Xi's approach to the economy was more of a continuation than a break from the past. Like his predecessors, Xi saw the market as a powerful force, essential to China's national rejuvenation, but also recognized its potential to be destructive and undermine the Party's goals.

In his early years, Xi went through a cycle of selectively embracing economic reforms and then backtracking when those reforms created financial and economic instability. In this respect, the early years of his rule echoed the approaches of Deng, Jiang, and Hu, all of whom went through alternating cycles of supporting reform and imposing new economic restrictions. However, in the years following the 2017–2018 crackdown, Xi notably broke with tradition and did not shift back toward loosening economic restrictions.

This shift marked a departure from the Party's historical approach to managing the economy. It was driven by events that fundamentally reshaped Xi's view of the challenges facing China. The benign and open international economic system that had welcomed China in at the start of reforms in the late 1970s was gone. In its place, China faced an intense strategic and economic conflict with the United States and its allies. Furthermore, the COVID-19 pandemic had recently exposed how vulnerable the global economy was to major disruptions. The world had become significantly more threatening and fraught with risk than ever before.

As a result, Xi's approach to the economy remained focused on risks and control. The prospect of intense competition with another superpower necessitated further strengthening the Party's control over the economy. The Party had to direct economic resources toward making China self-reliant and immune to foreign pressure. There would be less tolerance for economic instability and internal threats that might undermine the Party's efforts to address the challenge presented by the United States. The ebb and flow of economic liberalization that defined the prior forty years of economic reform was disrupted by the prospect of geostrategic competition with the world's superpower. The next chapter will analyze how this disruption to the historical cycle of reform would profoundly impact the economy.

Notes

1. Chun Han Wong, *Party of One: The Rise of Xi Jinping and China's Superpower Future* (Avid Reader Press/Simon & Schuster, 2023).
2. "Xi Jinping's Moment," *Lowy Institute for International Policy*, October 2017, https://www.jstor.org/stable/pdf/resrep10198.pdf.
3. Kerry Brown, *CEO, China: The Rise of Xi Jinping* (I.B. Tauris, 2016).
4. Joseph Torigian, "Xi Jinping and Ideology," *The Wilson Center*, May 31, 2022, https://www.wilsoncenter.org/sites/default/files/media/uploads/documents/Torigian_Xi%20Jinping%20and%20Ideology.pdf.
5. Carrie Gracie, "The Thoughts of Chairman Xi," *BBC News*, October 13, 2017, https://www.bbc.co.uk/news/resources/idt-sh/Thoughts_Chairman_Xi.
6. Chun Han Wong, *Party of One: The Rise of Xi Jinping and China's Superpower Future* (Avid Reader Press/Simon & Schuster, 2023).
7. Evan Osnos, "How Xi Jinping Took Control of China," *The New Yorker*, March 30, 2015, https://www.newyorker.com/magazine/2015/04/06/born-red.
8. Joseph Torigian, "Xi Jinping and Ideology," *The Wilson Center*, May 31, 2022, https://www.wilsoncenter.org/sites/default/files/media/uploads/documents/Torigian_Xi%20Jinping%20and%20Ideology.pdf.
9. Lin Chen, "How General Secretary Xi Jinping Interprets the Relationship Between Politics and Business (习近平总书记如何诠释政商关系)," *People's Forum* (人民论坛网), November 8, 2016, http://www.rmlt.com.cn/2016/1108/442446.shtml.

10. Kerry Brown, *CEO, China: The Rise of Xi Jinping* (I.B. Tauris, 2016).
11. Cheng Li, "China's Team of Rivals," *Brookings Institution*, February 17, 2009, https://www.brookings.edu/articles/chinas-team-of-rivals/.
12. Joseph Kahn, "Politburo in China Gets Four New Members," *The New York Times*, October 22, 2007, https://www.nytimes.com/2007/10/22/world/asia/22china.html.
13. Austin Ramzy, "A Chinese Leader Talks Tough to Foreigners | TIME.Com," *TIME.Com*, February 13, 2009, https://world.time.com/2009/02/13/a-chinese-leader-talks-tough-to-foreigners/.
14. Cheng Li and Eve Cary, "The Last Year of Hu's Leadership: Hu's to Blame?" *Jamestown Foundation*, December 20, 2011, https://jamestown.org/program/the-last-year-of-hus-leadership-hus-to-blame/.
15. Chen Ting and James Kai-sing Kung, "Busting the "Princelings": The Campaign Against Corruption in China's Primary Land Market," *The Quarterly Journal of Economics* 134, Issue 1 (February 2019): 185–226, https://doi.org/10.1093/qje/qjy027.
16. Chen and Kung, "Busting the "Princelings,"" 185–226, https://doi.org/10.1093/qje/qjy027.
17. David Barboza and Sharon LaFraniere, "'Princelings' in China Use Family Ties to Gain Riches," *The New York Times*, May 17, 2012, https://www.nytimes.com/2012/05/18/world/asia/china-princelings-using-family-ties-to-gain-riches.html.
18. Chun Han Wong, *Party of One: The Rise of Xi Jinping and China's Superpower Future* (Avid Reader Press/Simon & Schuster, 2023).
19. Rush Doshi, *The Long Game: China's Grand Strategy to Displace American Order* (Oxford University Press, 2021).
20. "The Central Economic Work Conference Was Held, Hu Jintao and Wen Jiabao Delivered Important Speeches (中央经济工作会议举行 胡锦涛、温家宝作重要讲话)," *State Administration of Grain* (国家粮食局), December 14, 2009, http://www.lswz.gov.cn/html/zhuanti/n16/n3615/n3631/4425878.html.

21. "Document 9: A ChinaFile Translation," *ChinaFile*, October 30, 2015, https://www.chinafile.com/document-9-chinafile-translation.
22. "China Takes Aim at Western Ideas," *The New York Times*, August 13, 2019, https://www.nytimes.com/2013/08/20/world/asia/chinas-new-leadership-takes-hard-line-in-secret-memo.html.
23. Sharon LaFraniere, "China Puts Joblessness for Migrants at 20 Million," *The New York Times*, February 3, 2009, https://www.nytimes.com/2009/02/03/world/asia/03china.html.
24. CEIC Data, accessed August 8, 2023. Measured as the increase in Aggregate Financing Stock between December 31, 2008 and December 31, 2011.
25. Xiao Gang, "Regulating Shadow Banking," *China Daily*, October 12, 2012, http://www.chinadaily.com.cn/opinion/2012-10/12/content_15812305.htm.
26. Ryan Rutkowski, "New National Audit on Local Government Borrowing in China: Three Years Later, Little Progress," *Peterson Institute for International Economics*, October 24, 2019, https://www.piie.com/blogs/china-economic-watch/new-national-audit-local-government-borrowing-china-three-years-later.
27. Jinping Xi, "Apply the New Development Philosophy in Full," *The Governance of China* IV, January 11, 2021, http://en.qstheory.cn/2023-06/12/c_893605.htm.
28. Barry Naughton, "After the Third Plenum: Economic Reform Revival Moves Toward Implementation," *Hoover Institution*, March 14, 2014, https://www.hoover.org/research/after-third-plenum-economic-reform-revival-moves-toward-implementation.
29. "Communiqué of The Third Plenary Session of the 18th Central Committee of the CPC (中国共产党十八届三中全会公报)," *China.Org.Cn*, January 16, 2014, http://www.china.org.cn/chinese/2014-01/16/content_31213800_3.htm.
30. "Decision of the Central Committee of the Communist Party of China on Some Major Issues Concerning Comprehensively Deepening the Reform," *China.Org.Cn*, January 16, 2014, http://www.china.org.cn/china/third_plenary_session/2014-01/16/content_31212602.htm.
31. "Decision of the Central Committee," 2014.

32. See Nicholas Borst, "Economic Reform in the Third Plenum: Balancing State and Market," *The Jamestown Foundation*, November 20, 2013, https://jamestown.org/program/economic-reform-in-the-third-plenum-balancing-state-and-market/, Daniel Rosen, "Avoiding the Blind Alley: China's Economic Overhaul and Its Global Implications," *The Asia Society*, October 2014, https://asiasociety.org/files/pdf/AvoidingtheBlindAlley_FullReport.pdf, Barry Naughton, "After the Third Plenum: Economic Reform Revival Moves Toward Implementation," *Hoover Institution*, March 14, 2014, https://www.hoover.org/research/after-third-plenum-economic-reform-revival-moves-toward-implementation, and Arthur Kroeber, "Xi Jinping's Ambitious Agenda for Economic Reform in China | Brookings," *Brookings Institution*, November 17, 2013, https://www.brookings.edu/articles/xi-jinpings-ambitious-agenda-for-economic-reform-in-china/.
33. "Communiqué of The Third Plenary Session of the 18th Central Committee of the CPC (中国共产党十八届三中全会公报)," *China.Org.Cn*, January 16, 2014, http://www.china.org.cn/chinese/2014-01/16/content_31213800_3.htm.
34. "Communiqué of The Third Plenary Session," 2014.
35. "Decision of the Central Committee of the Communist Party of China on Some Major Issues Concerning Comprehensively Deepening the Reform," *China.Org.Cn*, January 16, 2014, http://www.china.org.cn/china/third_plenary_session/2014-01/16/content_31212602.htm.
36. "Explanatory Notes for the 'Decision of the CCCPC on Some Major Issues Concerning Comprehensively Deepening the Reform' (关于《中共中央关于全面深化改革若干重大问题的决定》的说明)," *China.Org.Cn*, January 16, 2014, http://www.china.org.cn/chinese/2014-01/16/content_31215162_8.htm.
37. "Explanatory Notes," 2014.
38. "Explanatory Notes," 2014.
39. "Explanatory Notes," 2014.
40. "Explanatory Notes," 2014.
41. Jing Du, "Fighting Against the Black Swan and Grey Rhino Has Become Popular Recently (和 '黑天鹅'对着干 '灰犀牛'最近火了!)," *Xinhua*, July 19, 2017, http://www.xinhuanet.com/world/2017-07/19/c_129659332.htm.

42. Logan Wright and Daniel Rosen, "Credit and Credibility: Risks to China's Economic Resilience," *Center for Strategic and International Studies*, October 2018, https://csis-website-prod.s3.amazonaws.com/s3fs-public/publication/181003_Creditand Credibility_final.PDF.
43. Tianlei Huang, "Chinese Local Governments' Reliance on Land Revenue Drops as the Property Downturn Drags On," *The Peterson Institute for International Economics*, July 5, 2024, https://www.piie.com/research/piie-charts/2024/chinese-local-governments-reliance-land-revenue-drops-property-downturn.
44. "Notice on Further Strengthening the Work of Shantytown Reconstruction (国务院办公厅关于进一步加强 棚户区改造工作的通知)," *The Central People's Government of the People's Republic of China* (中华人民共和国中央人民政府), August 4, 2014, https://www.gov.cn/zhengce/content/2014-08/04/content_8951.htm.
45. "China to Accelerate Shantytown Redevelopment," *China Daily*, May 25, 2017, https://www.chinadaily.com.cn/china/2017-05/25/content_29488730.htm.
46. Thomas Orlik, *China: The Bubble That Never Pops* (Oxford University Press, 2020).
47. "Full Transcript: Interview With Chinese President Xi Jinping," *The Wall Street Journal*, September 14, 2015, https://www.wsj.com/articles/full-transcript-interview-with-chinese-president-xi-jinping-1442894700.
48. "People's Republic of China: Staff Report for the 2015 Article IV Consultation," *International Monetary Fund*, August 14, 2015, https://www.imf.org/en/Publications/CR/Issues/2016/12/31/Peoples-Republic-of-China-Staff-Report-for-the-2015-Article-IV-Consultation-43197.
49. Reyu Wang, "4000 Points Is the Beginning of the A-share Bull Market (4000点才是A股牛市的开端)," *People's Daily*, April 21, 2015, https://finance.sina.cn/stock/ggyj/2015-04-21/detail-icczmvun9987467.d.html?from=wap.
50. Gang Xiao, "Reform Bull Market Is Established, the Market Is Not Short of Money ('改革牛'成立 市场不差钱)," *People's Daily*, June 13, 2015, http://politics.people.com.cn/n/2015/0613/c1001-27149624.html.

51. "The China Securities Regulatory Commission Will Investigate Off-Market Capital Raising Again and Companies Involved in Manipulating Securities Transactions (证监会再查场外配资 个别公司涉操纵证券交易)," *People's Daily*, July 13, 2015, http://politics.people.com.cn/n/2015/0713/c70731-27294868.html.
52. Koh Gui Qing and Kazunori Takada, "China Stems Stocks Rout, but Market Faces Lengthy Hangover," *Reuters*, July 9, 2015, https://www.reuters.com/article/us-china-markets-idUSKCN0PI2RT20150709.
53. Tri Vi Dang, Wei Li, and Yongqin Wang, "Managing China's Stock Markets: The Economics of the National Team," *Social Science Research Network*, January 2020, https://doi.org/10.2139/ssrn.3546411.
54. Neil Gough, "China's Stock Exchanges Crack Down on Short-Selling," *The New York Times*, August 4, 2015, https://www.nytimes.com/2015/08/05/business/dealbook/chinese-shares-rise-sharply-after-government-cracks-down-on-short-selling.html.
55. Shen Hong, Wei Gu, and Shen Hong, "In China's Widening Stock Crackdown, It's 'Kill the Chicken to Scare the Monkey,'" *The Wall Street Journal*, November 12, 2015, https://www.wsj.com/articles/in-chinas-widening-stock-crackdown-its-kill-the-chicken-to-scare-the-monkey-1447355146.
56. Michael Forsythe, "Chinese Manager of Highflying Funds Is Arrested in Insider Trading Case," *The New York Times*, November 2, 2015, https://www.nytimes.com/2015/11/03/business/international/xu-xiang-zexi-insider-trading-arrest-china.html.
57. Meg Rithmire, *Precarious Ties Business and the State in Authoritarian Asia* (Oxford University Press, 2024).
58. "The PBC Announcement on Improving Quotation of the Central Parity of RMB against US Dollar," *The People's Bank of China*, August 11, 2015, http://www.pbc.gov.cn/english/130721/2941603/index.html.
59. Max Zenglein, "China's Caution about Loosening Cross-Border Capital Flows," *Mercator Institute for China Studies*, June 19, 2019, https://merics.org/en/report/chinas-caution-about-loosening-cross-border-capital-flows.

Woher, so wäre zu fragen, sollte denn die Zuversicht der Jünger stammen, mit der sie sich erkühnt hätten, zur bekräftigenden Ausschmückung ihrer Zuversicht die dann ja offenbar tatsachenwidrigen Behauptungen über Begegnungen mit dem Auferstandenen zu erzählen? Die biblischen Texte sprechen im Kontext der Osterereignisse zunächst von Angst, Zweifel, Unverständnis, Verzagtheit und Unglauben der Jünger. Erst die personale Erfahrung mit dem Auferstandenen, auch wenn sie literarisch recht unterschiedlichen Ausdruck gefunden hat – man vergleiche etwa die im Johannesevangelium erzählte Erfahrung der Maria von Magdala (Joh 20,1–18) und die von ihm selbst brieflich mitgeteilte Erfahrung des Paulus (1 Kor 15,1–8) –, befähigt die Jünger und die Apostel zum Zeugnis für Auferstehung und neues Leben.

Mag auch dieses oder jenes Element an den neutestamentlich mitgeteilten Ostererfahrungen dem Erzählungsmodus von Visionen oder Epiphanien ähneln, der Sache nach handelt es sich allerdings weniger um bloß innersubjektive Wahrnehmungen, sondern vielmehr um die konkreten auch intersubjektiv vermittelten Erfahrungen von Begegnungen mit dem Auferweckten bzw. dem Auferstandenen.

Eine Rekonstruktion des Wie der Auferstehung bzw. Auferweckung Jesu ist aus den neutestamentlichen Texten nicht zu erheben; es gibt keinen unmittelbaren Tat- oder Ereigniszeugen für die Auferstehung oder Auferweckung Jesu, der einen Tatsachenbericht vorlegen könnte. Es lässt sich auch keine fahrplanmäßig nachvollziehbare Vorstellung vom Ablauf der Ostererscheinungen rekonstruieren. Hinsichtlich des Wie gibt es also eine nicht hintergehbare Dürftigkeit der Quellen.

Dagegen hält Kessler aber andererseits das Dass und das Was der Erscheinungen fest:

„Das Daß und Was der Erscheinungen aber tritt mit umso größerer Klarheit hervor. Das vom Historiker postulierte, den Osterglauben mit seiner ganzen Dynamik auslösende, rätselhafte ‚Etwas' ist nach den als glaubwürdig erwiesenen neutestamentlichen Zeugnissen das gegenüber Leben und Sterben Jesu neue ganz außergewöhnliche Erlebnis der Begegnung und Selbstbekundung des Auferweckten selber."[40]

Ein empirisch-historisches ‚Packende' des sich in diesen Erscheinungen bekundenden, aber doch unfassbar bleibenden Ereignisses ist nur indirekt in den tiefgreifenden und folgenreichen Auswirkungen im

Leben der Jünger und Apostel zu sehen. Hier sind beide Ebenen, die subjektiv-existentielle und die objektiv-historische Ebene betroffen.

Ein traditionalistisch-fundamentalistischer Objektivismus, der ein supranaturales Mirakel verdinglichen und ins Historisch-Faktische verlegen möchte, bietet gerade keine Gewähr für die Bewahrung des theologischen Kerns von Ostern, sondern setzt ihn aufs Spiel. Dieser auferweckende Gott soll objektiv in der Geschichte ankommen und zugleich ohne das Subjektive des Menschen auskommen. Das ist wohl kaum möglich.

Mit anderem Vorzeichen versucht ein modernistisch-psychologisierender Subjektivismus die Anstößigkeit des Osterereignisses dadurch zu entschärfen, dass er es zu einem rein innerpsychischen Befreiungs- und Verlebendigungserlebnis ohne Bezug zur Geschichte degradiert.

Ein solcher ‚Psycho-Gott' ohne Geschichtsrelevanz erleichtert allenfalls dem einen oder anderen Menschen und das auch nur zeitweilig das Lebensschicksal, er enthebt die Toten der Geschichte aber nicht ihres Todesschicksals, sondern belässt sie im Tod. Die Anstößigkeit des Osterglaubens wird dadurch behoben, dass dieser mit Ausnahme der psychologischen jeglicher Wirklichkeitsannahme enthoben und damit entleert wird.

Der Gedanke an die seit jeher mit dem Auferstehungsglauben verbundene ausgleichende Gerechtigkeit bleibt auf der Strecke, wenn man den Gott der Geschichte zum Gott mit bloß innerpsychischer Zuständigkeit degradiert. Wenn Gott kein Gott der Geschichte ist, ist auch Geschichte nicht mehr als Heilsgeschichte zu interpretieren.

Ist die Auferstehung Jesu ein äußeres historisches Faktum und also gänzlich unserer Raum-Zeit zuzuordnen, oder ist sie ein innerpsychisch-existentielles Geschehen mit allenfalls indirekten Auswirkungen auf die Geschichte? Plakativ gefragt: Ist das Grab faktisch leer, oder erscheint es den Osterzeugen nur wie leer?

Auch wenn die Geschichten um das leere Grab im Detail voneinander abweichen, so ist doch das einhellige Zeugnis der Heiligen Schrift darüber, dass das Grab leer gewesen sei, zunächst einmal zur Kenntnis zu nehmen und zu respektieren. Aber damit ist die Historizität der Auferstehung oder gar die Verlagerung des Auferstehungsgeschehens als Ganzes in ein pures historisches Diesseits nicht belegt.

Die sich gerade des historisch so hart erscheinenden Faktums des leeren Grabes bedienenden Gegner des Auferstehungsglaubens knüp-

21, 2021, https://www.wsj.com/articles/how-china-vanke-chiefs-state-savior-could-be-his-undoing-1469127600.
79. Hui Qu and Han Wei, "Baoneng Continues Retreat From Vanke After High-Profile Purchases," *Caixin*, December 20, 2019, https://www.caixinglobal.com/2019-12-20/baoneng-continues-retreat-from-vanke-after-high-profile-purchases-101496099.html
80. "China Vanke Moves to End Potential Takeover Battle," *MarketWatch*, December 21 2015, https://www.marketwatch.com/story/china-vanke-moves-to-end-potential-takeover-battle-2015-12-21
81. Daniel Ren, "Baoneng Hits Back at Vanke Takeover Funding Claims," *South China Morning Post*, December 29, 2015, https://www.scmp.com/business/companies/article/1895913/baoneng-hits-back-vanke-takeover-funding-claims.
82. Frank Tang, "China's Muddled Regulatory Battlefront Against Stock Market 'Monsters'" *South China Morning Post*, December 11, 2016, https://www.scmp.com/news/china/economy/article/2053563/battling-beasts-black-stock-market-lagoon
83. Summer Zhen and Xie Yu, "Shenzhen Tycoon Yao Zhenhua Barred from Insurance Industry for 10 Years," *South China Morning Post*, February 24, 2017, https://www.scmp.com/business/companies/article/2073818/shenzhen-tycoon-yao-zhenhua-barred-insurance-industry-10-years.
84. Wendy Wu, "Private Chinese Insurer Follows Failed Vanke Takeover Bid with Plan to Set Up Communist Party Committee," *South China Morning Post*, July 20, 2017, https://www.scmp.com/news/china/economy/article/2103342/private-chinese-insurer-follows-failed-vanke-takeover-bid-plan
85. "Shenzhen Metro to Have Most Voting Rights at Vanke After Proxy Deal," *Reuters*, March 16, 2017, https://www.reuters.com/article/us-vanke-m-a-board/shenzhen-metro-to-have-most-voting-rights-at-vanke-after-proxy-deal-idINKBN16O0BF
86. Barry Naughton, "State Enterprise Reform Today," in *China's 40 Years of Reform and Development: 1978–2018*, edited by Ross Garnaut, Ligang Song, and Cai Fang (Australia: ANU Press, 2018), http://www.jstor.org/stable/j.ctv5cgbnk.28.

87. "Xi Jinping Emphasized: Uphold the Party's Leadership over State-Owned Enterprises Unswervingly and Create a New Situation in Party Building in State-Owned Enterprises (习近平强调:坚持党对国有企业的领导不动摇 开创国有企业党的建设新局面)," *Central People's Government of the Central People's Republic of China* (中央人民共和国中央人民政府), October 11, 2016, https://www.gov.cn/xinwen/2016-10/11/content_5117541.htm..
88. Wendy Leutert, n.d., "Challenges Ahead in China's Reform of State-Owned Enterprises," *Asia Policy*, no. 21: 83–99, https://www.brookings.edu/wp-content/uploads/2016/07/Wendy-Leutert-Challenges-ahead-in-Chinas-reform-of-stateowned-enterprises.pdf.
89. "Guiding Opinion on Deepening the Reform of SOEs (国务院关于深化国有企业改革的指导意见," *Central Committee of the Communist Party of China and the State Council of the People's Republic of China*, August 24, 2015, http://www.gov.cn/zhengce/2015-09/13/content_2930440.htm.
90. Wendy Leutert, n.d., "Challenges Ahead in China's Reform of State-Owned Enterprises," *Asia Policy*, no. 21: 83–99, https://www.brookings.edu/wp-content/uploads/2016/07/Wendy-Leutert-Challenges-ahead-in-Chinas-reform-of-stateowned-enterprises.pdf.
91. "Guiding Opinion on the Classification on the Definition and Classification of SOEs (关于国有企业功能界定与分类的指导意见)," *Chinese State-owned Assets Supervision and Administration Commission, Ministry of Finance, and National Development and Reform Commission*, December 30, 2015, http://www.mof.gov.cn/zhengwuxinxi/zhengcefabu/201512/t20151230_1638704.htm.
92. "Deepening the Classification Reform of State-Owned Enterprises, SASAC Clarifies the Main Direction of Reform and Development of Three Types of Enterprises (深化国有企业分类改革 国资委明确三类企业改革发展主攻方向)," *Xinhua*, April 21, 2021, https://www.gov.cn/xinwen/2021-04/28/content_5603657.htm.
93. Competitive neutrality "implies that no business entity is advantaged (or disadvantaged) solely because of its ownership," See Antonio Capobianco and Hans Christiansen, "Competitive Neutrality and SOEs: Challenges and Policy Options," *OECD*,

May 1, 2011, https://www.oecd-ilibrary.org/governance/competitive-neutrality-and-state-owned-enterprises_5kg9xfgjdhg6-en.
94. Nicholas Lardy, *The State Strikes Back: The End of Economic Reform in China?* (Washington, D.C.: The Peterson Institute for International Economics, 2019).
95. "SOE Reform: 'Four Beams and Eight Pillars' Implemented – Three Year Action Plan Launched (国企改革: "四梁八柱"落地三年行动开启)," *Guangming Daily*, October 13, 2020, http://www.gov.cn/zhengce/2020-10/13/content_5556937.htm.
96. "Special Announcement of China Unicom on the Relevant Circumstances of Mixed Ownership Reform (中国联通关于混合所有制改革有关情况的专项公告)," *China Unicom*, April 20, 2017, https://www.chinaunicom-a.com/api/doccenter/doc_file/getFile?original=1503246735688.pdf&hashCode=QmQdVUMUUHwze81DYxPLUvX61BBWD99GGyQgyu7KxT9LuE&contentType=application%2Fpdf%3Bcharset%3Dutf-8.
97. Clare Jim and Julie Zhu, "State-owned China Unicom to raise $12 billion from Alibaba, Tencent, others," *Reuters*, August 16, 2017, https://www.reuters.com/article/us-china-unicom-results/state-owned-china-unicom-to-raise-12-billion-from-alibaba-tencent-others-idUSKCN1AW0JP.
98. Wind Information, accessed September 14, 2023.
99. "Special Announcement of China Unicom on the Relevant Circumstances of Mixed Ownership Reform (中国联通关于混合所有制改革有关情况的专项公告)," *China Unicom*, April 20, 2017, https://www.chinaunicom-a.com/api/doccenter/doc_file/getFile?original=1503246735688.pdf&hashCode=QmQdVUMUUHwze81DYxPLUvX61BBWD99GGyQgyu7KxT9LuE&contentType=application%2Fpdf%3Bcharset%3Dutf-8.
100. "2017 Annual Report," *China Unicom*, 2018, https://www.chinaunicom.com.hk/en/ir/reports.php?year=2017.
101. As measured by the 2022 annual return on assets and equity. Wind Information, accessed September 14, 2023.
102. Nicholas Lardy, *The State Strikes Back: The End of Economic Reform in China?* (Washington, D.C.: The Peterson Institute for International Economics, 2019).
103. "National Energy Group Officially Established (国家能源集团正式成立)," *Central People's Government of the People's*

Republic of China (中华人民共和国中央人民政府), November 29, 2017, https://www.gov.cn/xinwen/2017-11/29/content_5243073.htm.

104. Cecilia Springer, Dinah Shi, and Aaditee Kudrimoti, "The Political Economy of Coal: The Case of China," In *The Political Economy of Coal*, edited by Michael Jakob and Jan C. Steckel, *Routledge*, https://doi.org/10.4324/9781003044543..

105. Michael Forsythe, "China Curbs Plans for More Coal-Fired Power Plants," *The New York Times*, April 25, 2016, https://www.nytimes.com/2016/04/26/business/energy-environment/china-coal.html.

106. "The State Council's Opinions on Resolving Overcapacity in the Coal Industry and Achieving Development by Overcoming Difficulties (国务院关于煤炭行业化解过剩产能 实现脱困发展的意见)," *Central People's Government of the People's Republic of China* (中华人民共和国中央人民政府), February 5, 2016, https://www.gov.cn/zhengce/content/2016-02/05/content_5039686.htm.

107. "Economic Daily: 'Giant' Emerges and Integration is a Matter of Course(经济日报:'巨无霸'横空出世 一体化水到渠成-国务院国有资产监督管理委员会)," *Economic Daily* (经济日报), August 29, 2017, http://www.sasac.gov.cn/n2588025/n2588139/c7798317/content.html.

108. "Factbox: Shenhua and Guodian—China's Latest State Marriage," *Reuters*, 29 August 2017, https://www.reuters.com/article/us-china-power-shenhua-guodian-factbox-idUSKCN1B918I.

109. "About Us Profile," China Energy Investment Corporation, Accessed February 2 2021, http://www.ceic.com.cn/gjnyjtwwEn/jtgk/chnjtjs.shtml.

110. "Guiding Opinions of the General Office of the State Council on Promoting the Structural Adjustment and Reorganization of Central Enterprises (国务院办公厅关于推动中央企业 结构调整与重组的指导意见)," *Central People's Government of the People's Republic of China* (中华人民共和国中央人民政府), July 26, 2016, https://www.gov.cn/zhengce/content/2016-07/26/content_5095050.htm.

111. "The Path of a Chinese Temasek Is Beginning to Emerge (国版淡马锡路径初现)," China Securities Journal, January 27,

2014, https://www.cs.com.cn/xwzx/jr/201401/t20140127_4294816.html.

112. "A New Group of 11 Central Enterprises for the State-owned Capital Investment Companies for Pilot Program Launched (新一批11家中央企业国有资本投资公司试点启动) *People's Daily*, January 8, 2019, http://www.gov.cn/xinwen/2019-01/08/content_5355718.htm.

113. "Implementing Opinion on Promoting State-owned Capital Investment and Operation Companies (国务院推进国有资本投资, 运营公司改革试点的实施意见)," *State Council of the People's Republic of China*, July 14, 2018.

114. Meg Rithmire, *Precarious Ties Business and the State in Authoritarian Asia* (Oxford University Press, 2024).

115. "Core Technology Depends on One's Own Efforts: President Xi," *People's Daily*, April 19, 2018, http://en.people.cn/n3/2018/0419/c90000-9451186.html.

116. "Opinions Regarding Strengthening the Leading Role of Enterprises in Innovation and Comprehensively Promoting Enterprises Innovation Ability (国务院办公厅关于强化企业技术创新主体地位全面提升企业创新能力的意见)," *Central People's Government of the People's Republic of China* (中华人民共和国中央人民政府), February 4, 2013, http://www.gov.cn/zhengce/content/2013-02/04/content_5547.htm.

117. Tai Ming Cheung, Thomas Mahnken, Deborah Seligsohn, Kevin Pollpeter, Eric Anderson, and Fan Yang, "Planning for Innovation: Understanding China's Plans for Technological, Energy, Industrial and Defense Development," *The University of California Institute on Global Conflict and Cooperation*, July 28, 2016, https://www.uscc.gov/Research/planning-innovation-understanding-china%E2%80%99s-plans-technological-energy-industrial-and-defense.

118. "Made in China 2025: Global Ambitions Built on Local Protections," *U.S. Chamber of Commerce*, March 16, 2017, https://www.uschamber.com/sites/default/files/final_made_in_china_2025_report_full.pdf

119. Tao Wang, *Making Sense of China's Economy* (Routledge, 2023).

120. Bonnie Glaser, "Made in China 2025 and the Future of American Industry," *Senate Small Business and Entrepreneurship*

Committee, February 27, 2019, https://www.sbc.senate.gov/public/_cache/files/0/9/090fe492-3ed9-4a1a-b6c1-ebdecec39858/1AB7520770B9032F388CC9E94C79321B.glaser-testimony.pdf..

121. "Made in China 2025: Global Ambitions Built on Local Protections," *U.S. Chamber of Commerce*, March 16, 2017, https://www.uschamber.com/sites/default/files/final_made_in_china_2025_report_full.pdf

122. "Circular of the State Council on the Issuance of Made in China 2025 (国务院关于印发《中国制造2025》的通知)," *Central People's Government of the People's Republic of China* (中华人民共和国中央人民政府), May 8, 2015, https://www.gov.cn/zhengce/content/2015-05/19/content_9784.htm.

123. "Circular of the State Council," 2015.

124. Max Zenglein and Anna Holzmann, "Evolving Made in China 2025," *Mercator Institute for China Studies*, July 2019, https://kritisches-netzwerk.de/sites/default/files/merics_-_evolving_made_in_china_2025_-_chinas_industrial_policy_in_the_quest_for_global_tech_leadership_-_2._juli_2019_-_80_seiten.pdf.

125. Zenglein and Holzmann, "Evolving Made in China 2025," 2019.

126. Allen Lu, "Challenges and Opportunities for China in the Semiconductor Industry," *Semi*, August 4, 2015, https://www.semi.org/en/challenges-and-opportunities-china-semiconductor-industry..

127. "Findings of the Investigation into China's Acts, Policies, and Practices Related to Technology Transfer, Intellectual Property, and Innovation Under Sect. 201 of the Trade Act of 1974," *The United States Trade Representative*, March 20, 2018, https://ustr.gov/sites/default/files/Section%20301%20FINAL.PDF.

128. Dieter Ernst, "From Catching Up to Forging Ahead: China's New Role in the Semiconductor Industry," *The East–West Center*, May 2016, https://www.eastwestcenter.org/sites/default/files/filemanager/Research_Program/Ernst%202016.pdf.

129. "About Us—Zhao Weiguo," n.d. *Tsinghua Holdings*, Accessed October 12, 2023, http://en.thholding.com.cn/2016-08/08/c_55163.htm.

130. Gerry Shih and Noel Randewich, "Intel to Invest Up to $1.5 Bln in Two Chinese Mobile Chipmakers," *Reuters*, September 26,

2014, https://www.reuters.com/article/spreadtrum-m-a-intel/intel-to-invest-up-to-1-5-bln-in-two-chinese-mobile-chipmakers-idINKCN0HL0CA20140926.
131. Paul Mozur and Quentin Hardy, "Micron Technology Is Said to Be Takeover Target of Chinese Company," *The New York Times*, July 15, 2015, https://www.nytimes.com/2015/07/15/business/international/micron-technology-is-said-to-be-takeover-target-of-chinese-company.html.
132. Greg Roumeliotis and Liana B. Baker, "Exclusive: Micron Does Not Believe Deal with Tsinghua Is Possible—Sources," *Reuters*, July 21, 2015, https://www.reuters.com/article/us-micron-m-a-tsinghua-exclusive/exclusive-micron-does-not-believe-deal-with-tsinghua-is-possible-sources-idUSKCN0PU1X120150721.
133. Arash Massoudi and James Fontanella-Khan, "Tsinghua Kills $3.8bn Investment Plan in Western Digital," *Financial Times*, February 23, 2016, https://www.ft.com/content/c235a154-da37-11e5-98fd-06d75973fe09.
134. J.R. Wu, "Chinese Tech Giant's Taiwan Deals Unravel as Powertech Calls Off Share Pact," *Reuters*, January 13, 2017, https://www.reuters.com/article/us-powertech-tech-tsinghua/chinese-tech-giants-taiwan-deals-unravel-as-powertech-calls-off-share-pact-idUSKBN14X1BA.
135. Chris Miller, *Chip War: The Fight for the World's Most Critical Technology* (Scribner, 2022).
136. "The Acquisition of Linxens," n.d., https://www.datenna.com/articles/the-acquisition-of-linxens.
137. "SK Hynix Says Rejected Tsinghua Unigroup Collaboration Offer," *Reuters*, November 27, 2015, https://www.reuters.com/article/sk-hynix-tsinghuaunigroup/sk-hynix-says-rejected-tsinghua-unigroup-collaboration-offer-idUSL3N13M13J20151127.
138. Chris Miller, *Chip War: The Fight for the World's Most Critical Technology* (Scribner, 2022).
139. Tao Wang, *Making Sense of China's Economy* (Routledge, 2023).
140. Josh Horwitz, "China's Chip Conglomerate Unigroup Gets State-Backed Investors, Alibaba out of Deal," *Reuters*, December 10, 2021, https://www.reuters.com/markets/europe/chinas-chip-conglomerate-unigroup-gets-state-backed-investors-alibaba-out-deal-2021-12-10/.

141. "Former Chip Guru at Tsinghua Unigroup Pleads Guilty in Corruption Trial After Beijing's Anti-Graft Push," *South China Morning Post*, September 29, 2023, https://finance.yahoo.com/news/former-chip-guru-tsinghua-unigroup-093000734.html.
142. "China Watchdog Says Is Probing the Head of Chip-Focused Big Fund," *Reuters*, August 1, 2022, https://www.reuters.com/world/china/china-watchdog-says-is-probing-head-chip-focused-big-fund-2022-08-01/.
143. Max Zenglein and Anna Holzmann, "Evolving Made in China 2025," *Mercator Institute for China Studies*, July 2019, https://kritisches-netzwerk.de/sites/default/files/merics_-_evolving_made_in_china_2025_-_chinas_industrial_policy_in_the_quest_for_global_tech_leadership_-_2._juli_2019_-_80_seiten.pdf.
144. Karen Sutter, Andres Schwarzenberg, and Michael Sutherland, "China's 'One Belt, One Road' Initiative: Economic Issues," *Congressional Research Service*, September 27, 2023, https://crsreports.congress.gov/product/pdf/IF/IF11735.
145. Wendy Leutert, "State-Owned Enterprises in Contemporary China," *The Routledge Handbook of SOEs*, May 28, 2020, https://static1.squarespace.com/static/578f7e4ac534a5c08c478743/t/5e781bb364f35a2e28936903/1584929716451/State-Owned+Enterprises+in+Contemporary+China_Leutert+%28*Accepted+Version%29+.pdf.
146. Kai Schultz, "Sri Lanka, Struggling with Debt, Hands a Major Port to China," *The New York Times*, December 12, 2017, https://www.nytimes.com/2017/12/12/world/asia/sri-lanka-china-port.html.
147. "China Merchants Port Holdings Company Limited," n.d., https://www.cmport.com.hk/enTouch/business/Infor.aspx?id=10007513.
148. "Chinese State-Owned Firm to Build Major Sri Lanka Port Complex," *South China Morning Post*, May 1, 2023, https://www.scmp.com/news/asia/south-asia/article/3219050/chinese-state-owned-firm-build-major-sri-lanka-port-complex.
149. Iain Marlow, "China's $1 Billion White Elephant," *Bloomberg.Com*, April 18, 2018, https://www.bloomberg.com/news/articles/2018-04-17/china-s-1-billion-white-elephant-the-port-ships-don-t-use#xj4y7vzkg.

150. George Lauriat, "Commentary: AJOT's Top 100 Container Ports.," *American Journal of Transportation*, June 27, 2023, https://www.ajot.com/premium/ajot-commentary-ajots-top-100-container-ports.
151. Wind Information, accessed October 12, 2023.
152. Xiaojun Li and Ka Zeng, "To Join or Not To Join? How Chinese Firms View the Belt and Road Initiative," *UBC*, June 2019, https://www.academia.edu/35054271/To_Join_or_Not_To_Join_How_Chinese_Firms_View_the_Belt_and_Road_Initiative.
153. "Country Garden's Forest City: Growth through Overseas Expansion," *Knowledge at Wharton*, March 2018, https://knowledge.wharton.upenn.edu/article/country-gardens-forest-city-growth-overseas-expansion/.
154. A. Ananthalakshmi and Xinghui Kok, "'Seeing Is Believing': Country Garden's Malaysia Project in Spotlight," *Reuters*, September 14, 2023, https://www.reuters.com/markets/asia/seeing-is-believing-country-gardens-malaysia-project-spotlight-2023-09-13/.
155. "Country Garden's Forest City: A Global Feast Under the 'Belt and Road' Strategy (碧桂园森林城市:'一带一路'战略下的全球盛宴)," *People's Daily*, October 24, 2016, http://house.people.com.cn/n1/2016/1024/c164220-28803064.html.
156. Xinghui Kok and A. Ananthalakshmi, "'Seeing Is Believing': Country Garden's Malaysia Project in Spotlight," *Reuters*, September 14, 2023, https://www.reuters.com/markets/asia/seeing-is-believing-country-gardens-malaysia-project-spotlight-2023-09-13/.
157. Shibani Mahtani, "A Would-Be City in the Malaysian Jungle Is Caught in a Growing Rift Between China and Its Neighbors," *Washington Post*, September 11, 2018, https://www.washingtonpost.com/world/asia_pacific/a-would-be-city-in-the-malaysian-jungle-is-caught-in-a-growing-rift-between-china-and-its-neighbors/2018/09/10/d705cb18-b031-11e8-9a6a-565d92a3585d_story.html.
158. Sebastian Horn et al., "Debt Distress on China's Belt and Road," *AEA Papers and Proceedings* 113 (May 1, 2023): 131–34, https://doi.org/10.1257/pandp.20231004.

159. There are many types party organizations, ranging from smaller branches to larger committee This text will use "party committee" as a general term for party organizations within companies.
160. Zemin Jiang, "In Accordance with the Requirements of Three Represents, Earnestly Strengthen Party Building (按照'三个代表'要求,切实加强党的建设)," May 14, 2000, http://www.reformdata.org/2000/0514/4655.shtml.
161. Xianchu Zhang, "Integration of CCP Leadership with Corporate Governance," *China Perspectives* 2019 (1): 5563, https://doi.org/10.4000/chinaperspectives.8770.
162. "Authorized Release: Regulations on the Work of Party Groups of the Communist Party of China—Trial Implementation (授权发布:中国共产党党组工作条例(试行))," *Xinhua*, June 16, 2015, http://www.xinhuanet.com//politics/2015-06/16/c_1115638059.htm.
163. "Guiding Opinion on Deepening the Reform of SOEs (国务院关于深化国有企业改革的指导意见)," Central Committee of the Communist Party of China and the State Council of the People's Republic of China, August 24, 2015, http://www.gov.cn/zhengce/2015-09/13/content_2930440.htm.
164. "Constitution of the Communist Party of China," *Xinhua*, 24 October 2017, http://www.xinhuanet.com/english/download/Constitution_of_the_Communist_Party_of_China.pdf.
165. A leading party organization, or Leading Party members' group, is a more organized and influential version of a grassroots party organization. Rather than electing its members, the membership of these groups is approved by a higher-level party organization. See "New CPC regulation stresses the role of leading Party members' groups," *Xinhua*, May 30, 2015, http://en.people.cn/n/2015/0530/c90785-8899822.html.
166. "Constitution of the Communist Party of China," *Xinhua*, 24 October 2017, http://www.xinhuanet.com/english/download/Constitution_of_the_Communist_Party_of_China.pdf.
167. "Code of Corporate Governance for Listed Companies," *China Securities Regulatory Commission*, 2018, http://www.csrc.gov.cn/pub/csrc_en/laws/rfdm/DepartmentRules/201904/P020190415336431477120.pdf
168. See Lauren Yu-Hsin Lin and Curtis J. Milhaupt, "Party Building or Noisy Signaling? The Contours of Political Conformity

in Chinese Corporate Governance," *Journal of Legal Studies*, December 22, 2020, https://papers.ssrn.com/sol3/papers.cfm?abstract_id=3510342; and see John Zhuang Liu and Angela Huyue Zhang, "Ownership and Political Control: Evidence from Charter Amendments," *International Review of Law and Economics*, July 22, 2019, https://papers.ssrn.com/sol3/papers.cfm?abstract_id=3424079/

169. "An Analysis Report on the Current State of Party Building in Private Enterprises (我国民营企业党组织建设现状分析报告)," *All-China Federation of Industry and Commerce*, May 23, 2019, https://www.acfic.org.cn/fgdt1/zjgd/201905/t20190523_125262.html.

170. "Constitution of the Communist Party of China," *Xinhua*, October 24, 2017, http://www.xinhuanet.com/english/download/Constitution_of_the_Communist_Party_of_China.pdf.

171. "PRC Company Law (2018 Revision)," China Law and Practice, November 7, 2018, https://www.chinalawandpractice.com/2018/11/07/prc-company-law-2018-revision/.

172. Jinping Xi, "Unswervingly Adhering to China's Basic Economic System and Promoting the Healthy Development of All Kinds of Ownership Economies (习近平:毫不动摇坚持我国基本经济制度 推动各种所有制经济健康发展)," *People's Republic of China Central People's Government*, March 9, 2016, https://www.gov.cn/xinwen/2016-03/09/content_5051083.htm

173. Jinping Xi, "Unswervingly Adhering," 2016.

174. "Opinions on Creating a Better Development Environment to Support the Reform and Development of Private Enterprises (关于营造更好发展环境支持民营企业改革发展的意见)," *Central People's Government of the Central People's Republic of China* (中央人民共和国中央人民政府), December 22, 2019, http://www.gov.cn/zhengce/2019-12/22/content_5463137.htm.

175. Qing Ye, "Promoting the Organic Integration Between the Party's Leadership and the Governance of Private Enterprises (推动党的领导制度体系与民企治理体系有机融合)," All-China Federation of Industry and Commerce, 17 September 2020, https://www.acfic.org.cn/bhjj/ldzc/hzfhz/yq/yqgzhd/202009/t20200917_60940.html

176. Lauren Yu-Hsin Lin and Curtis J. Milhaupt, "Party Building or Noisy Signaling? The Contours of Political Conformity in Chinese Corporate Governance," *Journal of Legal Studies*, December 22, 2020, https://papers.ssrn.com/sol3/papers.cfm?abstract_id=3510342.
177. Kathy Gao, "China's Largest Smartphone Maker Xiaomi Sets up Communist Party Committee," *South China Morning Post*, June 29, 2015, https://www.scmp.com/news/china/policies-politics/article/1828191/chinas-largest-smartphone-maker-xiaomi-sets-communist.
178. "Xiaomi's Establishment of a Party Committee Should Be Applauded by Society (小米成立党委应得到社会的掌声)," *People's Daily*, July 1, 2015, http://politics.people.com.cn/n/2015/0701/c70731-27236699.html.
179. "Why Do Private and Foreign Companies Have to Establish Party Committees? Most Party Committee Leaders Are Part-time (民企外企为何都要建党委?党委领导多为兼职)," *Xinhua*, July 6, 2015, http://www.xinhuanet.com/politics/2015-07/06/c_1115820681.htm.
180. "Xiaomi Corporation V. U.S. Department Of Defense Et Al, No. 1:2021cv00280 - Document 21 (D.D.C. 2021)," *Justia Law*, n.d., https://law.justia.com/cases/federal/district-courts/district-of-columbia/dcdce/1:2021cv00280/226816/21/.
181. "Chamber Stance on the Governance of Joint Ventures and the Role of Party Organisations," *The European Chamber of Commerce in China*, November 3, 2017, https://www.europeanchamber.com.cn/en/press-releases/2583/chamber_stance_on_the_governance_of_joint_ventures_and_the_role_of_party_organisations.
182. Alexandra Stevenson, "China's Communists Rewrite the Rules for Foreign Businesses," *The New York Times*, April 13, 2018, https://www.nytimes.com/2018/04/13/business/china-communist-party-foreign-businesses.html.

183. "Decision of the Central Committee of the Communist Party of China on Some Major Issues Concerning Comprehensively Deepening the Reform," *China.Org.Cn*, January 16, 2014, http://www.china.org.cn/china/third_plenary_session/2014-01/16/content_31212602.htm.
184. Li Yuan, "China Wants to Own Small Stake in Web Firms," *The Wall Street Journal*, April 28, 2016, https://www.wsj.com/articles/china-wants-to-own-small-stake-in-web-firms-1461781500.
185. Lingling Wei, "China's New Way to Control Its Biggest Companies: Golden Shares," *The Wall Street Journal*, March 8, 2023, https://www.wsj.com/articles/xi-jinpings-subtle-strategy-to-control-chinas-biggest-companies-ad001a63.
186. "China Acquires 'Golden Shares' in Two Alibaba Units," *Reuters*, January 13, 2023, https://www.reuters.com/technology/china-moving-take-golden-shares-alibaba-tencent-units-ft-2023-01-13/. See also Josh Ye, "Beijing Takes 'Golden Share' in a Tencent Subsidiary, Records Show," *Reuters*, October 19, 2023, https://www.reuters.com/world/china/beijing-takes-golden-share-tencent-subsidiary-records-show-2023-10-19.
187. Grady McGregor, "Golden Grip," *The Wire China*, April 2023, https://www.thewirechina.com/2023/04/02/golden-grip-golden-shares/.
188. "Company Introduction," *China Internet Investment Fund*, Accessed September 21, 2024, n.d., http://www.ciifund.cn/zwt/gsjj/gsjj.shtml.
189. "USTR Announces Initiation of Section 301 Investigation of China," *United States Trade Representative*, n.d., https://ustr.gov/about-us/policy-offices/press-office/press-releases/2017/august/ustr-announces-initiation-section.
190. "Findings of the Investigation into China's Acts, Policies, and Practices Related to Technology Transfer, Intellectual Property, and Innovation Under Sect. 201 of the Trade Act of 1974," *The United States Trade Representative*, March 20, 2018, https://ustr.gov/sites/default/files/Section%20301%20FINAL.PDF.
191. "Remarks by President Trump at Signing of a Presidential Memorandum Targeting China's Economic Aggression—The White House," The White House, March 22, 2018, https://trumpwhitehouse.archives.gov/briefings-statements/remarks-president-trump-signing-presidential-memorandum-targeting-chinas-economic-aggression/.

192. Chad Brown, "US-China Trade War Tariffs: An Up-to-Date Chart," The Peterson Institute for International Economics, April 6, 2023, https://www.piie.com/research/piie-charts/2019/us-china-trade-war-tariffs-date-chart.
193. "Remarks by President Trump at Signing of a Presidential Memorandum Targeting China's Economic Aggression – The White House," *The White House*, March 22, 2018, https://trumpwhitehouse.archives.gov/briefings-statements/remarks-president-trump-signing-presidential-memorandum-targeting-chinas-economic-aggression/.
194. Paul Mozur and Ana Swanson, "Chinese Tech Company Blocked From Buying American Components," *The New York Times*, April 16, 2018, https://www.nytimes.com/2018/04/16/technology/chinese-tech-company-blocked-from-buying-american-components.html.
195. Andrew Restuccia and Lindsay Wise, "Trump Signs Hong Kong Sanctions Bill, Pivots to Criticizing Biden," *The Wall Street Journal*, July 15, 2020, https://www.wsj.com/articles/trump-signs-hong-kong-sanctions-bill-11594762613.
196. Sarah Zheng, "John Bolton Book Reveals 'Xi Jinping's Personal Appeals to Donald Trump' on Huawei and ZTE," *South China Morning Post*, June 28, 2020, https://www.scmp.com/news/china/diplomacy/article/3090902/john-bolton-book-reveals-xi-jinpings-personal-appeals-donald.
197. "Addition of Entities to the Entity List," *Federal Register*, May 21, 2019, https://www.bis.doc.gov/index.php/documents/regulations-docs/2394-huawei-and-affiliates-entity-list-rule/file.
198. Ana Swanson, "U.S. Delivers Another Blow to Huawei With New Tech Restrictions," *The New York Times*, March 15, 2020, https://www.nytimes.com/2020/05/15/business/economy/commerce-department-huawei.html.
199. Chris Miller, *Chip War: The Fight for the World's Most Critical Technology* (Scribner, 2022).
200. Martin Chorzempa, Mary Lovely, and Yuting (Christine) Wan, "The Rise of US Economic Sanctions on China: Analysis of a New PIIE Dataset," The Peterson Institute for International Economics, December 2024, https://www.piie.com/publications/policy-briefs/2024/rise-us-economic-sanctions-china-analysis-new-piie-dataset.

201. Andrew Restuccia and Lindsay Wise, "Trump Signs Hong Kong Sanctions Bill, Pivots to Criticizing Biden," *The Wall Street Journal*, July 15, 2020, https://www.wsj.com/articles/trump-signs-hong-kong-sanctions-bill-11594762613.
202. "Addressing the Threat From Securities Investments That Finance Communist Chinese Military Companies," *Federal Register*, November 17, 2020, https://www.federalregister.gov/documents/2020/11/17/2020-25459/addressing-the-threat-from-securities-investments-that-finance-communist-chinese-military-companies.
203. Ling Chen, "Changing State-Business Relations Under the U.S.-China Tech War," *The Wilson Center*, 2022, https://www.wilsoncenter.org/publication/changing-state-business-relations-under-us-china-tech-war.
204. "Outline of the 14th Five-Year Plan (2021–2025) for National Economic and Social Development and Vision 2035 of the People's Republic of China," *The People's Government of Fujian Province*, August 9, 2021, https://www.fujian.gov.cn/english/news/202108/t20210809_5665713.htm#C53.
205. "Outline of the 14th Five-Year Plan," 2021.
206. Jinping Xi, "Understanding the New Development Stage, Applying the New Development Philosophy, and Creating a New Development Dynamic," *Qiushi*, July 8, 2021, http://en.qstheory.cn/2021-07/08/c_641137.htm.
207. Jinping Xi, "Understanding the New Development Stage," 2021.
208. Jinping Xi, "Understanding the New Development Stage," 2021.
209. Jinping Xi, "Understanding the New Development Stage," 2021.
210. The term is also sometimes translated as New Development Concept.
211. Kevin Rudd, *The Avoidable War: The Dangers of a Catastrophic Conflict between the US and Xi Jinping's China* (PublicAffairs, 2022).
212. National Development and Reform Commission, "Implementing the New Development Philosophy to Compose a New Chapter in Socialist Modernization," *Qiushi*, October 28, 2022, http://en.qstheory.cn/2022-10/28/c_824275.htm.

213. CPC Central Committee, "Resolution of the CPC Central Committee on the Major Achievements and Historical Experience of the Party over the Past Century," *State Council of the People's Republic of China*, November 16, 2021, https://english.www.gov.cn/policies/latestreleases/202111/16/content_WS6193a935c6d0df57f98e50b0.html.
214. CPC Central Committee, "Implementing the New Development," 2022.
215. CPC Central Committee, "Implementing the New Development," 2022.
216. CPC Central Committee, "Implementing the New Development," 2022.
217. Shu Zhang and John Ruwitch, "Exclusive: Ant Financial Shifts Focus from Finance to Tech Services: Sources," *Reuters*, June 5, 2018, https://www.reuters.com/article/us-china-ant-financial-regulation-exclus/exclusive-ant-financial-shifts-focus-from-finance-to-tech-services-sources-idUSKCN1J10WV.
218. Martin Chorzempa, *The Cashless Revolution: China's Reinvention of Money and the End of America's Domination of Finance and Technology* (PublicAffairs, 2022).
219. Julie Zhu and Kane Wu, "Insight: Jack Ma, Trump and Xi: How Chinese Billionaire Flew Close to the Sun," *Reuters*, November 5, 2021, https://www.reuters.com/business/jack-ma-trump-xi-how-chinese-billionaire-flew-close-sun-2021-11-04/.
220. Martin Chorzempa, *The Cashless Revolution: China's Reinvention of Money and the End of America's Domination of Finance and Technology* (PublicAffairs, 2022).
221. Kevin Xu, "Jack Ma's Bund Finance Summit Speech," *Interconnected*, September 22, 2022, https://interconnected.blog/jack-ma-bund-finance-summit-speech/.
222. Jing Yang and Lingling Wei, "China's President Xi Jinping Personally Scuttled Jack Ma's Ant IPO," *The Wall Street Journal*, November 12, 2020, https://www.wsj.com/articles/china-president-xi-jinping-halted-jack-ma-ant-ipo-11605203556.
223. Arjun Kharpal, "Alibaba Shares Dive 7% as Ant Group's Record $34.5 Billion IPO Is Suspended," *CNBC*, November

4, 2020, https://www.cnbc.com/2020/11/03/ant-group-ipo-in-shanghai-suspended.html.
224. "With Alibaba Investigation, China Gets Tougher on Tech," *The New York Times*, December 23, 2020, https://www.nytimes.com/2020/12/23/business/alibaba-antitrust-jack-ma.html.
225. "Pan Gongsheng, Vice Governor of the People's Bank of China, Answered a Reporter's Question on the Financial Management Department's Interview with Ant Group about the Situation (中国人民银行副行长潘功胜就金融管理部门约谈蚂蚁集团有关情况答记者问)," *The People's Bank of China*, December 27, 2020, http://www.pbc.gov.cn/goutongjiaoliu/113456/113469/4153479/index.html.
226. "Pan Gongsheng," 2020.
227. Laura He, "How Much Did Jack Ma's Speech Cost Ant Group? About $230 Billion," *CNN*, July 10, 2023, https://www.cnn.com/2023/07/10/investing/china-ant-group-valuation-jack-ma-intl-hnk/index.html.
228. Zichen Wang, "Beijing's Anti-Monopoly Findings on Alibaba: A Deep Dive," *Pekingnology*, April 11, 2021, https://www.pekingnology.com/p/beijings-anti-monopoly-findings-on.
229. Tony Munroe, "China Extends Crackdown on Jack Ma's Empire with Enforced Revamp of Ant Group," *Reuters*, October 31, 2022, https://www.reuters.com/business/chinas-ant-group-become-financial-holding-company-central-bank-2021-04-12/.
230. Emma Lee, "Ele.Me Fined $77,000 over Prices and Unlicensed Restaurants," *TechNode*, June 28, 2021, https://technode.com/2021/05/18/ele-me-fined-77000-over-prices-and-unlicensed-restaurants/.
231. Julie Zhu, "EXCLUSIVE Chinese State Firms to Take Big Stake in Ant's Credit-Scoring JV-Sources," *Reuters*, September 1, 2021, https://www.reuters.com/technology/exclusive-chinese-state-firms-take-big-stake-ants-credit-scoring-jv-sources-2021-09-01/.
232. "China Regulator Fines Alibaba, Tencent for Disclosure Violations," *Reuters*, July 10, 2022, https://www.reuters.com/world/china/china-regulator-fines-alibaba-tencent-disclosure-violations-2022-07-10/.
233. "Ant Group Execs Step down as Alibaba Partners as China's Regulatory Scrutiny Pushes Firms to Seek Distance," *CNBC*,

July 26, 2022, https://www.cnbc.com/2022/07/26/ant-group-execs-step-down-as-alibaba-partners-amid-regulatory-scrutiny.html.
234. "Ant Group Announces Further Corporate Governance Optimization," *Ant Group*, Accessed January 7, 2023, n.d., https://www.antgroup.com/en/notices/1.
235. "China's Alibaba to Break Up Empire into Six Units as Jack Ma Returns Home," *Reuters*, March 29, 2023, https://www.reuters.com/markets/deals/alibaba-splits-into-six-units-that-may-pursue-individual-ipos-bloomberg-news-2023-03-28/
236. "China Hits Alibaba Affiliate Ant Group with $985 Million Fine for Violating Various Regulations," *CNBC*, July 7, 2023, https://www.cnbc.com/2023/07/07/china-hits-alibaba-affiliate-ant-group-hit-with-985-million-fine.html.
237. Sophie Yu, Tony Munroe, and Sophie Yu, "Learn from Alibaba Penalty, China Warns Internet Firms," *Reuters*, October 31, 2022, https://www.reuters.com/technology/china-warns-online-platform-companies-halt-anti-competitive-practices-2021-04-13/.
238. "China Fines Tech Giants for Failing to Report 43 Old Deals," *Reuters*, November 20, 2021, https://www.reuters.com/technology/china-finds-43-anti-trust-law-violations-involving-alibaba-baidu-jdcom-2021-11-20/.
239. "China Declares All Crypto-Currency Transactions Illegal," *BBC News*, September 24, 2021, https://www.bbc.com/news/technology-58678907.
240. Keith Zhai and Liza Lin, "China Fines Ride-Hailing Giant Didi $1.2 Billion, Citing Cybersecurity Breaches," *The Wall Street Journal*, July 21, 2022, https://www.wsj.com/articles/china-fines-ride-hailing-giant-didi-1-2-billion-citing-cybersecurity-breaches-11658393088.
241. The Three Red Lines policy sets out balance sheet rules that real estate developers must adhere to or face restrictions on their ability to borrow. The regulations require developers to maintain a liabilities-to-assets ratio of less than 70%, a net debt-to-equity ratio of less than 100%, and a cash-to-short-term-debt ratio of greater than 1. "What China's Three Red Lines Mean for Property Firms," *Bloomberg*, October 8, 2020.

242. "The Political Bureau of the CPC Central Committee Held a Meeting Chaired by Xi Jinping (中共中央政治局召开会议 习近平主持)," *Xinhua*, December 11, 2020, http://www.xinhuanet.com/politics/2020-12/11/c_1126850644.htm.
243. "Interpretation of the Spirit of the Central Economic Work Conference: To Prevent the Disorderly Expansion of Capital (解读中央经济工作会议精神:防止资本无序扩张)," *Economic Daily*, December 27, 2020, https://www.gov.cn/xinwen/2020-12/27/content_5573663.htm.
244. "Interpretation of the Spirit," 2020.
245. "Insisting on Regulating, Standardizing, and Promoting Development—Both Hands Must Be Hard (坚持监管规范和促进发展两手并重、两手都要硬)," *People's Daily*, September 8, 2021, http://opinion.people.com.cn/n1/2021/0908/c1003-32220675.html.
246. Jinping Xi, "Guide and Regulate the Capital Market," *The Governance of China* IV, April 29, 2022, http://en.qstheory.cn/2023-07/03/c_898781.htm

CHAPTER 4

China's Economic Contradictions

Since the start of the Reform and Opening Period in the late 1970s, China's economic policy has been defined by a tension between the Party's political goals and the necessity of embracing the market to restore the economy. Over the decades, the balance between these competing priorities has shifted and evolved in response to events. However, the Party has maintained a consistent approach of selectively embracing market forces while seeking to manage and limit their undesired impacts.

As discussed in Chapter 2, in the 1990s and 2000s, the Chinese private sector grew and displaced large portions of the state economy. The Party feared that a Chinese economy completely dominated by the private sector would weaken its control and create social instability. In reaction to these developments, the government pushed new policies with the intention of preserving the power and influence of SOEs from the mid-2000s onwards. The Party continuously sought to shape economic outcomes through regulatory interventionism and preferential support for the state sector. As a result, China has transformed into a mixed economy in which a large private sector exists alongside a still powerful state sector. Private companies drive most of China's growth and market forces shape many industries, but SOEs continue to dominate many of the "commanding heights" of the economy, particularly industries viewed as sensitive or strategic. To echo Chen Yun's comments from four decades ago, the cage has grown larger but there is still a cage.

Chapter 3 highlighted how Xi Jinping continued the approach of his predecessors for the economy during his initial years in office. However, in reaction to growing risks throughout the economy, Xi Jinping began to use his unprecedented hold on power to realign economic policy. These efforts further accelerated as political and economic tensions with the United States increased. Xi started intervening more forcefully and across more parts of the economy than his predecessors. Xi's policies represent an escalation of prior efforts to control the economy and ensure the continued influence of SOEs. Motivating the intensification of interventions under Xi was a desire to promote stability, control, and self-reliance in the economy in preparation for a proacted competition with the United States.

However, Xi's heavy-handed approach is now running into limitations. Recent policies have upset the delicate balance between the state and the market that permitted China's economic growth miracle. Government policy has overly constricted the space necessary for the private sector to grow and thrive. As a result, China's economic trajectory has changed, and the country is facing a protracted slowdown in growth. Whether this slowdown is irreversible depends on the capacity of the Party to change course and adjust its approach.

China's leaders discuss policy as a balancing act between two seemingly contradictory goals. Xi Jinping frequently describes the Party's approach as seeking to "manage well" the contradictions between competing objectives.[1] Over the past decade, Xi has prioritized three main goals in economic policy—stability, control, and self-reliance. However, Xi and the Party have lost sight of the significant economic tradeoffs that result from overprioritizing these goals. These tradeoffs include lower growth, weaker innovation, and less integration with the global economy. Excessive pursuit of stability can distort economic policy and impede growth. The Party's efforts to control the commanding heights of the economy and the flow of information have hindered the development of the private sector, setting back efforts to make China into a more innovative economy. China's massive efforts to achieve self-reliance threaten to undermine its access to global markets and foreign technology. Table 1 summarizes these tradeoffs as the three principal contradictions that shape China's economic policy.

This chapter will explore each of these contradictions in detail. It will examine several recent examples of government intervention in the economy to achieve one the goals of stability, control, and self-reliance.

Table 1 Primary contradictions of chinese economic policy

Contradiction	Tension
Growth vs. Stability	Policies that promote economic stability may constrain growth
Innovation vs. Control	Policies that promote Party control over critical industries may damage private sector innovation
Global Integration vs. Self-reliance	Policies that promote economic self-reliance may lead to foreign economic restrictions against China

Each of these cases will illuminate how and why the Party intervenes in the economy to pursue its goals. Furthermore, these examples also reveal how excessive intervention by the Party has damaged the economy with respect to growth, innovation, or global integration. The conclusion in the next chapter will explore what China's economic future holds if the Party persists with its current approach.

1 Growth vs. Stability

The tradeoff between growth and stability is one of the key contradictions shaping the Party's economic policies. Economic growth is essential to Xi's vision of a national rejuvenation for China. The Party has defined establishing a moderately prosperous society, *xiǎokāng shèhuì* (小康社会) as a core component of China's efforts to achieve national rejuvenation. Echoing this, Xi has stated that the principal contradiction facing China is "unbalanced and inadequate development and the people's ever-growing needs for a better life."[2] Additionally, a large and flourishing economy has important implications for the Party's desire to restore China's position among the world's great powers. A strong economy allows China to fund a world-class army and use trade and investment as tools of international influence.

For these reasons, the Party seeks robust economic growth. However, the Party also has long had an intense fixation on stability, which has grown even more extreme under Xi. As tensions with the United States have increased, Xi has declared that "security is the foundation of development and stability is the prerequisite for prosperity."[3] In 2018, Xi made his views on economic stability clear, calling for the "Six Stabilities," a stable financial system, foreign trade, foreign investment, domestic investment, and economic expectations.[4] Recent economic policy documents, such as the Central Economic Work Conference readout, are replete with references to maintaining stability.[5]

The concept of stability is broad and extends beyond economics into social issues. Xi explicitly states in his speeches that social and economic stability are deeply entwined. According to Xi, social stability can only be maintained by improving employment, education, healthcare, food safety, and the housing market.[6] Companies and industries seen as negatively influencing these areas or exacerbating social inequalities threaten social stability. The Party fears that instability, whether it be economic or social, undermines its legitimacy and, if left unaddressed, could threaten its grip on power.

The dilemma for the Party is that efforts to maintain stability can come at the cost of economic growth. Modern capitalist economies alternate between periods of growth and recession. Capitalism's "animal spirits" can lead to rapid growth but also result in overinvestment and speculation. This creates a boom-and-bust cycle where excessive growth eventually leads to a pullback and correction. Capitalism also requires "creative destruction," whereby new industries disrupt and displace old ones. This often leads to adverse economic shocks for the workers and companies in the industries being displaced. The economic cycles of a market-driven economy conflict with the Party's notion of economic and social stability.

The Party aggressively intervenes in the economy against perceived threats to stability. It does so frequently and in a variety of different forms. The Party directs regulators to manage price volatility for critical commodities and resources, commands regulators to defuse sources of financial instability, uses the balance sheet of state entities to arrest declines in the stock market, cracks down on sources of perceived social problems, and directs banks to bailout struggling industries. While all governments do these activities to some extent, China does so with a scale and intensity unmatched by other major economies.

While China often succeeds in suppressing sources of instability, it can create unintended consequences such as stunting the formation of industries, distorting the flow of capital, and sometimes creating even new sources of instability problems. This section of the chapter will look at some recent examples of government intervention to achieve goals related to stability and the consequences of those interventions. These examples will highlight that the obsessive pursuit of stability often undermines the goal of economic growth.

1.1 Case Studies of Government Intervention for Stability

1.1.1 Intervening in Resource Markets to Limit Price Increases

The Party has shown little tolerance for price volatility in strategic commodities and other vital resources. The Party deems a wide variety of commodities to be strategic, even some surprising ones such as pork.[7] The Party believes that price fluctuations above what it deems appropriate could damage the economy and lead to economic stability. As a result, authorities frequently intervene to manage price volatility, using both formal and informal tools. One formal tool is introducing new supplies in the market to lower prices, such as releasing pork from the nation's strategic pork reserve. Conversely, the government may also purchase commodities to increase prices when they fall below a level viewed as acceptable.

This type of activity is not uncommon among governments around the world. Many countries maintain subsidies to lower prices of essential food staples and energy inputs. Where China differs is in the scale and scope of its interventions and the harsh response directed at companies, individuals, and even data providers, which are seen as supporting speculative trading activity. The Party intervenes often across a wide variety of different commodity markets in the name of maintaining economic stability.

An example of the Party's overreaching efforts to manage prices occurred in 2021 as global commodity prices, including coal, metals, and food staples, began to rise. In early 2021, inflation began driving price increases for commodities, including copper, aluminum, and zinc. The government released quantities of these materials from its strategic reserves to lower prices.[8] China's Ministry of Industry and Information Technology promised to stabilize prices and punish speculation.[9]

When these actions failed to stem the increase in commodity prices, the Party shifted toward punitive action vowing to punish hoarders and speculators and investigate commodity pricing services.[10] Executives from large mining firms were summoned to a meeting with the National Development and Reform Commission (NDRC) and threatened with punishment for speculation and monopolist behavior.[11] The government began investigating what it deemed as transactions that did not serve the real economy, causing traders to pull back from the market for fear of being targeted.[12] In June of 2022, the NDRC proposed a new series of regulations to crack down on what it viewed as improper behavior by non-government price index providers.[13] In early 2022, similar investigations occurred into the trading of iron ore.[14] Regulators went after platforms that publish price information for "false price information."[15]

In 2021, the Party's efforts to manage coal prices and energy prices paid to coal power plant operators exposed the shortcomings of the overemphasis on stabilizing prices. Despite a push to develop renewable energy, coal remains an extremely important commodity for China, with coal-fired power plants producing nearly 60% of the country's total electricity.[16] Though coal is a globally traded commodity, China attempts to manage the domestic price of coal through guidance to coal producers and via its control over state-owned power plants and grid operators. The NDRC issues a "reasonable" price range for coal and manages energy prices for the industrial sector and households by setting the tariff paid to coal power plants.[17] Regulations only allow contracts between power plants and end-users to fluctuate 10% above the price.

As shown in Fig. 1, coal prices began to spike in the latter half of 2021 as China and the global economy recovered from the COVID-19 pandemic. As coal prices began to soar, the Chinese government cajoled coal producers to avoid speculative behavior. Several coal pricing indices were suspended after a significant surge in coal prices.[18] The government then guided coal and metals producers, many of whom are state-owned, to increase output and avoid "unreasonable" price increases.[19]

Despite the clear domestic and global trend in coal prices, Chinese regulators refused to adjust the energy tariff paid to power plants. By the fall of 2021, coal prices had risen to a level where it was no longer profitable for many power plants to operate. Power plant operators faced dramatically higher costs due to the increase in coal prices, while their end tariff payment barely adjusted. As a result, coal power plants across the country began to cease operations for suspiciously timed repairs, and 20 provinces were forced into rolling blackouts.[20] The blackouts impacted the operations of Chinese factories, and Chinese households were forced to ration power.

In response to the power crisis, Chinese regulators made some modest moves toward relaxing energy price controls. The price paid to coal power plants was allowed to increase to 20% above the set price, compared to the

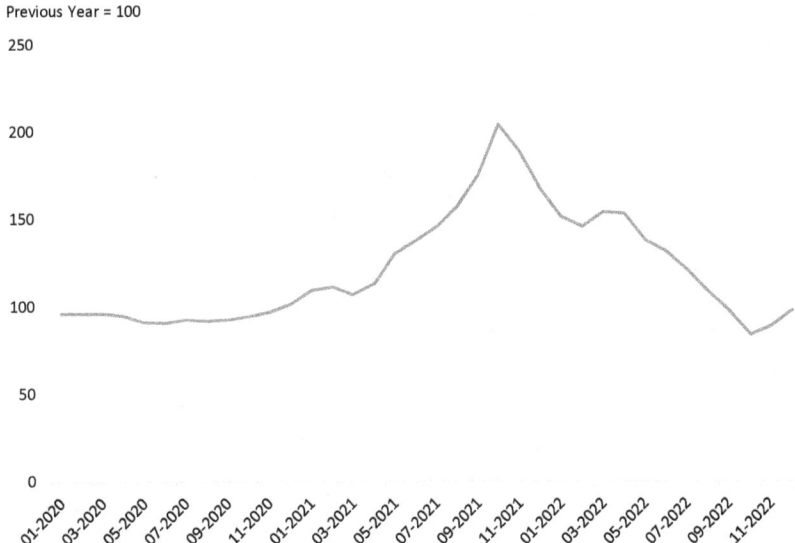

Fig. 1 China coal price producer price index, 2020–2022 (*Source* China National Bureau of Statistics)

prior 10% limit.[21] However, the Party also took steps to increase its intervention in the coal market. In October 2021, regulators and government bodies in China issued 71 new power-related documents with instructions to the industry.[22] Coal miners were ordered to boost output "regardless of cost" and cap prices.[23] Regulators promised punitive action against traders engaged in "speculation." State power plants were told to build up coal inventory regardless of cost.

Even as the crisis subsided, the government remained heavily involved in managing coal prices, with the NDRC issuing a new "reasonable" price range for coal and began issuing new guaranteed payments for coal power plants based on capacity.[24] The Party has not given up on its efforts to manage key commodity and input prices despite the risk that this can create unintended and destabilizing impacts on the economy.

1.1.2 Intervening in Industries to Reduce Economic Risks

The Party will often intervene in industries abruptly and in a draconian fashion when it senses a risk to the economy. One recent example is the draconian actions taken to address the country's housing bubble. Both Chinese and foreign economists have long warned about the potential economic dangers of a real estate bubble.[25] There were many signs that the growth of China's housing market had become unsustainable and a source of financial risks. First, according to international comparisons, the share of the Chinese economy dependent on real estate was extraordinary.[26] This means that any downturn in the property market could lead to a sharp slowdown in growth. Second, the price of homes had increased to extremely unaffordable levels for the typical Chinese household. This issue grew in potency as a source of social discontent, as many Chinese families felt they were priced out of affordable housing. Finally, due to their large and highly leveraged balance sheet, Chinese property developers emerged as serious financial risks. A sharp downturn in the property market could lead to large-scale defaults by property developers and possibly result in a financial crisis.

The combination of these risks led the Party to undertake a dramatic shift in China's housing policy. In 2016, Xi began using the slogan, "Housing is for living, not speculation," to signal his intentions to crack down on the housing market and China's overextended developers.[27] In late 2016 and 2017, new restrictions on purchasing investment properties were enacted, and down payment and mortgage requirements were increased.[28]

Despite restrictions, investment and leverage in the property sector continued to grow. Over the years, many of China's real estate developers have grown both large and reckless. Between 2015 and 2021, the total liabilities of Chinese real estate enterprises more than doubled, reaching RMB 91 trillion, or around $12.7 trillion.[29] They borrowed heavily from banks, issued onshore and offshore bonds, and took on high-interest-rate debts from shadow banks to fund an aggressive accumulation of land holdings. Their balance sheets were further stretched by a dishonest practice of using funds from the presale of apartments from one project to fund another. Any disruption in the market would lead to developers not having enough money to complete the projects that homebuyers had already paid for.

Evergrande was emblematic of these behaviors. The company's balance sheet swelled in the late 2010s, growing from $77 billion in 2014 to $352 billion in 2020.[30] The company had thousands of real estate projects in hundreds of cities across China.[31] Evergrande heavily engaged in the abuse of presale funds to finance its projects. It also used borrowed funds to expand into unrelated business lines, such as electric vehicles, wealth management, and food and drinks. Behind closed doors, Evergrande engaged in other highly questionable practices, such as pressuring employees to invest in the company's investment products and delaying payments to suppliers to cover financial shortfalls. Evergrande was not alone in the practices, with many of China's most prominent developers adopting similar tactics to grow as large as possible.

Given their egregious and risky business practices, it is understandable that Chinese policymakers would target real estate developers for a crackdown. In 2020, the Chinese government decided to push ahead with a significant restructuring of the property sector. One of the most important policies issued during this period was the Three Red Lines, a set of balance sheet constraints for property developers intended to force deleveraging. The policy sets out balance sheet rules that real estate developers must adhere to or face restrictions on their ability to borrow. They require developers to maintain a liabilities-to-assets ratio of less than 70%, a net-debt-to-equity ratio of less than 100%, and a cash-to-short-term-debt ratio of greater than 1.

China Securities Journal, an influential media outlet controlled by China's financial regulators, described the policy as forcing developers to "lose weight" by selling assets and strengthening their financial position.[32] However, the policy quickly led to a very different outcome. Large developers violating one or more of the three red lines soon found themselves cut off from new credit and fell into financial distress. As shown in Fig. 2, funding for real estate developers began to collapse in 2021 as the effects of the Three Red Lines became fully felt.

While the riskiest and most overleveraged property developers ran into trouble first, it soon impacted the entire real estate sector. When property developers could no longer obtain financing, they stopped working on new and ongoing projects. This created panic among buyers who had prepurchased homes and feared they would not receive a completed home. In turn, they stopped making mortgage payments, further increasing stress in the property market.

To avert a deep crisis in the property sector, the Chinese government moved to undo some of the damage caused by the Three Red Lines. The central government began telling banks to restore funding to real estate developers and commanded local governments to restart stalled development projects. However, it was too late to prevent a major slump in the market that impacted the entire economy. Further compounding

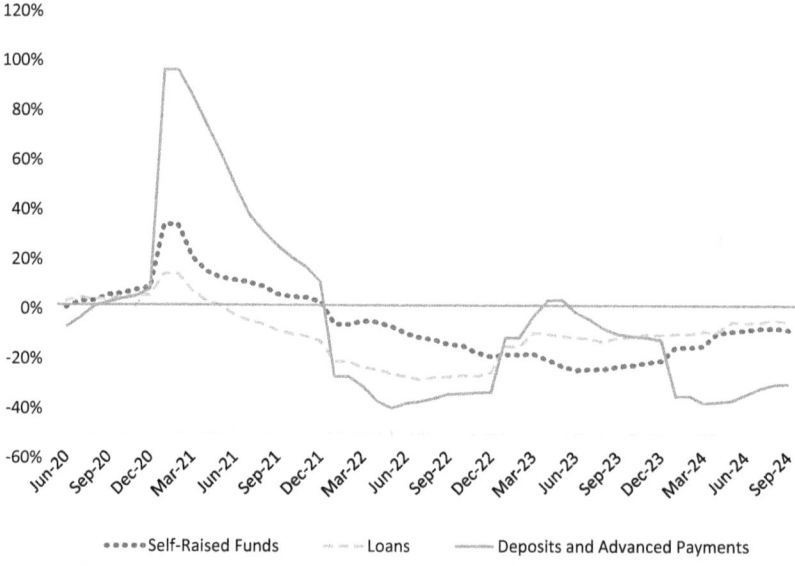

Fig. 2 Real estate developer major source of funds, June 2020–September 2024 (YoY, YTD) (*Source* China National Bureau of Statistics)

the problem, the housing market decline intensified at the same time the Chinese economy was suffering from the effects of strict COVID lockdowns.

In just a few short years, many of China's most private developers went bankrupt or were forced into restructuring. In contrast, many state-owned developers survived due to support from the government. As a result, the real estate sector underwent a form of nationalization as private developers disappeared and only state-owned developers remained. Evergrande's politically connected founder, Xu Jiayin, also was arrested by authorities.

With an iron fist, the Party had struck at the perceived economic risks presented by the housing bubble. However, somewhat ironically, its efforts to address these risks triggered a sharp economic slowdown and led to the collapse of many private firms. The core of the problem was that the Party's approach was blunt, inflexible, and poorly timed. Instead of implementing market-based reforms to address the distortions in the housing market, the Party relied on heavy-handed regulatory measures. The desire to preserve stability came at a tremendous cost to economic growth.

1.1.3   Intervening in Industries to Address Social Discontent

The Party will often intervene when it believes that an industry is contributing to social negative pressures. In the summer of 2021, China began an aggressive crackdown on the private education industry. Regulators had hinted at changes to the rules for the industry for many years. Most education institutions in China are state-owned and tightly controlled by the Party. Despite being an egalitarian system in theory, the educational system in China is rife with inequalities. There is fierce competition to get into the best schools in China, starting with elite primary schools and extending to the university system. Parents view these schools as a ladder for their children to find good jobs after graduation. Grades, test scores, and social connections are the critical determinants for determining which students are admitted to the best schools.

In the mid-2000s, a private education industry sprouted up to provide after-school tutoring and test preparation classes. Intense pressure to achieve good grades and test scores led to significant out-of-pocket expenses for parents and grueling hours for students who spent nights and weekends taking prep classes in addition to their regular schooling. As early as 2018, regulators began proposing new guidelines to address problems in the industry.[33] Xi began to take a personal interest in the issue with a view to addressing an issue of growing social discontent and inequity.[34]

In the summer of 2021, Chinese regulators released the "Opinions on Further Reducing the Homework Burden and Off-Campus Training Burden of Students in Compulsory Education," or the Double Reduction Policy for short. Xi presided over a meeting approving the reform, signifying his personal approval of the policy. Presented as a response to the concerns of overburdened students and anxious parents, the Double Reduction Policy implemented a massive regulatory overhaul for the private education system.[35] Localities were instructed to review and cancel business licenses for online educational services teaching students in compulsory education (primary and middle school) and providing subject-based training (i.e., the core academic curriculum). Existing subject-based training institutions were required to re-register as non-profits. Furthermore, subject-based training institutions were prohibited from listing on the stock market or accepting investment from foreign entities.

The impact of the Double Reduction Policy on China's private education sector was devastating. New Oriental, one of the largest companies, fired 60,000 employees after its operating income fell by 80%. As shown in Fig. 3, the share prices of three leading private education companies, New Oriental, TAL Group, and Gaotu, fell precipitously due to the regulatory changes. Other firms, like Wall Street English and Juren Education, closed operations.[36]

The Double Reduction Policy decimated the private education industry in China. The surviving companies had to radically restructure their businesses, such as education for adults and technical training. New Oriental was able to partially reinvent itself as a live-streaming company, with former instructors selling produce and other goods while delivering

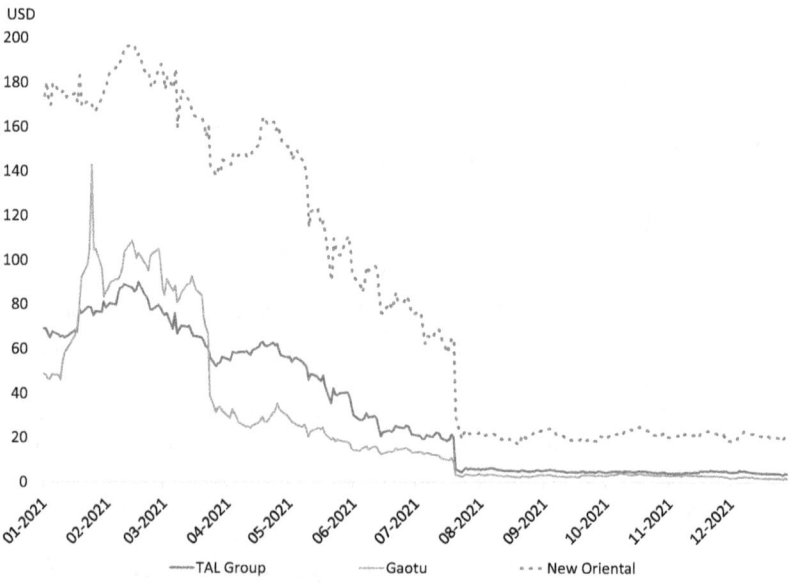

Fig. 3 Chinese private education stock prices, January–December 2021 (*Source* Bloomberg)

lessons on various topics.³⁷ While the Party had been responding to legitimate social concerns around education, it reacted in such a draconian way that it decimated a once-thriving private industry. Rather than seek to reform the sector and make it more inclusive, regulators effectively outlawed it.

While the Party undertook these actions in the name of preserving social stability, it appears to have failed to fully stamp out private tutoring. The private education industry has been driven into the underground economy. Several years after the crackdown, the Ministry of Education launched a crackdown on unlicensed tutoring services, indicating that parents were still finding a way to procure additional tutoring for their children.³⁸ The Party's pursuit of stability damaged the economy without achieving its original goal.

1.1.4 Intervening in Capital Markets to Reduce Volatility

Chinese policymakers frequently intervene in the stock market during periods of capital market volatility. These interventions stem from a fear that stock market volatility will create larger instability in the economy and that declining share prices will create social discontent among China's millions of retail traders. In the last decade, Chinese policymakers have orchestrated major interventions in 2015–2016, 2018, and 2023–2034.

Each of these interventions shares several common tactics. The first is the mobilization of the "National Team," a group of state-linked entities to support prices by purchasing shares in the market. The primary members of the national team are listed in Table 2.

Central Huijin, a state-owned investment holding company, is the most prominent national team member. A subsidiary of China's sovereign wealth fund, China Investment Corporation, Central Huijin holds significant ownership stakes in large state-owned banks, including ICBC, Bank of China, Agricultural Bank of China, and China Construction Bank. Huijin mobilizes the vast financial assets at its disposal to purchase shares during severe market drawdowns. For example, state media reported in February 2024 that Central Huijin had pledged to increase its purchases in the A-Share market, aiming to bolster the stability and health of the stock market.⁴⁰ The security regulator declared that it was facilitating Central Huijin's efforts and called for public and private funds, state-owned enterprises, securities and insurance companies, pension funds, and others to increase their market participation.⁴¹ The regulator also strongly

Table 2 China national team members

Entity name	Channels
Central Huijin	Purchasing securities via Central Huijin Investment and Central Huijin Asset Management
China Securities Finance Corporation	Purchasing securities directly and via state-linked asset management plans
State Administration of Foreign Exchange (SAFE)	Purchasing securities through Buttonwood, Beijing Kunteng, and Beijing Fengshan investment platforms
Mutual Funds	Purchasing securities via state-linked mutual funds
State-Owned Insurance Companies	Purchasing securities directly
State-Owned Enterprises	Purchasing securities directly

Source Goldman Sachs,[39] Author

encouraged other market participants to buy shares. A UBS report estimated that in the first two months of 2024, the national team may have purchased more than RMB 410 billion ($57 billion) in domestic shares.[42] Another estimate pegged the purchases by Central Huijin alone at $45.5 billion in the first quarter of 2024.[43] The national team's efforts were even greater in 2015 when it purchased around RMB 1.25 trillion ($174 billion) worth of shares, around 7.7% of the entire market's free float.[44]

If securities purchases by the national team represent the "carrot" of government intervention in the capital market, the "stick" is defined by draconian restrictions designed to prevent a decline in share prices. Regulators use several levers of control. The first is to limit new initial public offerings (IPOs) under the notion that IPOs divert capital away from existing securities, depressing share prices. The securities regulator has frequently taken this step during periods of market volatility.

Another method used by regulators to combat market volatility is to guide large institutional investors in limiting their selling activity.[45] Directors and other large shareholders in companies are told they are not permitted to reduce their shareholding.[46] In more severe instances, regulators will go directly after market participants seen as engaging in undesirable activities. The most common activity is putting restrictions on activities such as short selling.[47] Regulators also target individual traders, such as "malicious" short sellers or insiders selling their shares.[48] Some traders have been explicitly told that they cannot sell shares. Authorities have also censored the accounts of analysts and media outlets that publish negative coverage of the economy and, in some instances, arrested those involved. For example, in the wake of the stock market crash in 2015, nearly 200 people were arrested for the crime of "spreading rumors," including Wang Xiaolu, a journalist at the prominent financial magazine Caijing.[49]

Efforts to stabilize markets and mitigate volatility have been costly and largely unsuccessful. In the three instances of market interventions over the past decade, prices continued to fall for months after regulators intervened. For example, as shown in Fig. 4, it took almost two and half years for the CSI 300 index to return to its July 2015 levels, when the national team began its intervention. The national team and other market participants pressured to buy shares often suffer losses on their holdings, at least in the short run.

The larger impact of these policies has been to distort the development of China's capital markets and create problems of moral hazard. Returns from China's stock market have severely lagged the development of the overall economy. Since the start of Xi Jinping's reign in 2012 to 2023, GDP increased by 134%, while the Shanghai Stock Exchange Index returned 31%.[51] These numbers are a stunning indictment of China's mismanagement of its stock markets. Moreover, constant intervention by regulators creates expectations by investors that every downturn will see

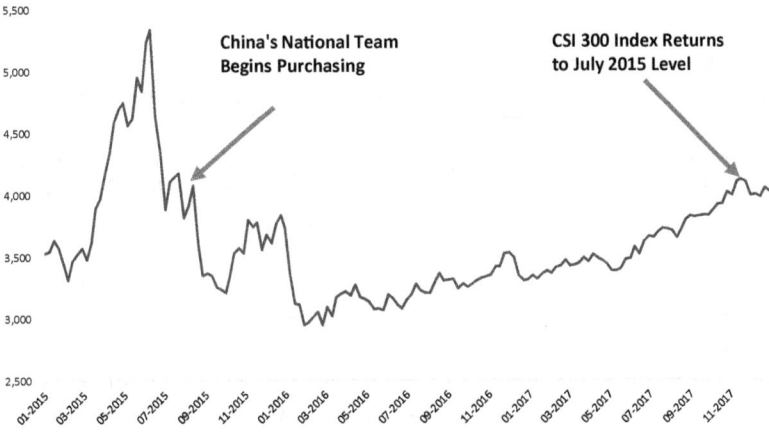

Fig. 4 China CSI 300 index, 2015–2017 (*Source* Bloomberg[50])

activity by the national team to support prices. This creates the risk of moral hazard, where investors take increasingly speculative bets, knowing regulators will act if the market falls too sharply.

1.1.5 Directing Banks to Prevent Financial Instability

The Party frequently instructs financial institutions to use their balance sheets to support troubled borrowers and industries. This process is referred to as "national service," whereby financial institutions make loans and investments according to the government's directions, often at great cost to their own profitability.

The Party has long viewed financial institutions as a key tool for directing financial resources. After taking power in 1949, the Party nationalized the private banking sector and created a "monobank," with the People's Bank of China serving as the central bank, policy bank, and commercial bank. The lending activity of the PBOC was closely linked to policy goals and economic plans created by the Ministry of Finance and State Planning Commission. There was no central bank independence, and the central bank operated as a subdepartment of the Ministry of Finance.

Policymakers set lending targets for various industries, and then loans were made to SOEs at fixed and highly subsidized interest rates. Loan targets were akin to budget allocations, and repayment was not prioritized. Nonperforming loans were rolled over or repaid with newly borrowed funds, a process called evergreening. Given that the state banks were often lending to SOEs "regardless of their risks or profitability, simply to meet the goals of the government," it is unsurprising that the banking system was rife with inefficiency and the misallocation of resources.[52]

Over the decades, the banking sector in China has become increasingly efficient and commercially oriented. As outlined in Chapter 2, a key reform was to allow a variety of different types of banks to be established. In the 1980s, the People's Bank of China was transformed into a modern central bank, and large state-owned commercial banks were established. Around that time, a variety of regional banks controlled by local governments and state-owned enterprises were also created. By the 1990s, these regional banks had grown quickly and become full-service banks with nationwide operations. By the 2000s, China had thousands of different banks, including a small number of private banks. This diverse ecosystem of banks fostered competition for borrowers and deposits.

The Party also gradually eased its control of interest rates in the name of improving the efficiency of lending. The process of interest rate liberalization unfolded across multiple decades. In the late 1990s, China began to introduce a degree of flexibility around the benchmark lending rate, letting banks make loans up to a specific percentage above or below the benchmark rate, varying by sector. Later on, regulators loosened controls on interest rates paid to depositors. By 2015, most explicit interest rate controls had been lifted. However, regulators continued to exert significant influence over lending and deposit rates through a variety of tools, ranging from window guidance to targeted relending facilities.

Despite these reforms, the Party has retained its ability to selectively intervene and direct financial institutions to lend to specific companies and industries. This frequently manifests as an effort to prevent messy bankruptcies that could be destabilizing economically. Bankruptcy is a politicized process in China in which courts, regulators, and ultimately, the Party must approve any large bankruptcies. Clear evidence of this interference is China's extraordinarily low bankruptcy rate, around 20% of the rate of the United States.[53] In the case of large bankruptcies, the government pushed for creditor committees to be formed to manage the process. State-owned financial institutions are inevitably large and influential members of these committees. The Party uses its influence through these state-owned financial institutions and through other methods of guidance to reduce bankruptcies and limit their social and economic impact. This is especially true when bankruptcies involve a state-owned enterprise.[54]

There are two recent examples of government intervention to direct financial institutions in the name of stability. The first is related to local government debt. Chinese local governments have on-balance sheet bonds, off-balance sheet bonds, and bank loans linked to local government financing vehicles (LGFVs). In October 2023, news agencies reported that the People's Bank of China directed banks to extend loans, adjust repayment terms, and reduce interest to provide a lifeline to struggling local governments.[55] Separately, the government also reportedly maintains a whitelist of approved LGFVs to which banks are encouraged to lend. The motivation behind directing banks to continue to direct credit to local governments (and their off-balance sheet vehicles) is a fear that their bankruptcies could lead to economic instability. One particularly egregious example of this involved Zunyi Road and Bridge

Construction Group, an LGFV located in Guizhou province. The creditor committee for Zunyi Road and Bridge agreed to restructure $2.26 billion in outstanding bank loans from five years to twenty-five years, with reduced interest and no principal repayment for ten years.[56] The generous terms of this restructuring deal granted to the LGFV were undoubtedly the result of government efforts to avoid bankruptcy.

The second recent example of government direction to financial institutions is property developers. After imposing policies like the Three Red Lines (described earlier in the chapter), many of China's property developers fell into financial distress. In November 2022, the central bank and banking regulator issued a 16-point rescue plan for real estate developers, which included guidance to financial institutions to continue making loans to property developers and extend current loans that could not be paid back.[57] Those policies were extended again in July of 2023 as liquidity problems for property developers continued.[58] In early 2024, the government became even more involved in directing loans to the property market. It directed 170 city governments across China to develop a "whitelist" of more than 3,000 approved property projects for banks to lend to.[59] Local officials pressured banks to make loans for these projects despite the fact that many of them did not meet the banks' lending criteria and might result in even more nonperforming loans.[60] As with directed lending to LGFVs, the guidance to continue lending to property developers is motivated by a desire to avoid further economic instability as a result of the property market slowdown. If developers continue to go bankrupt and leave unfinished projects, it would further damage homebuyer confidence and lead to a broader economic slump.

The Party's interventions to direct financial institutions may help prevent economic instability in the short term, but over the long run, they distort the flow of capital throughout the economy. Studies have shown that China's SOE borrowers receive preferential financing rates relative to the private sector despite being significantly less efficient than private firms.[61] Moreover, there is worrying evidence this distortion in lending in favor of SOEs is stunting the growth of private firms and leading to an overall decrease in business dynamism in China.[62] Perhaps most tellingly, as shown in Fig. 5, China's banking sector trades at an enormous discount to book value relative to emerging market banks as a whole and U.S. banks. Chinese banks trading significantly below a book value of one implies that investors believe that the bank's net assets are worth less than what is stated in the banks' financials. This stems from a belief that

Chinese banks will incur significant costs associated with complying with their national service requirements. If national service lending is pushed too far, it could create significant risks for the banking system.

In summary, the Party's overriding desire for economic and social stability brings about significant tradeoffs. China's government has actively intervened in a wide variety of industries in the name of defusing economic, financial, and social risks. It has often done so in a draconian manner, crushing perceived risks with little attention paid to the consequences that might result. In the past, China's rapid economic growth, driven by structural factors such as a growing labor force, urbanization, and global trade integration, helped mitigate the negative consequences of government interventions aimed at maintaining stability. However, the damaging impacts of these interventions have become more pronounced as the economy has slowed. Unfortunately, statements from Xi that "stability is the prerequisite for prosperity" indicate that China's leader does not see the tradeoff between his desire for stability and the growth of the economy.

Fig. 5 Bank price-to-book ratios, 2015–2023 (*Source* Bloomberg[63])

2 Innovation vs. Control

Xi and other Party officials constantly speak of the need for China to pursue an innovation-driven economic development model. According to Xi, China must unleash "new quality productive forces," a shorthand for developing new industries and technologies, to grow its economy.[64] Economic innovation is essential to the mission of China's national rejuvenation for both economic and strategic reasons. Innovation is a prerequisite for the Chinese economy to keep growing and avoid the middle-income trap. The middle-income trap refers to the tendency of fast-growing, developing economies to slow significantly as they reach middle-income status. This is often due to these countries failing to develop more advanced and higher value-added industries. These countries remain stuck in a lower and less lucrative position within the global supply chain network. This middle-income trap can also be toxic for social and political stability as stagnating economic growth generates widespread discontent. Previously rapidly growing countries like Thailand, Mexico, and South Africa are emblematic of the middle-income trap. While their economies continue to grow, it is at a pace too slow for them to catch-up with the high-income countries.

Beyond economic growth, innovation is important for China's national security. In a 2014 speech, Xi declared that "science and technology form the basis of a country's strength and prosperity" and "changes in the balance of world political and economic power."[65] China must rejuvenate the country through science, education, and innovation-led growth.[66] An innovative Chinese economy is one that is powerful and less susceptible to foreign pressures, such as the growing number of technology restrictions imposed by the United States.

The Party's dilemma is that creating an innovative economy requires the cooperation of private firms. Efforts to make SOEs more innovative have largely been unsuccessful. Xi and the Party have acknowledged the critical role of the private sector in driving innovation, declaring that private firms are responsible for 70% of technological innovation.[67] This number is likely an underestimate of the private sector's true contribution. Therefore, the Party has no choice but to turn to private companies to lead innovation within the Chinese economy.

This reliance on the private sector for innovation creates the second fundamental contradiction for the Chinese economy: innovation vs.

control. As discussed in Chapters 2 and 3, control is a driving motivation behind the Party's economic policy. The Party has never given up its efforts to control the economy's commanding heights. This includes key and strategically important industries. It also encompasses control over the flow of information and critical economic inputs, such as credit. Large concentrations of power and influence not controlled by the Party need to be eliminated or coopted.

When the Party feels its control over the economy is threatened, it intervenes in many different ways. The Party will pressure companies to establish Party committees, accept golden share investments, or give their data to the government. The Party will also enact new regulations to weaken the market power of private firms or prevent them from entering a state-dominated industry. In some instances, the Party will force the restructuring or breakup of a private company that is threatening state control over an industry. The Party will also orchestrate mergers and targeted bailouts for SOEs to reinforce their dominance of an industry. Finally, the Party will intervene when private companies begin to have too much influence over the flow of information within society.

The dilemma is that these efforts to retain control often impede the development of the private sector, upon which the Party relies for innovation. Interventions to reassert control or degrade the power and influence of a private company often damage not only that company but the entire industry in which it operates. The next section will cover several examples of interventions in the name of control and explore their impact on China's efforts to create an innovation-driven economy.

2.1 *Case Studies of Government Intervention for Control*

2.1.1 *Establishing Party Structures Within a Company*

When a private company in China begins to wield significant power and influence within the economy or society, the Party will often intervene to establish or strengthen Party structures within that company. While connections between corporations and the government are common throughout the world, the direct embedding of a political party within a company's governance structure takes this to a new level. The Party does this because a powerful private company that is not under the control of the Party is viewed as a potential threat because of its ability to act independently. Strengthening Party structures within a company is a way to gain eyes and ears into a company's activities and prevent it from engaging in activities the Party views undesirable or threatening. As discussed in Chapter 3, Party committees are one of the key tools used to achieve this control. As required by the Party's constitution, all companies with three or more employees who are Party members must facilitate the establishment of a Party committee. As a company grows, its Party committee may also increase in size and complexity.

Tencent is one of the most prominent examples of a private company growing to a size and level of influence that prompted intervention by the Party to establish greater control. Founded in the late 1990s, Tencent developed a messaging platform called QQ. This messaging platform grew rapidly and became a popular communications tool for young internet users. Tencent also had significant success with the online and mobile phone games it has released, attracting hundreds of millions of players. The company's most successful product, WeChat, was launched in 2011. Like QQ, WeChat was a messaging platform, but it had much broader functionality. Acting as a "super app," WeChat allowed users to make payments, book tickets, pay bills, and a wide range of other functions. WeChat quickly became a dominant platform on the Chinese internet, with companies building "mini apps" to function within WeChat. By the mid-2010s, Tencent was one of the key firms shaping the Chinese internet and had control over major channels of communication, commerce, and finance.

Tencent was initially classified as an imitator of Western tech firms. It was accused of copying Microsoft's instant messenger platform early in its history. The company's initial strategy was to take products popular in the West and adapt them to the Chinese market. That changed as the company grew and evolved. With the launch of WeChat, Tencent created a new model of a social media app. Compared to Western competitors like Facebook, WeChat offered much more functionality and deeper integration into the real economy. Rather than an imitator, Tencent became one of China's most innovative companies, with Western business schools writing articles about Tencent's impressive ability to innovate.[68]

Given its importance, the Party has long prioritized having strong Party organizations within Tencent. As early as 2003, Tencent had a Party branch.[69] In 2011, the original Party branch was upgraded to a Party committee, with 12 general Party branches and 106 Party branches, with a total of 5,593 Party members.[70] By 2018, the number of branches had grown to 116, with a total of 7,915 Party members.[71] Tencent's Party committee is made up of its senior management.[72] The Party committee and its subordinate branches conduct training for all Party members within the company, such as studying Xi Jinping's speeches and how to "adhere to the correct guidance of public opinion" in managing messaging platforms.[73] Such correct guidance includes promoting core socialist values, safeguarding national security information, and fighting the spread of "illegal information."[74] As of 2016, Tencent had set up a 6,000-square-meter "Party member activity venue," assigned three full-time Party cades and 360 part-time Party cadres, and allocated more than RMB 1 million in special funds for Party building work.[75] In 2017, a new statue with a hammer and sickle was installed in front of Tencent's headquarters, proclaiming, "Follow our Party, Start Your Business."[76] While more recent statistics have not been made public, it's reasonable to assume that the scale and resources dedicated to the company's Party committee have only increased since then in line with Tencent's growth (Table 3).

Despite the large-scale Party organizations operating in Tencent, the company has still not been able to avoid scrutiny by the government. The Party felt that its level of control was insufficient, and Tencent was among the many Chinese companies swept up in the crackdown in 2021. There were allegations that it was misusing its user data.[78] Over the next several years, Tencent faced a torrent of regulatory action. The State Administration for Market Regulation blocked the company from merging two of its video streaming apps, Douyu and Huya.[79] Furthermore, Tencent Music Entertainment was banned from having exclusive rights to music libraries. Tencent was blocked from sending out updates for any of its apps before receiving approval from government regulators.[80] In addition, regulators halted the approval of new video games and drastically limited the amount of time that minors were allowed to play.[81] The company was fined for previous acquisitions that regulators said violated antitrust provisions.[82] Tencent's financial businesses were subject to new restrictions, forcing a scale back of its operations, and Tencent was forced to reorganize as a financial holding company.[83]

Table 3 Levels of Party organizations within companies

Level of Party organization	Number of members
Party Committee	More than 100
General Party Branch	50–100
Party Branch	3–50

Source CSIS[77]

There is little public information about what actions were taken by Tencent's internal party committees during the crackdown. However, their impact can be felt from how quicky the company reversed course. Statements from Tencent's leadership adopted an apologetic and conciliatory tone. Ma Huateng, founder and chief executive of Tencent, reportedly told employees that Tencent should not challenge the banks.[84] He also commented that Tencent's apps "served society" and "assisted the real economy," echoing the Party's demands.[85] In 2022, the company issued its first sustainable social value report, separate from the existing environmental social and governance (ESG) reports it already produces. In the report, Ma praised a common vision based on national needs, government guidance, and concerns about people's livelihoods.[86] The report outlines Tencent's efforts to support various government initiatives.

By the end of the regulatory crackdown, the Party had firmly brought Tencent under control. The company's growth slowed significantly and its market capitalization fell 75% from its peak, as shown in Fig. 6. The company also opened its platform to competitors and divested several large stakes in other Chinese companies. These days, Tencent operates more cautiously, fearful of provoking the Party's ire again. Whether the company can again replicate its earlier success at innovation is uncertain.

2.1.2 Intervention to Prevent Private Companies from Dominating an Industry

The Party frequently intervenes when it believes a private company has become overly influential in an important industry. The payments sector serves as a prime example of such intervention. Historically, China's payments system has been tightly linked to state-own banks and state-controlled payments infrastructure. As the Chinese economy developed, electronic retail payments became increasingly important. In 2002, a consortium of state-owned banks launched UnionPay to unify the country's growing number of credit and debit card networks, many of which were not interoperable. Dai Xianlong, the central bank governor, presided over the launch ceremony of the new entity.[87] UnionPay was anointed with a de facto monopoly on the card payments network in China. The company's senior leadership was dominated by former central bank officials.

To further entrench its position, the Chinese government protected UnionPay from foreign competition, making it difficult for Visa and

Fig. 6 Tencent market capitalization, 2019–2023 (*Source* Bloomberg)

Mastercard to operate in the Chinese market. This was in direct contravention of commitments made by China during its World Trade Organization membership negotiations.[88]

UnionPay was primarily focused on real-world transactions, such as those in restaurants, hotels, and retail. That left an opening for private companies to offer payment services to China's nascent but rapidly growing e-commerce industry. Both Tencent and Alibaba began offering online payment services. Tencent explored payments involving digital currencies in 2002, and Alibaba launched Alipay in 2004. The Chinese government initially adopted a wait-and-see attitude toward the development of private payment companies, avoiding regulations that would have squelched the new industry.[89] The central bank began issuing licenses to third-party payment providers in 2011.

As e-commerce in China continued developing, Alipay and Tencent became significant players in the online payments sector. Both companies created digital wallets that allowed users to store funds, send payments, and even purchase financial products. Alipay and Tencent soon began to threaten UnionPay's monopoly on in-person card payments by allowing users to pay in retail stores, restaurants, and other locations by scanning a QR code with their mobile phones. Figure 7 shows the rapid growth of non-bank internet payment transactions and the value of those transactions over the last decade.

The rapid growth of the two private payments companies generated fierce reactions from UnionPay and the state banks. UnionPay was strongly opposed to Tencent and Alipay offering both in-person payments.[90] The banks were worried that Tencent and Alipay were beginning to compete directly with them by offering financial services such as credit, investing, and insurance via their apps.

In addition to these commercial concerns, the Party was concerned that private companies dominated payments, a critical node of the economy. Yi Gang, China's central bank governor, articulated these concerns clearly. He criticized private payment companies for competing with banks in the deposit business, abusing their access to information on consumers and businesses, capturing an excessively high market share

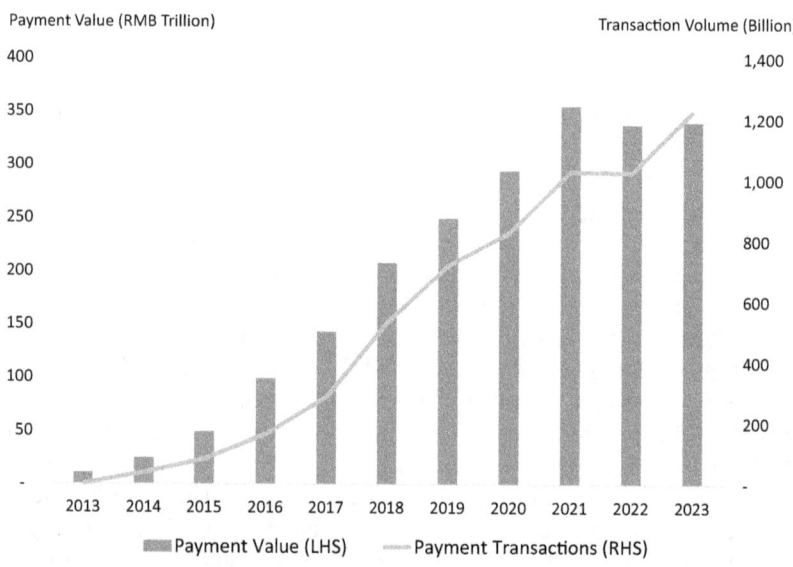

Fig. 7 Value and transaction volume of non-bank payments (*Source* The People's Bank of China)

of the payments industry, failing to adhere to money laundering requirements, and acting as an unofficial central bank by doing their own netting and clearing.[91]

In 2017, the central bank created the NetsUnion Clearing Corporation, commonly known as NetsUnion. As a public-private partnership, NetsUnion was capitalized by the central bank, with smaller contributions from a variety of private players, including Alibaba and Tencent. However, it was evident that this new clearing system was a direct reassertion of control over the private payments system created by Alibaba and Tencent. By regulation, all payments would now need to flow through NetsUnion instead of circulating within the two companies' platforms. Moreover, the central bank would have direct access to the data associated with every transaction. Soon afterward, new regulations were released that required all customer funds held by private payment companies to be deposited with the central bank, removing a key source of revenue for Alibaba and Tencent, which had made money on customer float.[92]

As discussed in Chapter 3, Ant would undergo a lengthy and severe regulatory crackdown. The Party blocked the company's IPO, forcing it to restructure and devolve key parts of its business, most notably consumer lending. Ant's consumer ratings arm, Zhima Credit, was split off, and state investors took ownership stakes.[93] Regulators ordered Zhima to share its trove of information on consumer with the central bank's credit rating platform, Baihang Credit Services Platform. Following the crackdown, Jack Ma relinquished most of his voting rights in Ant and was declared no longer a controlling shareholder.[94]

Payments in China are still innovative in many respects. The country has transitioned to a near-cashless economy much quicker than many would have predicted. Tencent and Alipay still maintain dominant market shares in online and mobile payments. However, both companies have reached a regulatory ceiling on the scope of activities in which they can engage. The Party will not allow the creation of privately run payment networks due to its desire to monitor and control key financial flows within the economy. Private companies that offer financial services that compete directly with the state banks will face regulatory scrutiny. Large collections of information about transactions must be shared with the state. Innovation is often difficult to quantify. However, one example of this industry's diminished prospects is that Ant announced a valuation in 2023 that was 75% lower than the IPO price it was targeting in 2020.[95]

Meanwhile, UnionPay persists as a quasi-monopoly in bank card transactions, earning a fee from Tencent and Alibaba every time a payment involving a bank card occurs on their platforms.

2.1.3 Bailouts or Mergers to Preserve State Control

The Party has long sought to consolidate state control over critical industries. The Chinese government strengthens SOEs through a variety of tools, including subsidies, capital injections, and orchestrated mergers. The subsidies provided to SOEs are significant, including direct financial payments, access to cheap land, preferential lending rates, and capital. Government guidance funds, such as China Reform Holdings and China Structural Adjustment Fund, are tasked with bailing out and restructuring weak SOEs. Perhaps the most significant tool used by the Party to strengthen state control over critical industries is mergers between SOEs. Unlike business mergers in the United States, which are determined by a company's shareholders or management, the Party orchestrates SOE mergers in China.

Orchestrating mergers to strengthen SOEs was a major feature of the "Grasp the Large, Release the Small" policy of the late 1990s. As part of the reforms, China let smaller SOEs go out of business while simultaneously consolidating and merging SOEs in specific sectors. As discussed in Chapter 2, the goal was to preserve and strengthen SOEs in strategically important areas of the economy. That process continued for many years, with the number of centrally owned SOEs steadily decreasing through mergers. This approach was again renewed in the 2015 Guiding Opinion on State-Owned Enterprise Reform, which kicked off a round of SOE mega-mergers. Between 2003 and 2019, the number of central SOEs supervised by the State-owned Assets Supervision and Administration Commission (SASAC) decreased from 196 to 96.[96] Meanwhile, as shown in Fig. 8, the total assets of central enterprises have expanded rapidly since 2001. Meanwhile, efficiency, as measured by return on assets, has fallen to low levels, hovering around 3% for much of the last decade.[97]

The pattern of mergers among SOEs since Xi took office shows that the Party has been trying to reinforce the strength of SOEs in the energy, food production, transportation, and logistics sectors.[98] This has the effect of squelching competition from private firms in the sectors, which ultimately has a negative impact on both efficiency and innovation.

The Party's focus on logistics is evident in the steady stream of new policies introduced for the sector. In 2019, the NDRC issued "Opinions

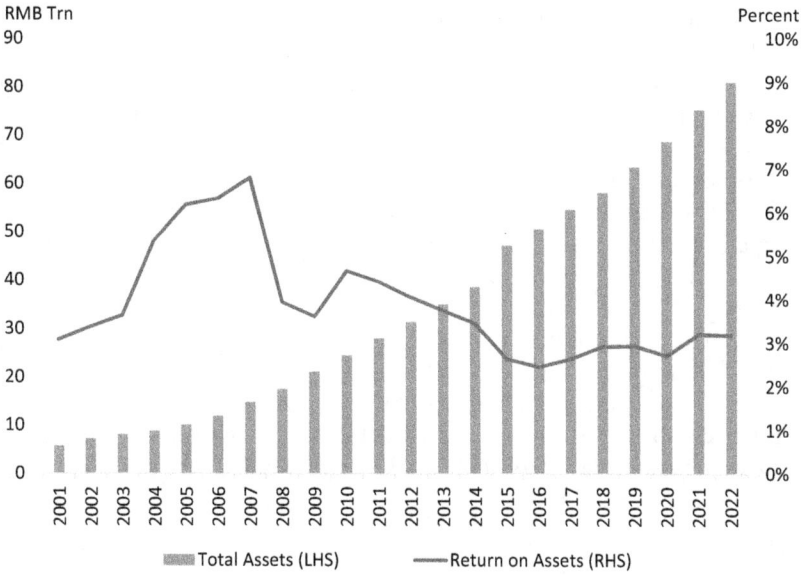

Fig. 8 Total assets and return on assets of central SOEs (*Source* China Ministry of Finance)

on Promoting High-Quality Development of Logistics and Promoting a Strong Domestic Market."[99] In the document, logistics is referred to as a "foundation, strategic, and leading industry" for the national economy. It calls for integrating logistics with manufacturing to improve efficiency and strengthen supply chains. The document specifies the creation of national logistics hubs to support major strategic priorities, such as the Belt and Road Initiative and economic integration between Guangdong, Hong Kong, and Macao. The opinion calls for creating new models of logistics powered by the internet and addressing shortcomings in intermodal logistics (i.e., rail, water, and road). In 2020, Xi Jinping began to talk about the concept of Dual Circulation, the need to break down transportation bottlenecks that hindered the development of China's domestic market, and vigorously develop the smart logistics industry.[100] Party news outlets have begun stressing China's goal of becoming a transportation and logistics "superpower."[101]

Ironically, it is the Party's domination of a critical part of the transportation and logistics sector that undermines these goals. As shown in Fig. 9, highway freight accounts for the vast majority of freight volume in China and it is an area led by private firms. The relatively open highway freight sector has spawned many thriving private market players. Private companies such as SF, ZTO Express, EMS, JDL, Full Truck Alliance, and Cainiao have made China's delivery and logistics industry extremely competitive. It has also created innovation, with China's last-mile delivery services cited for their speed and efficiency in delivering e-commerce purchases.[102]

In contrast, through monopolies and mergers, the Party has ensured that SOEs dominate water, air, and railway transportation and logistics. In 2015, state conglomerate China Merchants Group merged with state logistics companies Sinotrans and CSC Holding Company. In 2016, the Party orchestrated the merger of two SOEs, COSCO and China Shipping,

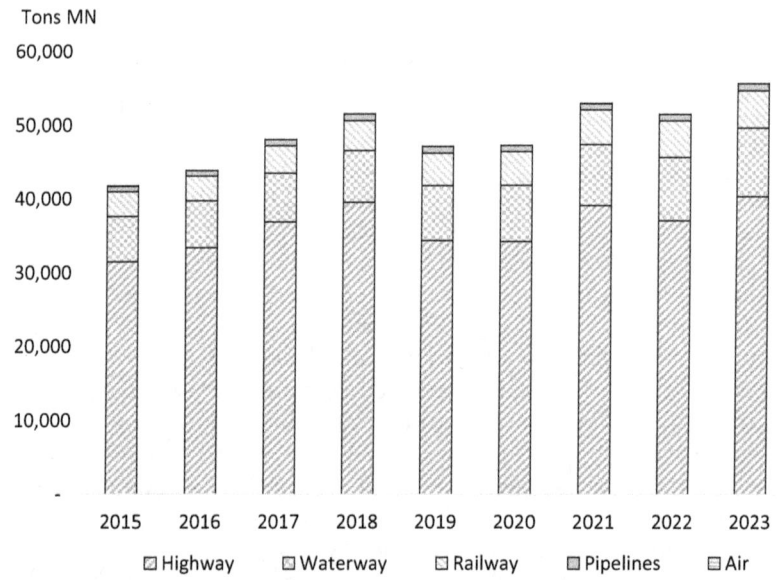

Fig. 9 Freight transportation in China (*Sources* China Ministry of Transport, Civil Aviation Administration of China, China Railway Corporation, China National Railway Administration, China National Bureau of Statistics)

to create the largest shipping logistics company in the world, China Cosco Shipping.[103] Both companies had been facing financial pressure due to a downturn in the global shipping industry. In 2021, the Party orchestrated the creation of a new entity, China Logistics Group, through the merger of China Railway Materials Group and four companies that are subsidiaries of China Chengtong Holdings, a central holding company that manages the China Structural Reform Fund. China Chengtong's website declares that it will operate "under the guidance of Xi Jinping Thought on Socialism with Chinese Characteristics" and will pursue goals for the SOEs under its guidance, including "strengthening the Party's leadership."[104] SASAC took a 38.8% share, and a group of three state-owned strategic investors, China Eastern Airlines, China COSCO Shipping, and China Merchants Group, took stakes in the group worth a total of 22%.[105] The effect of this merger was further consolidation of the logistics structure among a handful of SOEs.

The results of this government intervention can be seen in the skewed structure of the logistics industry. China's dynamic and innovative private logistics firms are limited in their ability to expand outside of road delivery and the sector remains fragmented. SOEs remain in control of rail, air, and waterway transportation and logistics. This creates significant inefficacies for the economy. For example, the state-owned railroad companies are seen as "bureaucratic, slow to respond, and fraught with restrictions that hinder efficient operation."[106] Despite numerous policy initiatives, China has struggled to establish efficient intermodal logistics between road, rail, sea, and air.

Another indication of the stranglehold the Party has enacted on logistics is that despite private firms handling the bulk of freight transportation in the country, five out of China's top seven logistics companies by revenue are state-owned.[107] Maintaining control over critical transportation is essential to the Party's control over the commanding heights of the economy. Unfortunately, the Party's approach has forestalled the rise of more efficient private firms and stifled innovation in the logistics industry in China. China's logistics spending is among the highest in the world,[108] but much of it is channeled through enormous state-owned conglomerates that are shielded from private competition.

2.1.4 Intervening to Control the Flow of Information

Managing the flow of information is essential to the Party's control over China. It is one of the key mechanisms by which the Party manages public opinion. Within China's borders, censorship and guidance to media outlets are used to create a narrative that conforms to the Party's official perspective on all matters. This includes the suppression of any news or viewpoints that conflict with the Party's agenda. Private media outlets in China have faced a litany of different restrictions. According to the Negative List for Market Access, a catalog put out by the NDRC on which sectors are permitted to receive private investment, the media industry is essentially reserved for SOEs[109]:

> Non-public capital shall not engage in the business of news gathering, editing, and broadcasting. Non-public capital shall not invest in the establishment and operation of news organizations, including but not limited to news agencies, newspapers and periodicals, radio and television broadcasting organizations, radio and television stations, and Internet news and information collection, compilation, and release service organizations.
> Non-public capital shall not operate the layout, frequency, channels, columns, and public accounts of news organizations. Non-public capital shall not be engaged in live broadcasting of political, economic, military, diplomatic, major social, cultural, scientific and, technological, health, education, sports, and other activities and events related to political direction, public opinion orientation, and value orientation.
> Non-public capital shall not introduce news released by foreign subjects.
> Non-public capital shall not hold forum summits and award selection activities in the field of news and public opinion.

These regulations on private investment in the media have been in place since 2005. Despite these restrictions, a few private media outlets have persisted, notably the financial and economic news site Caixin. The Party has recently tightened the screws on private media by adding the provision on non-public capital being banned from holding forum summits and award selection activities, a money-making opportunity for many media outlets. Caixin and the Economic Observer, another prominent private media outlet, were targeted for further restrictions when the Cyberspace Administration of China was removed from the list of media outlets that websites in China can republish, curtailing the distribution of their content.[110]

With the rise of social media platforms in China, the Party's hold on controlling news flow has weakened. News feeds driven by algorithms on social media platforms have become immensely popular. Algorithms promote news stories based on a variety of factors and are often heavily influenced by user likes and engagement. This can often lead to stories being promoted that conflict with what the Party would like to be highlighted. As a result, the Party has begun to intervene directly in managing news and media algorithms.

One notable instance of this intervention occurred in 2018 when regulators criticized Jinri Toutiao and Kuaishou, two of the most popular platforms, for allowing users to upload "inappropriate content."[111] The head of Kuaishou apologized and stated that the company would only recommend content "in keeping with the country's laws and regulations, and with social norms."[112] Soon after, four popular news apps, Jinri Toutiao, Tiantian Kuaibao, Netease News, and Ifeng News, were temporarily removed from app stores.[113] Bytedance, which owns Jinri Toutiao, apologized, stating that "This entire time, we've been overemphasizing the value of technology without realizing that technology must be guided by socialist core values."[114]

Countries worldwide have restrictions on media platforms to deal with the problems of obscene content. In that sense, Chinese regulators are similar in their approach to cracking down on lewd or violent social media posts. However, the Party goes well beyond this in its desire to intervene deeply in the flow of news and social media stories to impose political and ideological constraints. In 2021, the Party's propaganda department introduced new guidelines for Chinese content creators to "adhere to the correct direction" and "strengthen the research and guidance of network algorithms, carry out comprehensive management of network algorithm recommendations, and do not provide dissemination channels for erroneous content."[115]

In March 2022, the effort to regulate algorithms expanded significantly. China passed Regulations on the Administration of Internet Information Service Recommendation Algorithms to, among other things, "carry forward Core Socialist Values" and "preserve national security."[116] The regulations require registration of any algorithms that have "public opinion properties" or the "capacity for social mobilization" and for the companies producing these algorithms to "carry out security assessments in accordance with relevant state provisions."[117] News algorithms were prohibited from transmitting news information from outlets "not within the scope provided by the state."[118] A wide range of China's most prominent platform companies, including Tencent, Alibaba, and Bytedance, registered algorithms with the Cyberspace Administration of China (CAC).[119]

China has also reacted to the spread of new large language model-based artificial intelligence with increased controls. Chinese companies were instructed not to offer ChatGPT-based services to their users because of concerns that the model's unfiltered replies conflict with censorship rules.[120] Chinese companies have created their own AI models, but due to censorship restrictions, they cannot discuss many issues related to domestic and international politics, such as answering whether Xi Jinping is a good leader.[121] In 2023, China released Draft Measures for the Management of Generative Artificial Intelligence Services that declare that "content generated through the use of generative AI shall reflect Core Socialist Values" and may not contain content related to the subversion of state power, overturning of the socialist system, incitement of separatism, or harm national unity, among other requirements.[122] Like algorithms, new generative AI products must be submitted to the Cyberspace Administration of China for a security assessment.[123] According to one report, generative AI models must answer tens of thousands of preselected questions by the government designed to test whether the model provides politically approved answers, and models must also decline to answer thousands of questions deemed to be politically sensitive, such as those critical of the Party.[124]

Chinese companies have certainly been successful and innovative in adapting algorithms to drive the growth of social media platforms. Douyin and its international variant TikTok are a clear example of that success, with collectively more than a billion active monthly users. However, recent efforts to control algorithms, including news recommendation algorithms and artificial intelligence, threaten to stifle that innovation. Private companies in this area succeeded before the Party stepped in to regulate. It is unclear whether they can continue to do so in the new environment of strict oversight. In the realm of news outlets, China has largely controlled the flow of information at the expense of suppressing the creation of a private media industry. Tightly controlled state news agencies dominate China's media landscape, leaving little room for creativity and innovation.

In summary, the Party's demand for control over industries and the flow of information has had a damaging impact on innovation and economic dynamism. The difficult business environment created by Party interventions has contributed to a collapse in new startup companies, a key ingredient for innovation.[125] Many of China's most promising private companies have been stifled as the Party has sought to inject itself into their corporate structures. Industries that were ripe for disruption by new private entrants have been consolidated under SOE control through mergers and other forms of government support. The free flow of information, essential to any modern economy, has been restricted and distorted by a media industry that operates under tight Party control. While China continues to show sparks of dynamism in certain industries, overall, the economy's innovative potential has been limited by policies that promote control over other priorities.

3 Global Integration vs. Self-Reliance

Self-reliance has long been a priority for the Party. During the days of Mao, the Party prioritized self-reliance in a variety of critical industries. The motivation for doing so was that foreign adversaries would refuse to trade with China for essential resources and technology. This was certainly the case during the Korean War when many Western nations stopped trading with China. Mao began emphasizing self-reliance even more after the Sino-Soviet split in the early 1960s. Until then, the Chinese economy had relied heavily on Soviet aid and technical assistance. After the split, both Soviet advisors and financial assistance were withdrawn, leaving significant parts of the Chinese economy in the lurch. China was forced to develop domestic capabilities, but it was often costly and resulted in inefficient and technologically backward industries.

During the Reform and Opening period, which began in the late 1970s, the Party underwent a significant shift in its approach to trade. Western countries had become increasingly open to trade with China, and the Party began to actively embrace trade as a driver of economic growth. China actively sought to integrate itself into global supply chains, using its vast low-cost labor base to attract manufacturing investment. Deng and others in the Party embraced trade as a means to strengthen China's economy and the Party's legitimacy.[126] Trade could give China access to technology and manufacturing, which the Party viewed as necessary for China to modernize its economy.

China's integration into the global economy accelerated throughout the 1980s due to trade and foreign investment. However, the Tiananmen Massacre in 1989 led to a new round of trade restrictions and sanctions from Western nations. These restrictions remained in effect during much of the 1990s but were eventually relaxed as Western nations decided to once again embrace trade with China. The country's international economic integration accelerated after its accession to the World Trade Organization in 2001. The 2000s witnessed a rapid expansion of China's trade with the world, propelling the country to the status of a global manufacturing powerhouse. By 2009, China had become the world's largest exporter, a remarkable feat considering its minimal trade with the rest of the world just three decades earlier.[127]

After Xi Jinping took office, he began revitalizing efforts to develop self-reliance in strategic industries. The most well-publicized of these efforts was the Made in China 2025 program, which set explicit targets for domestic production in various high-tech sectors. This effort created a backlash from many of China's largest trading partners, who viewed the domestic production goals outlined in Made in China 2025 as a plan to replace foreign companies with Chinese ones.

From Xi and the Party's perspective, recent events have made the need for self-reliance indisputable. With the onset of the U.S.-China Trade War, China has faced severe and growing restrictions on its ability to access foreign technology. U.S. policymakers have taken steps to limit China's access to strategic technologies and stunt the growth of key sectors, such as semiconductors. Additionally, China, like many countries, experienced supply chain shocks arising from the COVID-19 pandemic. These supply chain shocks were disruptive for China's manufacturing sector continues to rely on a wide variety of foreign inputs.

In response to these pressures, Xi has accelerated the Party's efforts to develop self-reliance in strategic industries. Xi has ordered officials to create backup plans for critical industries to ensure there is at least one alternative source for every important product and material.[128] This is done to insulate the Chinese economy from global economic shocks and reduce the ability of foreign powers to use economic pressure on the country.

This approach, however, highlights the third of China's major economic contradictions: global integration vs. self-sufficiency. China wishes to remain integrated in the global economy and retain access to international export markets. Trade is still crucial for the economy, and China relies on imports for many vital resources, including food and energy. Moreover, despite efforts to develop indigenous technology sources, China remains dependent on the United States and its allies for many critical technologies. Xi and the Party's aggressive pursuit of self-reliance has led to a backlash from the rest of the world. Many of China's trading partners view these efforts as a way to cut them out of the Chinese market and steal their technology and intellectual property. The dilemma for the Party is that the push for self-reliance has created a countervailing reaction in China's foreign trade partners. The country is now facing growing barriers to overseas trade. If pushed too far, China may find itself cut off from the global markets it needs for growth and the key foreign resources it depends upon for its economic development. Thus, China's efforts to achieve self-reliance could create the scenario that the Party wishes to avoid.

3.1 Case Studies of Government Intervention for Self-Reliance

3.1.1 Industrial Policy to Create Domestic Industries

For decades, China has sought to use industrial policy to foster domestic industries. These efforts have been motivated by a desire to move up the global value chain and to reduce reliance on foreign imports, especially in industries viewed by the Party as strategic. The automobile industry has long been viewed as strategic by the Party, with many state-owned automakers being established in the 1950s. After the start of economic reforms, China allowed foreign automakers to set up manufacturing within the country but limited foreign ownership of automotive companies to 50%. This forced foreign firms to partner with a Chinese company through a joint venture. The goal behind this structure was to leverage access to China's domestic market to force foreign automakers to share technology and manufacturing know-how in hopes that it would benefit China's domestic auto industry.

This strategy for the automotive industry produced mixed results. China's imports of foreign vehicles dropped significantly, but foreign brands remained dominant in most market segments.[129] Foreign investment restrictions ensured that brands such as Honda, Toyota, General Motors, and Volkswagen had to work with Chinese joint venture partners for domestic production. However, using these restrictions as a tool to propel forward the domestic auto industry was unsuccessful for many years. China's wholly domestic brands were not major players globally. Until quite recently, Chinese car exports were largely confined to lower-end segments, particularly compact cars.

As technology began to develop for electric vehicles, Chinese policymakers identified an opportunity to leapfrog ahead in a new emerging industry.[130] The Made in China 2025 Plan, launched in 2015, identifies new energy vehicles, which include battery and plug-in hybrid vehicles, as a sector to "energetically promote break through development" and seek the creation of "independent brands at internationally advanced levels."[131] The plan set a goal of having domestic new energy vehicle producers increase their market share to 80% by 2025.[132] The Mid-to-Long-Term Automotive Industry Plan, issued in 2017, set a goal for Chinese domestic brands to begin exporting EVs.[133]

To achieve this, the Chinese government has spent vast sums to support the domestic electric vehicle and battery industries in a manner that largely excluded foreign manufacturers. The central government rolled out a subsidy for passenger electric vehicles according to their battery range starting in 2016.[134] Local governments in China had their own corresponding subsidies for vehicles purchased in their municipalities. Electric vehicles also received an exemption from the vehicle purchase tax, consumption tax, and vehicle and vessel tax. The Chinese government also invested in infrastructure for electric vehicles and funded research for the industry. One report estimates that total government support for the electric vehicle industry between 2009 and 2023 was worth more than $230 billion, even excluding item such as support from government guidance funds and subsidized land for manufacturers.[135] According to the Chinese government's estimates, these tax incentives may reach RMB 520 billion ($72 billion) between 2024 and 2027.[136]

Because batteries are the most expensive component of an electric car, the Chinese government has also undertaken large-scale finance support for domestic battery makers and protected them from foreign competition. One estimate puts the amount of state support for China's two largest battery makers, BYD and CATL, at $6.8 billion between 2015 and 2020.[137] Foreign battery makers have had trouble gaining entry to the Chinese market. In 2016, Samsung and LG, who were leading electric battery makers at the time, were excluded for several years from the Chinese Ministry of Industry and Information Technology's Whitelist of batteries that were eligible for state subsidies.[138]

BYD is at the center of much of the industrial policy for the EV and battery industries. The company is remarkable in that in the span of a few short years, it has surpassed Tesla to become the world's largest electric vehicle maker. It has done so through grit, innovation, and a business model that most competitors cannot replicate. BYD is both a battery maker and a car manufacturer, giving it scale and cost efficiencies compared to its rivals. While the company's success is hard-fought, it has also received tremendous subsidies from the Chinese government.

The Shenzhen government awarded massive government procurement contracts for taxis and governments to BYD.[139] BYD has reported receiving $2 billion in direct subsidies between 2011 and 2021.[140] That number increased by another $1.7 billion in 2022 as BYD captured nearly 40% of the purchase subsidies offered by the government.[141] Indirect subsidies through low-cost capital, land, and other tax incentives add substantially to these amounts.

China's effort to create a domestic electric vehicle industry has generated significant backlash. As mentioned above, foreign automakers were forced to partner with domestic Chinese companies for the initial years of EV-focused industrial policy. Tesla was eventually able to enter the Chinese market without a Chinese partner, a special concession that was eventually granted to all foreign automakers. It produced its first cars out of its Shanghai factory in December 2019, after its domestic Chinese competitors had been protected from foreign competition for many years. So developed was the electric vehicle supply chain in China, that Tesla claims to use 95% domestic components in its Shanghai factory.[142] While Tesla has made inroads in the domestic Chinese market, it has also used its Shanghai factory as its primary vehicle export hub, exporting hundreds of thousands of vehicles, primarily to Europe.[143] Figure 10 shows the explosive growth of Chinese battery electric passenger cars over the past several years.

The rapid and state-supported growth of Chinese electric vehicle exports has led to trade countermeasures by Europe and the United States. In 2023, the European Union launched an anti-subsidy probe into Chinese electric vehicle imports. The probe alleges that "Chinese EV firms owe their competitive edge to government support and incentive policies."[144] Following the probe, the European Union announced additional tariffs on Chinese EVs, bringing the tariffs on some imported EVs to 45%.[145] The Trump Administration has put a 25 tariff on Chinese electric vehicles in the United States, a tariff that was subsequently raised by the Biden Administration to 100%. In 2022, the United States passed the Inflation Reduction Act, a major component of which were policies and subsidies aimed at jump-starting the domestic electric vehicle and battery industry. As part of the bill, the United States put in place new Foreign Entity of Concern guidelines that effectively exclude electric vehicles with Chinese-made batteries from receiving subsidies. In February 2024, the Biden Administration opened an investigation into whether Chinese cars pose a national security risk, and prominent U.S. politicians called for a

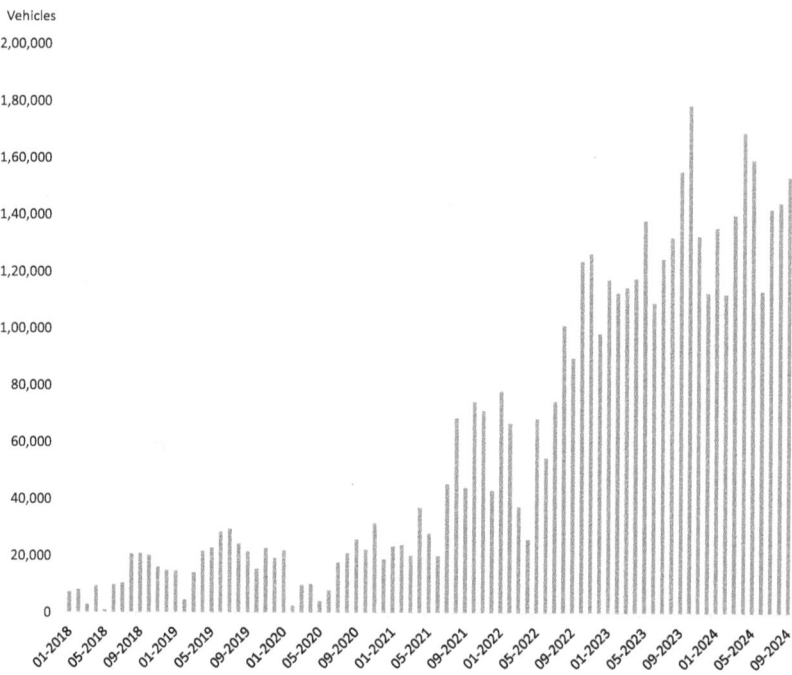

Fig. 10 China's exports of battery electric passenger cars, January 2018–September 2024 (*Source* China General Administration of Customs)

ban on Chinese electric vehicles.[146] Even countries outside of the EU and the United States have taken steps to limit Chinese electric vehicle imports. In June 2024, Turkey announced a new 40% tariff, set to be a minimum of at least $7,000 per vehicle, on Chinese car imports.[147]

China was early in identifying electric vehicles as a key strategic industry and succeeded in creating a largely self-sufficient electric vehicle industry. The Chinese government's financial support and industrial policy helped the EV industry grow to scale at a time when foreign competitors were largely absent or excluded from the domestic market. Now, Chinese EV companies have become global competitors in their own right. This has created a backlash from China's trading partners, who resent the heavy hand of the government in promoting this industry and the threat that Chinese auto exports represent to their domestic auto industries.

These export markets have become more critical now that the vehicle market in China has slowed, with total sales in 2023 only 4% higher than they were in 2017.[148] While EV sales continue to grow relative to gas cars, overcapacity has emerged as a major issue for the industry. In 2023, China's EV companies only utilized slightly more than half of their available production capacity. According to one estimate, Chinese EV manufacturers were on track to add capacity to produce 8 million more EVs per year by 2026, far greater than the projected increase in domestic demand.[149] As Chinese automakers grapple with this overcapacity problem, they face growing restrictions on exports of EVs to global markets.

3.1.2 Efforts to Establish Domestic Sources of Key Technologies
The Party has actively intervened in the Chinese economic to help establish domestic sources of strategic technologies. Beginning early in his term, Xi began prioritizing the development of key "chokepoint" technologies. As discussed in Chapters 2 and 3, Xi's efforts expand upon long-standing efforts by the Party to develop strategic technologies through top-down campaigns. Xi's initiatives, such as Made in China 2025, have focused on industries where China was dependent upon technology from foreign suppliers. These include integrated circuits, advanced communications technology, high-end manufacturing, aviation and aerospace, biotechnology, and others. In these sectors, the Chinese government has made a concerted effort to support the development of domestic sources of these technologies to reduce reliance on foreign countries.

The desire to do this stems from a fear that foreign countries can and will deny China access to these technologies. The Party believes that the United States and its allies will hold the Chinese economy hostage by refusing China access to the key technologies needed for the country to develop and move up the value chain. These fears have already manifested in many sectors, including semiconductors, artificial intelligence, and biotechnology, where the United States has imposed strong restrictions on technology transfer to China. The security implications of these technologies are as important as economic ones. Many of the technologies targeted for domestic development by the Party are dual-use in nature. Through a strategy known as military-civil fusion, the Party has sought to drive domestic industry to support the People's Liberation Army in becoming a world-class military power.

With the onset of the U.S.-China trade war in 2018, China's efforts to acquire strategic technologies have become even more assertive. In 2020, Xi declared he would "make technological self-reliance a strategic pillar of national development."[150] The Party describes this goal as requiring a whole-of-nation effort to break through technological bottlenecks imposed by the United States and its allies.

The means China uses to establish domestic sources of critical technologies range from relatively mundane to exceptional. One way to spur domestic innovation is to subsidize domestic firms in target industries. While China is not unique in this, it operates at an unprecedented scale. One study estimated that China's total industrial policy spending—such as below-market land sales, cheap credit, direct financial support, and tax incentives—was the largest in the world by a substantial margin, totaling nearly three times the amount spent by the United States.[151] Chinese firms also benefit from public procurement orders that favor domestic firms over foreign competition.

China uses its domestic market as a tool to gain access to foreign technologies. Historically, foreign investment restrictions in many industries required foreign companies seeking access to the Chinese market had to work with a Chinese joint venture partner. These joint ventures were designed to share the technology and know-how of the foreign partner with the Chinese firm. In some instances, the foreign firm was eventually cast aside as the Chinese firm developed the technology and expertise to compete on its own. This method of gaining access to foreign technology is controversial but used by many emerging markets. Over time, China has significantly reduced the number of industries where foreign investment is prohibited or subject to joint venture requirements, but restrictions still remain in important sectors such as telecommunications, technology, media, education, aviation, agriculture, and healthcare.

China has also sought to gain access to foreign trade in less legitimate ways. Government-sponsored efforts such as the Thousand Talents program seek to recruit foreign experts to work in China and share their expertise.[152] Foreign critics have accused the program of operating as a guise for intellectual property theft. China has also been charged by the United States and other Western nations with massive state-sponsored hacking efforts to steal trade secrets and technology of foreign firms.

Semiconductors and advanced communications technologies have long been strategic priorities for China. Both are important foundational technologies for modern economies and critical for national security. The

Made in China 2025 plan lists 5G technology and integrated circuit design as major priorities.[153] The 14th Five-Year Plan, which sets goals for the country's economy between 2021 and 2025, set ambitious targets for semiconductor advancements.[154]

One firm that has been at the forefront of many of China's efforts to gain access to critical technologies is Huawei. Though Huawei claims to be a private company, it has been tightly embraced by the Chinese government for many decades. The company has received significant support through subsidies, cheap credit, large state contracts, and protection from foreign competition. One estimate put the amount as high as $75 billion through 2019.[155] Huawei has also faced numerous allegations of economic espionage and foul play. Early in its life, Huawei lifted code directly from Cisco for its networking equipment. In 2020, the U.S. Justice Department unveiled charges against Huawei for stealing intellectual property from several American firms.[156]

By the mid-2010s, Huawei had succeeded in becoming the world's largest telecom equipment maker. The company also served as China's national champion in establishing domestic sources of cutting-edge communications technologies, such as 5G. Huawei was also important to China's efforts to develop domestically produced semiconductors through its chip design subsidiary HiSilicon. Huawei's success has helped support the creation of a domestic chip production ecosystem.[157]

However, Huawei's close links to the Chinese state have also generated a fierce backlash in overseas markets. As Xi accelerated China's efforts toward self-reliance, party control, and securitization of the economy, the United States began to view Huawei with greater skepticism.[158] In 2017, the U.S. government began imposing restrictions on Huawei, prohibiting the federal government from using its telecom equipment. In 2019, Huawei was added to the Commerce Department's Entity List, banning American firms from selling equipment to the company without a special waiver. In 2020, the U.S. State Department launched the Clean Networks Initiative to convince other nations to exclude Chinese companies, notably Huawei, from their domestic networks.[159]

Several European countries have also followed in America's footsteps regarding Huawei. In 2020, the United Kingdom banned Huawei equipment from its new 5G network.[160] Estonia, Denmark, France, Italy, Latvia, Lithuania, Portugal, Romania, and Sweden have taken steps to restrict Huawei.[161] The German Interior Ministry has proposed forcing telecom operators to stop using Chinese telecom equipment.[162] Even in countries that have historically been more open to China, such as Malaysia, Huawei has faced pushback and contract cancellations.[163]

The case of Huawei highlights the Party's dilemma in seeking to develop domestic sources of critical technologies. Huawei was tightly embraced by the Party and given significant support, which allowed it to emerge as a national champion. As a result, China made advances in both 5G technology and semiconductors that began to rival the advanced economies. However, these aggressive efforts to support Huawei also sowed the seeds for a fierce backlash against the company. This backlash has led to Huawei being excluded from many of the world's most important telecom markets and being targeted by export controls designed to restrict its ability to continue making technological advances.

These foreign restrictions severely disrupted the company, forcing it to sell subsidiaries and restructure its business lines. After years of rapid expansion, the company's overseas revenue growth plummeted in 2019, as shown in Fig. 11. By 2023, bolstered in part by Chinese government support, Huawei's domestic revenue had largely recovered. However, its overseas revenue remained substantially below its 2018 level, the year when U.S. actions against Huawei began.

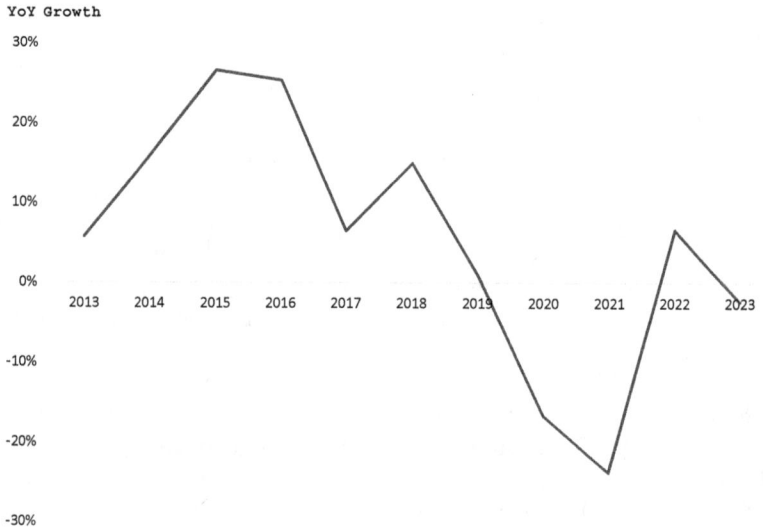

Fig. 11 Huawei overseas revenue growth (*Source* Company Annual Reports)

Given the deterioration relations between China and the United States and its allies, any Chinese telecom company seeking a global presence would have faced scrutiny. Nonetheless, the Party's overt efforts to support and promote Huawei into a national champion invited a foreign counter-response that has weakened the company's ability to become a global technology leader.

3.1.3 Efforts to Reduce Vulnerability to Foreign Financial Pressure

Xi Jinping and the Party have long held becoming a global financial power as a goal for China. The motivations behind this goal are both economic and political. The Party believes that a modern and powerful country must also be a financial power.[164] Xi has called for transforming China into a financial superpower with "a strong currency, a strong central bank, strong financial institutions, strong international financial centers, strong financial supervision and regulation, and a strong financial talent pool."[165]

Global financial integration is essential to this vision of China becoming a financial superpower. Integration with global capital markets will benefit the Chinese economy by facilitating trade and lowering the cost of capital. One of the major policies to achieve greater financial integration with the world has been to promote the internationalization of the renminbi. Establishing a greater international role for the renminbi would allow China to rely upon its own currency for cross-border trade and financial transactions. Countries that are able to trade and borrow in their own currency are less exposed to the challenges of fluctuating exchange rates. An internationalized currency can also reduce borrowing costs for companies and raise asset prices through foreign financial inflows. Nations with international currencies can typically finance their national debt in their own currencies, lowering the risks of a sovereign debt crisis. Being able to purchase key global resources, like oil and commodities, in a country's own currency can also help mitigate price volatility.

The Party views an international currency as a barometer of a country's overall power and prestige. Only a few nations can claim the combination of these factors, especially having a strong currency that is used globally. For the Party, this is important because China's main geopolitical rivals, the United States, the nations of the European Union, the United Kingdom, and Japan, all boast global currencies.

As much as the Party would like to achieve global financial integration, it also insists on a financial system that is self-reliant and resilient against foreign influence. According to Xi Jinping, China must build a financial system with "an independent, controllable, secure, and efficient financial infrastructure system," that operates autonomously and is "free from control and intervention by external forces."[166] This means controlling inflows and outflows of capital so that China has a buffer against global financial instability.

Maintaining buffers against foreign financial influence requires control over many aspects of the financial system. China tightly regulates its currency, allowing it to only trade within a prescribed range. Both the central bank and the state-owned banks are involved in helping maintain the Party's desired exchange rate. This control also requires restricting the access of foreigners to onshore capital markets, limiting offshore debt, and maintaining foreign ownership limits to prevent foreign creditors from controlling too much of the country's financial assets. Periodically, the Party will undertake large crackdowns when cross-border financial flows become concerning. For example, in 2017, China targeted insurers and other Chinese companies that had started to accumulate significant overseas investments, compelling them to reduce their foreign assets through regulatory pressure. Similarly, in 2023, regulators undertook a crackdown on Chinese brokerages that were selling overseas securities to their clients.

In the instances when China has opened its financial system, it has adopted a number of unique structures, such as the Stock Connect. Officially announced by Li Keqiang in 2014, the Stock Connect established a trading link between the Shanghai and Hong Kong stock exchanges.[167] In 2016, a similar link was created between the Shenzhen and Hong Kong exchanges. These links enable foreign investors with a brokerage account in Hong Kong to buy shares of domestically listed Chinese companies, while mainland investors can purchase Hong Kong-listed stocks. However, the Stock Connect operates as a "closed loop," ensuring that capital flows are confined to this channel and cannot spread into other parts of the economy. This structure allows Chinese regulators to monitor, and if necessary, restrict capital flows during periods of volatility. Thus far, Chinese regulators have not restricted capital flows through the Stock Connect.

Another important component of a self-reliant financial system is limiting the ability of foreign countries, especially the United States, to exert pressure on China. One major focus is to reduce China's vulnerability to financial sanctions.[168] To achieve this, China has built alternatives to the existing financial infrastructures controlled by the United States and its allies. One example of this is China's Cross-Border Interbank Payments System (CIPS), which was launched in 2015. CIPS provides a clearing and settlement network for offshore renminbi payments. One important function of CIPS is that it provides China with an alternative to the SWIFT network, the global payments network that is under the control of the United States and its allies. During times of conflict, countries such as Iran and Russia have been kicked off the SWIFT network, damaging their ability to engage in international commerce. CIPS provides China with an alternative network that is closely controlled by the Chinese government. This control is accomplished through CIPS clearing banks, which are state-owned, and the central bank which provides liquidity to the network.

The contradiction embedded in the Party's approach is that the efforts to create a self-reliant financial system undermine the goal of achieving global financial integration. This is evident in the lack of progress in renminbi internationalization, the cornerstone of China's financial integration efforts. Despite China being the world's second-largest economy and the largest exporter, the renminbi has not emerged as a contender to either the dollar or the euro. As shown in Fig. 12, according to data from SWIFT, the renminbi accounted for less than 5% of global transactions.[169] The renminbi also has a low weight in foreign exchange reserves held by other countries. According to data from the People's Bank of China, the renminbi only accounted for 2.69% of global foreign exchange reserves.[170] The balance of offshore renminbi deposits has not grown significantly since 2015, when the People's Bank of China began to promote their growth.

What has held back renminbi internationalization to such a degree? The continued restriction on capital inflows and outflows is a major factor. For foreigners to want to hold large amounts of renminbi, they must be confident that they will be able to transact with few restrictions. Forcing foreign investment through carefully controlled channels such as the stock connect also limits China's attractiveness as an investment destination. This has resulted in foreigners having a low foreign ownership share of Chinese stocks and bonds.

With the continued deterioration in U.S.-China relations, the Party has reemphasized its desire for a self-reliant financial system. As China pushes

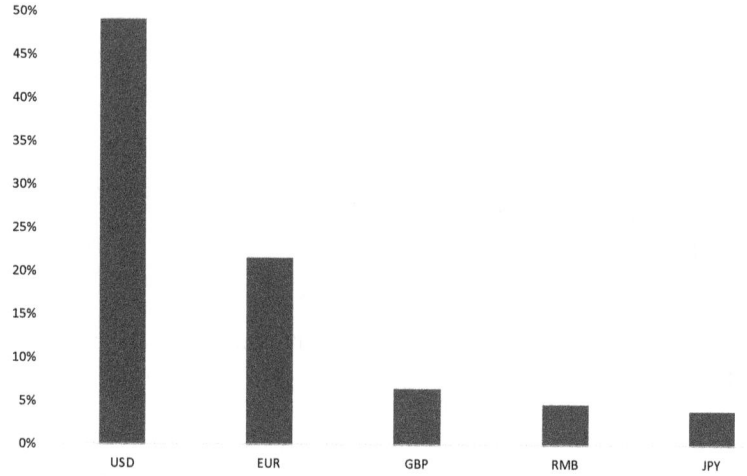

Fig. 12 Share of global payments by currency (September 2024) (*Source* SWIFT)

forward with this goal, it will further undermine efforts for global financial integration and establishing the renminbi as an international currency.

3.1.4 Efforts to Control Key Resources

One of China's primary motivations for pursuing integration into the global economy is to secure access to critical resources it lacks. Chinese leaders have long been concerned about insufficient domestic supplies of critical resources. Stretching back to the Going Out Policy of the early 2000s, the Chinese government has pushed companies, especially state-owned enterprises, to secure access to critical resources overseas through trade and investment. The highest priority resources were strategic commodities like oil, gas, and critical minerals. The Chinese government has also encouraged purchases of farmland in foreign countries to bolster the country's food supplies. In the mid-2010s, the push to gain access to critical natural resources was renewed again as part of the Belt and Road Initiative. Under the banner of the Belt and Road, China signed massive loan agreements with countries all over the world to gain access to natural resources. Many of these agreements were structured as loans from Chinese financial institutions that the borrowing country could repay with the sale of natural resources. These efforts to secure resources have accelerated recently given U.S.-China tensions. China has increased its strategic supplies of energy, metals, and food to guard against geopolitical threats.[171]

China's quest to secure natural resources abroad is intertwined with its efforts to tightly manage the production of domestic resources. In the name of self-reliance, China has attempted to consolidate its control over these resources to ensure domestic supplies remain uninterrupted. Control over these supplies can also be used as a strategic weapon by the Party against foreign adversaries. Rare earth elements are an example of such a resource. China possesses abundant supplies of these seventeen metallic elements, which are essential for a wide range of consumer and military electronic components. Deng Xiaoping is quoted as saying that "the Middle East has oil, China has rare earths."[172]

While rare earth minerals are not as rare as their name would imply, they are difficult to mine and process in a cost-effective manner. China has managed to corner the global rare earth industry, accounting for 55–70% of rare earth mining and 90% of processing.[173] Within the domestic rare earth industry, government industrial plans have consolidated production in a small number of firms.[174] China has also established a controlling position with other strategic minerals, accounting for 40% of copper, 59% of lithium, and 73% of cobalt refining globally.[175] Lacking plentiful domestic supplies of these critical minerals, Chinese companies have entered into long-term contracts with countries such as Chile, Argentina, Zimbabwe, the Democratic Republic of Congo (DRC), and Australia. In the DRC, which is the world's leading producer of cobalt, Chinese companies own or have interests in almost all the country's cobalt mines.[176]

China's government has taken actions over the past decade and a half to consolidate its hold on the rare earths industry. In 2011, the State Council issued the Opinions on Promoting the Sustainable and Healthy Development of the Rare Earth Industry, which called for greater consolidation and supervision over the industry and for controlling exports.[177] In 2021, China merged three state-owned enterprises, Minmentals Rare Earth, Chinalco Rare Earth, and China Southern Rare Earth Group, to create China Rare Earth Group. Operating as an SOE controlled by the central government, this new entity would control around 70% of China's rare earth production.[178] State media referred to the new company as a "super aircraft carrier" that is poised to strengthen China's position in the global industry.[179] According to the company's website, China Rare

Earth Group will be "guided by Xi Jinping's New Era of Socialism with Chinese Characteristics," help cultivate China as a "rare earth power," and "achieve supply chain security," among other goals.[180] In 2024, China announced new regulations for tracing rare earth products and unveiled new rules requiring companies involving in mining, processing, and exporting of rare earths to report their activities to the government or face potentially severe penalties.[181]

China has used its control over rare earths and other critical minerals to exert its geostrategic influence. In 2010, China reportedly limited the export of rare earths to Japan as punishment for clashes between the Japanese coast guard and Chinese fishermen in disputed waters.[182] In 2023, China banned the export of technology to extract and separate rare earth minerals.[183] The same year, it announced new export controls for several critical minerals. In 2024, China implemented a ban on the export of gallium, germanium, and antimony, to the United States in response to American restrictions on technology sales to China.[184]

China's concerted efforts to secure key resources undermine its pursuit of greater global economic integration. In the case of critical minerals and rare earths, China aggressively prioritized self-reliance, achieving dominance in both the supply and production of these resources. The Party was an active participant in this effort, guiding the industry toward greater consolidation and increasing its control over exports. These efforts have sparked a backlash from many countries worldwide, who feared that China's near monopoly would be used as a tool of geostrategic influence.

In response to these fears, many nations are now actively coordinating and subsidizing the reconfiguration of mineral supply chains to control against the threat posed by China. In 2022, the United States used the Defense Production Act to increase the mining, processing, and recycling of critical minerals in the country.[185] The United States, European Union, Japan, India, Korea the United Kingdom, and several other nations established the Minerals Security Partnership to develop new minerals supply chains among themselves in order to lessen China's grip on the industry.[186] The United States and its allies are now actively funding projects in Africa and Latin America designed to reduce Chinese firms' dominance in mining and processing critical minerals.

In summary, the Party's efforts to achieve self-reliance in various strategic industries have undermined the global economic integration that has been essential to China's economic development. Large-scale industrial policy to dominate emerging industries and resources has triggered a significant backlash by China's trading partners. Efforts to create a financial system immune to foreign pressure have stifled the growth of the RMB as an international currency. Initiatives to gain access to foreign technology through legitimate and illegitimate means have led Chinese companies to be excluded from critical global markets. The overwhelming focus on self-reliance has damaged China's economic links to the rest of the world and threatens its ability to continue to grow its economy through trade.

Notes

1. Jinping Xi, "Promoting Chinese-Style Modernization Requires Handling Major Relationships Well (推进中国式现代化需要处理好若干重大关系)," *Qiushi*, September 30, 2023, http://www.qstheory.cn/dukan/qs/2023-09/30/c_1129890528.htm.
2. Jinping Xi, "Secure a Decisive Victory in Building a Moderately Prosperous Society in All Respects and Strive for the Great Success of Socialism with Chinese Characteristics for a New Era," *China Daily*, October 18, 2017, https://www.chinadaily.com.cn/china/19thcpcnationalcongress/2017-11/04/content_34115212.htm.
3. Jinping Xi, "Full Text of Xi Jinping's Speech at First Session of 14th NPC," *State Council Information Office*, March 13, 2023, http://english.scio.gov.cn/m/topnews/2023-03/15/content_85168965.htm.
4. "Doing a Good Job in Employment Is the Key to Realizing the 'Six Stabilizers' and 'Six Guarantors' (做好就业工作是实现'六稳''六保'的关键)," *People's Republic of China Central People's Government* (中华人民共和国中央人民政府), October 4, 2020, https://www.gov.cn/xinwen/2020-10/04/content_5549252.htm.
5. "Xi Jinping, Li Keqiang Make Important Speeches at Central Economic Work Conference (中央经济工作会议举行 习近平李克强作重要讲话)," *People's Republic of China Central People's Government* (中华人民共和国中央人民政府), December 10, 2021, https://www.gov.cn/xinwen/2021-12/10/content_5659796.htm.

6. Jinping Xi, "Improve Prevention and Control Capabilities and Strive to Prevent and Resolve Major Risks to Maintain Sustained and Healthy Economic Development and Social Stability (提高防控能力着力防范化解重大风险 保持经济持续健康发展社会大局稳定)," *Xinhua*, January 21, 2019, http://www.xinhuanet.com/politics/2019-01/21/c_1124021712.htm.
7. Zhaolong Liao, "Now with Too Many Pigs, China Moves to Prop up Pork Prices," *Caixin Global*, June 30, 2021, https://www.caixinglobal.com/2021-06-30/now-with-too-many-pigs-china-moves-to-prop-up-pork-prices-101734281.html.
8. "Measures to Ensure Commodity Prices Stable," *State Council of the People's Republic of China*, July 20, 2021, http://english.www.gov.cn/statecouncil/ministries/202107/20/content_WS60f603b1c6d0df57f98dd3f3.html.
9. "China Intervenes to Manage Commodity Prices," *Reuters*, August 4, 2021, https://www.reuters.com/world/china/china-intervenes-manage-commodity-prices-2021-08-04/.
10. "Chinese Regulator Tells Businesses to Set Commodity Prices 'Reasonably,'" *Reuters*, September 10, 2021, https://www.reuters.com/article/china-commodities-regulator/chinese-regulator-tells-businesses-to-set-commodity-prices-reasonably-idUKL4N2QC2NH/.
11. "Economics and Trade Bulletin—June 2021," 2021, *U.S.-China Economic and Security Review Commission*, June 21, 2021, https://www.uscc.gov/sites/default/files/2021-06/June_2021_Trade_Bulletin.pdf.
12. "Crackdown Spooks Commodity Traders," *The Star*, August 3, 2023, https://www.thestar.com.my/business/business-news/2023/08/04/crackdown-spooks-commodity-traders.
13. "Order from the National Development and Reform Commission of the People's Republic of China (中华人民共和国国家发展和改革委员会令)," *National Development and Reform Commission*, June 12, 2021, https://www.ndrc.gov.cn/xxgk/zcfb/fzggwl/202106/t20210617_1283387.html.
14. "Chinese Regulators to Carry Out Joint Supervision and Investigations into Possible Speculation in the Iron Ore Market | Shanghai Non ferrous Metals," *SMM*, February 11, 2022,

https://news.metal.com/newscontent/101747333/chinese-regulators-to-carry-out-joint-supervision-and-investigations-into-possible-speculation-in-the-iron-ore-market.

15. Min Zhang and Gabriel Crossley, "China Warns Against Publishing False Iron Ore Information Amid Price Rally," *Reuters*, February 8, 2022, https://www.reuters.com/world/china/china-warns-against-publishing-false-iron-ore-price-information-2022-02-09/.

16. Gavin Maguire, "China Cuts Coal's Share of Electricity Output in H1 2024," Reuters, July 24, 2024, https://www.reuters.com/markets/commodities/china-cuts-coals-share-electricity-output-h1-2024-maguire-2024-07-24/.

17. Hao Feng, "New Pricing Could Spell Trouble for China's Coal Sector," *China Dialogue*, June 20, 2020, https://chinadialogue.net/en/energy/11759-new-pricing-could-spell-trouble-for-china-s-coal-sector/.

18. "China Intervenes to Manage Commodity Prices," *Reuters*, August 4, 2021, https://www.reuters.com/world/china/china-intervenes-manage-commodity-prices-2021-08-04/.

19. "China Says It Will Stabilise Commodity Market, Asks Coal Producers to Hike Output," *Reuters*, May 19, 2021, https://www.reuters.com/business/energy/china-says-it-will-stabilise-commodity-market-step-up-trade-stockpiling-2021-05-19/ and "Chinese Regulators Warn Metals Firms to Maintain Good Market Order," *Reuters*, May 21, 2021, https://www.reuters.com/business/energy/chinese-regulators-warn-metals-firms-maintain-good-market-order-2021-05-24/.

20. "2022 Annual Report to Congress," *U.S.-China Economic and Security Review Commission*, November 2022, https://www.uscc.gov/annual-report/2022-annual-report-congress.

21. Ouyang Shijia, "NDRC Studying Ways to Stabilize Coal Prices Over the Long Run," *China Daily*, October 26, 2021, https://global.chinadaily.com.cn/a/202110/26/WS61779a8aa310cdd39bc715b8.html.

22. "China Wields Political Might to Cool Coal Prices, but Winter Looms," *Reuters*, November 21, 2021, https://www.reuters.com/business/energy/china-wields-political-might-cool-coal-prices-winter-looms-2021-11-12/.

23. Reuters, "Major Coal Miners in China Vow to Boost Output and Cap Prices," CNBC, October 20, 2021, https://www.cnbc.com/2021/10/20/major-coal-miners-in-china-vow-to-boost-output-and-cap-prices.html.
24. "China Guides Coal-Price Band Upwards," *Fitch Ratings*, March 10, 2022, https://www.fitchratings.com/research/corporate-finance/china-guides-coal-price-band-upwards-10-03-2022 and Andrew Hayley and Colleen Howe, 2023, "China to Guarantee Payments to Coal Power Producers Based on Capacity," *Reuters*, November 23, 2023, https://www.reuters.com/world/china/china-guarantee-payments-its-coal-power-producers-based-capacity-2023-11-10/.
25. Nicholas Lardy, *Sustaining China's Economic Growth After the Global Financial Crisis* (Washington, DC: The Peterson Institute for International Economics, 2012).
26. Kenneth Rogoff and Yuanchen Yang, "Peak China Housing," *National Bureau of Economic Research*, August 2020, https://www.nber.org/system/files/working_papers/w27697/w27697.pdf.
27. "China's Xi Says to Maintain Principle Property Is Not for Speculation," *Reuters*, October 17, 2017, https://www.reuters.com/article/idUSKBN1CN0B5/.
28. Richard Koss and Xinrui Shi, "Stabilizing China's Housing Market," *IMF Working Papers* No. 089 (2018): 1, https://doi.org/10.5089/9781484348550.001.a001.
29. CEIC Data, accessed February 8, 2024.
30. Wind Information, accessed February 2, 2024.
31. Mariko Oi, "Evergrande: The Rise and Fall of the Property Giant's Billionaire Founder," *BBC*, September 29, 2023, https://www.bbc.com/news/business-66540794.
32. "The 'Three Red Lines' Are Hanging High, Real Estate Developers 'Stepping on the Lines' Are Busy Selling Assets to 'Slim Down' ('三道红线'高悬 '踩线'房企出售资产忙'瘦身')," *China Securities Journal*, September 30, 2020, https://www.cs.com.cn/fdc/202009/t20200930_6099145.html.
33. Yiming Zhong, "The Chinese Double Reduction Policy: Challenges to Private and Public Education Systems—The Cornell Policy Review," *The Cornell Policy Review*, June 4, 2023, https://www.cornellpolicyreview.com/the-chinese-double-reduction-policy-challenges-to-private-and-public-education-systems/.

34. Jinping Xi, "'Let's Care About These Education Issues Together' ('我们来共同关心这些教育问题')," *People's Daily*, March 7, 2021, http://cpc.people.com.cn/n1/2021/0307/c64094-320 44589.html.
35. "国务院办公厅关于优化生育政策促进人口长期均衡发展的决定" [Decision of the General Office of the State Council on Optimizing Birth Policies to Promote Long-term Balanced Population Development], *The State Council of the People's Republic of China*, July 24, 2021, https://www.gov.cn/zhengce/2021-07/24/content_5627132.htm.
36. Eduardo Jaramillo, "China's Radically Transformed Tutoring Market, One Year After Crackdown," *The China Project*, August 11, 2022, https://thechinaproject.com/2022/08/05/chinas-radically-transformed-tutoring-market-one-year-after-crackdown/.
37. Shen Lu, "Targeted by Beijing, One Chinese Tutoring Company Reinvents Itself With Live Streams Selling Groceries," *The Wall Street Journal*, July 13, 2022, https://www.wsj.com/articles/targeted-by-beijing-one-chinese-tutoring-company-reinvents-itself-with-live-streams-selling-groceries-11657704780.
38. "China to Impose Hefty Fines, Penalties for Illegal Education Tutors," *Reuters*, September 12, 2023, https://www.reuters.com/world/china/china-impose-hefty-fines-penalties-illegal-education-tutors-2023-09-13/.
39. Fu Si, Kinger Lau, Timothy Moe, Kevin Wang, "Meeting the New Chinese 'National Team'," *Goldman Sachs*, September 18, 2022.
40. "Central Huijin Investment Co Increases Holdings in China's A-Share Market ETFs," *Shanghai Stock Exchange*, February 6, 2024, https://english.sse.com.cn/news/newsrelease/voice/c/c_20240206_10750598.shtml.
41. "Central Huijin Investment Co," *Shanghai Stock Exchange*, 2024.
42. Meng Lei, Cathy Fang, Yu Sheng, Lynce Wang, and Robin Xu, "China Equity Strategy—How to Track and Quantify Inflow from the 'National Team'?," *UBS*, February 27, 2024.
43. "China's Sovereign Fund Poured $45 Billion into Stock Market in First Quarter," *Caixin Global*, April 25, 2024, https://www.caixinglobal.com/2024-04-25/chinas-sovereign-fund-poured-45-billion-into-stock-market-in-first-quarter-102189844.html.

44. Meng Lei, et al., "China Equity Strategy."
45. "China Expanding Stock Selling Restrictions to Insurers, Sources Say," *Bloomberg*, January 23, 2024, https://www.bloomberg.com/news/articles/2024-01-23/china-is-said-to-expand-stock-selling-restrictions-to-insurers.
46. "Good Things You Should Know About Today's A-Share Market (关于今日A股市场, 你应该知道的利好)," *China Securities Web*, July 9, 2015, https://www.gov.cn/xinwen/2015-07/09/content_2894594.htm.
47. "China Regulator Announces More Curbs on Short-Selling," *Reuters*, February 6, 2024, https://www.reuters.com/markets/asia/china-regulator-unveils-more-curbs-short-selling-2024-02-06/.
48. Yue, Quen, and Denise Jia, "CSRC Vows to Crack Down on Malicious Short Selling to Stabilize Stock Market," *Caixin Global*, February 7, 2024, https://www.caixinglobal.com/2024-02-07/csrc-vows-to-crack-down-on-malicious-short-selling-to-stabilize-stock-market-102164554.html.
49. Amie Tsang, "Caijing Journalist's Shaming Signals China's Growing Control Over News Media," *The New York Times*, September 6, 2015, https://www.nytimes.com/2015/09/07/business/media/caijing-journalists-shaming-signals-chinas-growing-control-over-news-media.html.
50. Data accessed February 28, 2024.
51. Data from CEIC, accessed February 22, 2024. GDP is measured from 2012 to 2023. Shanghai Stock Exchange Index return is measured from December 2012 to December 2023.
52. Zongyuan Zoe Liu, *Sovereign Funds: How the Communist Party of China Finances Its Global Ambitions* (Harvard University Press, 2023), 76, https://www.hup.harvard.edu/books/9780674271913.
53. "China's Economy Is a Mess. Why Aren't Firms Going Under?" *The Economist*, November 2, 2023, https://www.economist.com/finance-and-economics/2023/11/02/chinas-economy-is-a-mess-why-arent-firms-going-under.
54. "Reprofiling Bank Debt May Pose Rating Challenges for China SOEs," *Fitch Ratings*, March 26, 2021, https://www.fitchratings.com/research/international-public-finance/reprofiling-bank-debt-may-pose-rating-challenges-for-china-soes-26-03-2021.

55. "China Tells Banks to Roll Over Local Government Debts as Risks Mount," *Reuters*, October 17, 2023, https://www.reuters.com/world/china/china-instructs-banks-roll-over-local-government-debt-sources-2023-10-17/.
56. "LGFV Loan Restructurings May Rise in China's Weaker Regions," *Fitch Ratings*, January 18, 2023, https://www.fitchratings.com/research/banks/lgfv-loan-restructurings-may-rise-in-chinas-weaker-regions-18-01-2023.
57. "China Regulators Order More Financing Support for Property Firms," *Reuters*, November 13, 2022, https://www.reuters.com/markets/asia/china-regulators-urge-more-financing-support-property-firms-sources-2022-11-13/.
58. "China Central Bank Extends Policies for Financial Support of Real Estate Market," *Reuters*, July 10, 2023, https://www.reuters.com/article/idUSKBN2YQ0XA/.
59. "China Real-Estate Projects Set to Receive Loans Under 'Whitelist' Program," *The Wall Street Journal*, February 4, 2024, https://www.wsj.com/economy/housing/china-real-estate-projects-set-to-receive-loans-under-whitelist-program-d938b49e.
60. Xiaomeng Wu, Bo Chen, Liangtao Zhu, and Na Qing, "Why China's Project Whitelists Can't Cure Real Estate Slump," *Caixin Global*, April 18, 2024, https://www.caixinglobal.com/2024-04-18/in-depth-why-chinas-project-whitelists-cant-cure-real-estate-slump-102187733.html.
61. Emilia Jurzyk and Cian Ruane, "Resource Misallocation Among Listed Firms in China: The Evolving Role of State-Owned Enterprises," *IMF*, March 12, 2021, https://www.imf.org/en/Publications/WP/Issues/2021/03/12/Resource-Misallocation-Among-Listed-Firms-in-China-The-Evolving-Role-of-State-Owned-50167.
62. Diego Cerdeiro and Cian Ruane, "China's Declining Business Dynamism," *IMF*, February 18, 2022, https://www.imf.org/en/Publications/WP/Issues/2022/02/18/China-s-Declining-Business-Dynamism-513157.
63. Data was accessed from Bloomberg on February 28, 2025. The United States, Emerging Markets, and China are represented by the MSCI US Banks Index (MXUS0BK), the MSCI EM

Banks Index (MXEF0BK), and the MSCI China Banks Index (MXCN0BK).
64. "Xi Stresses Development of New Productive Forces, High-Quality Development," The State Council of the People's Republic of China, February 2, 2024, https://english.www.gov.cn/news/202402/02/content_WS65bcb13cc6d0868f4e8e3b8c.html.
65. Tai Ming Cheung, "Innovate to Dominate: The Rise of the Chinese Techno-Security State," in *Cornell University Press* (Cornell University Press, 2022), 22, https://doi.org/10.1515/9781501764356.
66. Tai Ming Cheung, *Innovate to Dominate*, 2022.
67. Jinping Xi, "Speech at the Private Enterprise Symposium (在民营企业座谈会上的讲话)," *Xinhua*, November 1, 2018, http://www.xinhuanet.com/politics/2018-11/01/c_1123649488.htm.
68. "Seven Lessons From Tencents Pony Ma," n.d. *London Business School*, September 17, 2018, https://www.london.edu/think/seven-lessons-from-tencents-pony-ma.
69. "Tencent: When the Penguin Wears the Party Emblem (腾讯：当'企鹅'戴上党徽)," *Xinhua*, April 2, 2018, http://www.xinhuanet.com/politics/2018-04/02/c_129842262.htm.
70. "Advanced Deeds of the Party Committee of Tencent Technology (腾讯科技 (深圳) 有限公司党委先进事迹)," *People's Daily*, July 1, 2016, http://dangjian.people.com.cn/n1/2016/0630/c117092-28513326.html.
71. "Tencent: When the Penguin Wears the Party Emblem," 2018.
72. Scott Livingston, "The New Challenge of Communist Corporate Governance," *Center for Strategic and International Studies (CSIS)*, January 2021, https://csis-website-prod.s3.amazonaws.com/s3fs-public/publication/210114_Livingston_New_Challenge.pdf.
73. "Advanced Deeds of the Party Committee of Tencent Technology (腾讯科技 (深圳) 有限公司党委先进事迹)," *People's Daily*, July 1, 2016, http://dangjian.people.com.cn/n1/2016/0630/c117092-28513326.html.
74. "Tencent: When the Penguin Wears the Party Emblem," 2018.
75. "Advanced Deeds of the Party Committee," 2016.

76. Josh Horwitz, "China's Communist Party Is All in on the Power of Technology," *Quartz*, July 20, 2022, https://qz.com/1102948/chinas-communist-party-is-all-in-on-the-power-of-technology-and-thats-tricky-for-its-tech-giants.
77. "The General Office of the Central Committee of the Chinese Communist Party Issues the Regulations on the Work of Grassroots Organizations of State-owned Enterprises of the Chinese Communist Party (for Trial Implementation) 中共中央印发了《中国共产党国有企业基层组织工作条例 (试行)》," *Interpret China—Center for Strategic and International Studies (CSIS)*, January 5, 2020, https://interpret.csis.org/translations/the-central-committee-of-the-communist-party-of-china-issues-the-regulations-on-the-work-of-grassroots-organizations-of-state-owned-enterprises-of-the-communist-party-of-china-for-trial-implementatio/.
78. Lulu Chen, *Influence Empire: Inside the Story of Tencent and China's Tech Ambition* (Hodder & Stoughton, 2022).
79. Dashveenjit Kaur, 2022, "Why Is China's Tech Crackdown Widening on Tencent?" *Tech Wire Asia*, April 11, 2022, https://techwireasia.com/04/2022/why-is-chinas-tech-crackdown-widening-on-tencent/.
80. Arjun Kharpal, 2021, "Tencent Must Get Approval From Chinese Regulators Before Publishing New Apps and Updates," *CNBC*, December 2, 2021, https://www.cnbc.com/2021/11/25/tencent-must-get-approval-from-regulators-before-publishing-new-apps.html.
81. Lu-Hai Liang, 2023, "Leveling Up," *The Wire China*, October 15, 2023, https://www.thewirechina.com/2023/10/15/leveling-up-tencent-honor-of-kings-gaming-china/.
82. Stephanie Yang and Jing Yang, "China Regulator Fines Tencent, Baidu, Others Over Investment Deals," *The Wall Street Journal*, March 12, 2021, https://www.wsj.com/articles/china-regulator-fines-tencent-baidu-others-over-investment-deals-11615553409.
83. Yuzhe Zhang, Yue He, and Meihan Luo, "Exclusive: Tencent Ordered to Set up Financial Holding Company," *Caixin Global*, May 26, 2021, https://www.caixinglobal.com/2021-05-26/exclusive-tencent-ordered-to-set-up-financial-holding-company-101718352.html.

84. "Tencent CEO Pony Ma Asks Fintech Unit to Cede Share in Payments Market to Avoid Challenging Banks," *South China Morning Post*, January 30, 2024, https://finance.yahoo.com/news/tencent-ceo-pony-ma-asks-093000731.html.
85. "What Tencent's Rebound Says About Prospects for China's Big Tech," *The Economist*, February 16, 2023, https://www.economist.com/what-tencents-rebound-says-about-prospects-for-chinas-big-tech.
86. "Tencent Sustainable Social Value Report 2021 (腾讯可续社会价值报告)," *Tencent*, May 2022, https://static.www.tencent.com/attachments/ssv/2021/TencentSSVReport2021.pdf.
87. "Remarks by Mr. Dai Xianglong, Governor of the PBC at the Opening Ceremony of China Unionpay," *People's Bank of China*, March 26, 2002, http://www.pbc.gov.cn/english/130721/2830453/index.html.
88. "DS413: China—Certain Measures Affecting Electronic Payment Services," *World Trade Organization*, July 13, 2013, https://www.wto.org/english/tratop_e/dispu_e/cases_e/ds413_e.htm.
89. Martin Chorzempa, *The Cashless Revolution: China's Reinvention of Money and the End of America's Domination of Finance and Technology*, Hachette UK, October 4, 2022.
90. Wei He, "Alipay to Discontinue Offline-Payment Service," *China Daily*, April 28, 2013, https://www.chinadaily.com.cn/bizchina/tech/2013-08/28/content_16925580.htm.
91. Bank for International Settlements, "Panel Discussion," *YouTube Video*, 1:05:57, June 30, 2019, https://www.youtube.com/watch?v=KMJDuRWKB5M.
92. Jia Chen and Wei He, "PBOC Reins in Funds of Payment Platforms," *China Daily*, January 15, 2019, https://www.chinadaily.com.cn/a/201901/15/WS5c3d169fa3106c65c34e4671.html.
93. Julie Zhu, 2021, "Chinese State Firms to Take Big Stake in Ant's Credit-Scoring JV-Sources," *Reuters*, September 1, 2021, https://www.reuters.com/technology/exclusive-chinese-state-firms-take-big-stake-ants-credit-scoring-jv-sources-2021-09-01/, Julie Zhu, "China to Push Its Tech Giants to Share Consumer Credit Data-Sources," *Reuters*, January 11, 2021, https://www.reuters.com/world/china/exclusive-china-push-its-tech-giants-share-consumer-credit-data-sources-2021-01-11/, and "Company Introduction." n.d. *Baihang Credit*, Accessed May 6, 2024, https://www.baihangcredit.com/main/about/profile.

94. Yingzhi Yang, Brenda Goh, and Kane Wu, "Ant Group Founder Jack Ma to Give Up Control in Key Revamp," *Reuters*, January 7, 2023, https://www.reuters.com/business/ant-group-says-jack-ma-relinquishes-control-company-2023-01-07/.
95. Julie Zhu and Joshe Ye, 2023, "Ant's Surprise Share Buyback Values Firm at Steep 75% Discount to IPO," *Reuters*, July 8, 2023, https://www.reuters.com/technology/ants-share-repurchase-plan-values-firm-nearly-79-bln-2023-07-08/.
96. "China Approves Restructuring of Two Central SOEs," *Xinhua*, July 8, 2019, http://www.xinhuanet.com/english/2019-07/08/c_138209090.htm.
97. While SASAC firms and central enterprises are often used interchangeably, the universe of central enterprises is larger and includes firms such as China Tobacco, China Post, and China Railways. See https://one.oecd.org/document/ECO/WKP(2019)5/En/pdf.
98. Sean O'Conner, "SOE Megamergers Signal New Direction in China's Economic Policy," *U.S.-China Economic and Security Review Commission*, May 24, 2018, https://www.uscc.gov/sites/default/files/Research/SOE%20Megamergers.pdf.
99. "Opinions on Promoting High-Quality Development of Logistics and Facilitating the Formation of a Strong Domestic Market (发展改革委等关于推动物流高质量发展促进形成强大国内市场的意见)," People's Republic of China Central People's Government (中华人民共和国中央人民政府), March 2, 2019, https://www.gov.cn/xinwen/2019-03/02/content_5370107.htm.
100. "加快由物流大国迈向物流强国 (Accelerating From a Large Logistics Country to a Strong Logistics Country)," *The National Committee of the Chinese People's Political Consultative Congress*, January 18, 2022, http://www.cppcc.gov.cn/zxww/2022/01/18/ARTI1642468805915147.shtml.
101. "The State Council Information Office Held a Conference on High-Quality Development of Transportation to Serve Chinese-style Modernization (国务院新闻办就交通运输高质量发展服务中国式现代化举行发布会)," *People's Republic of China Central People's Government* (中华人民共和国中央人民政府), February 28, 2024, https://www.gov.cn/lianbo/fabu/202402/content_6935136.htm.

102. Alan Amling and Patricia Daugherty, "Logistics and Distribution Innovation in China," *International Journal of Physical Distribution & Logistics Management* 3 (50), https://www.alanamling.com/wp-content/uploads/2021/04/Logistics-and-Distribution-Innovation-in-China.pdf.
103. Chris Dupin, "Merged China COSCO Shipping Corporation Limited Launched," *FreightWaves*, March 2, 2019, https://www.freightwaves.com/news/merged-china-cosco-shipping-corporation-limited-launched.
104. China Chengtong Holdings Group "Group Profile," Accessed March 21, 2024, http://www.checg.cn/cctgroupen/about_us/group_profile/index.html.
105. "China Logistics Group Co., Ltd. Was Officially Founded," *China Logistics*, December 7, 2021, https://www.chinalogisticsgroup.com.cn/en/news/2023/48508.shtml.
106. "In Depth: Logistics Is Getting Pricy in China, but Reform Will Be a Long Haul," *Caixin Global*, June 6, 2024, https://www.caixinglobal.com/2024-06-06/in-depth-logistics-is-getting-pricy-in-china-but-reform-will-be-a-long-haul-102203894.html.
107. "China Logistics Sector Blue Book—2023," *Fitch Ratings*, September 2023, https://www.fitchratings.com/research/corporate-finance/china-logistics-sector-blue-book-21-09-2023.
108. "In Depth: Logistics Is Getting Pricy in China, but Reform Will Be a Long Haul," *Caixin Global*, June 6, 2024, https://www.caixinglobal.com/2024-06-06/in-depth-logistics-is-getting-pricy-in-china-but-reform-will-be-a-long-haul-102203894.html.
109. "China's 2022 Negative List for Market Access: Here Are the Key Changes," *China Briefing News*, April 13, 2022, https://www.china-briefing.com/news/chinas-2022-negative-list-for-market-access-restrictions-cut-financial-sector-opening/.
110. "China Boots Caixin Financial News from Approved Media List | AP News," *AP News*, October 22, 2021, https://apnews.com/article/business-china-media-33c7ed65bd7bc9a7c0e4367225db6d95.
111. "Online Media Giant Bans New Users from Uploading Clips," *Caixin Global*, April 5, 2018, https://www.caixinglobal.com/2018-04-05/online-media-giant-bans-new-users-from-uploading-clips-101231084.html.

112. "Livestreaming App Apologizes After State TV Exposé of Teenage Mothers," *Caixin Global*, April 4, 2018, https://www.caixinglobal.com/2018-04-04/livestreaming-app-apologizes-after-state-tv-expos-of-teenage-mothers-101230695.html.
113. "Four News Apps Removed Amid Tightening Content Crackdown," *Caixin Global*, April 10, 2018, https://www.caixinglobal.com/2018-04-10/four-news-apps-removed-amid-tightening-content-crackdown-101232219.html.
114. Josh Chin, "New Target for China's Censors: Content Driven by Artificial Intelligence," *The Wall Street Journal*, April 11, 2018, https://www.wsj.com/articles/new-target-for-chinas-censors-content-driven-by-artificial-intelligence-1523446234.
115. "Guiding Opinions on Strengthening Literary and Artistic Criticism in the New Era (关于加强新时代文艺评论工作的指导意见)," *Xinhua*, August 2, 2021, http://www.xinhuanet.com/politics/2021-08/02/c_1127722893.htm.
116. "Internet Information Service Algorithm Recommendation Management Regulations (互联网信息服务算法推荐管理规定)," *China Law Translate*, January 4, 2022, https://www.chinalawtranslate.com/en/algorithms/.
117. "Internet Information Service," 2022.
118. "Internet Information Service," 2022.
119. Matt Sheehan and Sharon Du, "What China's Algorithm Registry Reveals About AI Governance," *Carnegie Endowment for International Peace*, December 9, 2022, https://carnegieendowment.org/2022/12/09/what-china-s-algorithm-registry-reveals-about-ai-governance-pub-88606.
120. Cissy Zhou, "China Tells Big Tech Companies Not to Offer ChatGPT Services," *Nikkei Asia*, February 22, 2023, https://asia.nikkei.com/Business/China-tech/China-tells-big-tech-companies-not-to-offer-ChatGPT-services.
121. Shen Lu, "China's AI Chatbots Clam Up When Asked About Xi Jinping's Leadership," *The Wall Street Journal*, March 15, 2023, https://www.wsj.com/articles/when-chatbots-run-up-against-chinas-censorship-f7ee1cea.
122. "Translation: Measures for the Management of Generative Artificial Intelligence Services (Draft for Comment)—April

2023—DigiChina," *DigiChina*, April 19, 2023, https://digichina.stanford.edu/work/translation-measures-for-the-management-of-generative-artificial-intelligence-services-draft-for-comment-april-2023/.
123. "Translation: Measures," 2023.
124. Liza Lin, "China Puts Power of State Behind AI—And Risks Strangling It," *The Wall Street Journal*, July 16, 2024, https://www.wsj.com/tech/china-puts-power-of-state-behind-aiand-risks-strangling-it-f045e11d.
125. Eleanor Olcott and Wang Xueqiao, "How China Has 'Throttled' Its Private Sector," *Financial Times*, September 25, 2024, https://www.ft.com/content/1e9e7544-974c-4662-a901-d30c4ab56eb7.
126. Neil Thomas, "Mao Redux: The Enduring Relevance of Self-Reliance in China—MacroPolo," *MacroPolo*, October 2, 2023, https://macropolo.org/analysis/china-self-reliance-xi-jinping-mao/.
127. "China Becomes World's No. 1 Exporter, Passing Germany," *The New York Times*, January 10, 2010, https://www.nytimes.com/2010/01/11/business/global/11chinatrade.html.
128. Steve Tsang and Olivia Cheung, *The Political Thought of Xi Jinping* (Oxford University Press, 2024). 122.
129. Scott Kennedy, "China's Risky Drive into New-Energy Vehicles," *Center for Strategic and International Studies*, November 2018, https://csis-website-prod.s3.amazonaws.com/s3fs-public/publication/181127_Kennedy_NEV_WEB_v3.pdf.
130. Tai Ming Cheung, Barry Naughton, and Eric Hagt, "China's Roadmap to Becoming a Science, Technology, and Innovation Great Power in the 2020s and Beyond: Assessing Its Medium- and Long-Term Strategies and Plans," *US Institute on Global Conflict and Cooperation*, July 2022, https://ucigcc.org/wp-content/uploads/2022/07/Ocea-revised-19-July-2022-1.pdf.
131. "Notice of the State Council on the Publication of 'Made in China 2025' (Translation)," *Center for Security and Emerging Technology*, March 8, 2022, https://cset.georgetown.edu/wp-content/uploads/t0432_made_in_china_2025_EN.pdf.
132. Kennedy, "China's Risky Drive," 2018.
133. Ilaria Mazzocco and Gregor Sebastian, "Electric Shock: Interpreting China's Electric Vehicle Export Boom," *Center for*

Strategic and International Studies, September 2023, https://csis-website-prod.s3.amazonaws.com/s3fs-public/2023-09/230914_%20Mazzocco_Electric_Shock_0.pdf.

134. Tong Zhang, Paul Burke, and Qi Wang, "Effectiveness of Electric Vehicle Subsidies in China: A Three-Dimensional Panel Study," *Australian National University*, January 2024, https://acde.crawford.anu.edu.au/publication/working-papers-trade-and-development/21867/effectiveness-electric-vehicle-subsidies.

135. Scott Kennedy, "The Chinese EV Dilemma: Subsidized Yet Striking," *Center for Strategic and International Studies*, June 20, 2024, https://www.csis.org/blogs/trustee-china-hand/chinese-ev-dilemma-subsidized-yet-striking.

136. "Vehicle Purchase Tax Reduction Policy for New Energy Vehicles Extended to the End of 2027 (新能源汽车车辆购置税减免政策延长至2027年年底)," *People's Republic of China Central People's Government* (中华人民共和国中央人民政府), June 21, 2023, https://www.gov.cn/zhengce/202306/content_6887717.htm.

137. Camille Boullenois, Agatha Kratz, and Reva Goujon, "Opening Salvo: The EU's Electric Vehicle Probe and What Comes Next," *Rhodium Group*, October 23, 2023, https://rhg.com/research/opening-salvo-the-eus-electric-vehicle-probe-and-what-comes-next.

138. In-Soo Nam, "Samsung SDI, LG Chem Face Setback in China on Electric-Car Batterie," *The Wall Street Journal*, June 21, 2016, https://www.wsj.com/articles/samsung-sdi-lg-chem-face-setback-in-china-on-electric-car-batteries-1466496080.

139. Gerard DiPippo, Ilaria Mazzocco, and Scott Kennedy, "Red Ink: Estimating Chinese Industrial Policy Spending in Comparative Perspective," *Center for Strategic and International Studies*, May 2022, https://csis-website-prod.s3.amazonaws.com/s3fs-public/publication/220523_DiPippo_Red_Ink.pdf.

140. Eliot Chen, "BYD'S Big International Bid," *The Wire China*, April 10, 2023, https://www.thewirechina.com/2023/01/01/byds-big-international-bid/.

141. Frank Bickenbach, Dirk Dohse, Rolf Langhammer, and Wan-Hsin Liu, "Foul Play? On the Scale and Scope of Industrial Subsidies in China," *Kiel Institute for the World Economy*, April

2024, https://www.ifw-kiel.de/fileadmin/Dateiverwaltung/ IfW-Publications/fis-import/bc6aff38-abfc-424a-b631-6d789e 992cf9-KPB173_en.pdf.
142. "Tesla's Shanghai Plant Delivers 947,000 Vehicles in 2023," *Xinhua*, January 1, 2024, https://english.news.cn/20240103/ ee7a313aa02141358c9f241f0db6034a/c.html.
143. "Tesla's Shanghai Plant," 2024.
144. "EU Anti-subsidy Probe into Electric Vehicle Imports From China," *European Parliament*, October 4, 2023, https://www.europarl.europa.eu/RegData/etudes/ATAG/2023/754553/EPRS_ATA(2023)754553_EN.pdf.
145. Melissa Eddy and Jenny Gross, "Europe Imposes Higher Tariffs on Electric Vehicles Made in China," *The New York Times*, October 30, 2024, https://www.nytimes.com/2024/10/30/business/european-union-china-electric-vehicle-tariffs.html.
146. Mariko Oi, "Biden Urged to Ban China-Made Electric Vehicles from the US," *BBC*, April 12, 2024, https://www.bbc.com/news/articles/cyerg64dn97o.
147. "Turkey Imposes 40% Tariff on Vehicle Imports from China," *Reuters*, June 8, 2024, https://www.reuters.com/business/autos-transportation/turkey-impose-40-additional-tariff-vehicle-imports-china-2024-06-08/.
148. China Association of Automobile Manufacturers, CEIC Data, accessed October 17, 2024.
149. Trina Chen, "China's Capacity—Imbalances, Inflections, and Beyond Cycles," Goldman Sachs, August 6, 2024, https://marquee.gs.com/content/research/en/reports/2024/08/06/aa42eca4-3376-4919-bebd-498eee1bfaa9.html.
150. Chris Buckley and Steven Lee Myers, "China's Leaders Vow Tech 'Self-Reliance,' Military Power and Economic Recovery," *The New York Times*, October 29, 2020, https://www.nytimes.com/2020/10/29/world/asia/china-five-year-plan-communist-party.html.
151. Gerard DiPippo, Ilaria Mazzocco, and Scott Kennedy, "Red Ink: Estimating Chinese Industrial Policy Spending in Comparative Perspective," *Center for Strategic and International Studies*, May 2022, https://csis-website-prod.s3.amazonaws.com/s3fs-public/publication/220523_DiPippo_Red_Ink.pdf.

152. Owen Daniels, "CSET Analyses of China's Technology Policies and Ecosystem: The PRC's Domestic Approach," *Center for Security and Emerging Technology*, September 2023, https://cset.georgetown.edu/wp-content/uploads/20230035_The-PRCs-Domestic-Approach.pdf.
153. "Notice of the State Council on the Publication of 'Made in China 2025' (Translation)," *Center for Security and Emerging Technology*, March 8, 2022, https://cset.georgetown.edu/wp-content/uploads/t0432_made_in_china_2025_EN.pdf.
154. "Outline of the People's Republic of China 14th Five-Year Plan for National Economic and Social Development and Long-Range Objectives for 2035 (Translation)," *Center for Security and Emerging Technology*, May 12, 2021, https://cset.georgetown.edu/wp-content/uploads/t0284_14th_Five_Year_Plan_EN.pdf.
155. Chuin-Wei Yap, "State Support Helped Fuel Huawei's Global Rise," *The Wall Street Journal*, December 25, 2019, https://www.wsj.com/articles/state-support-helped-fuel-huaweis-global-rise-11577280736.
156. As of this writing, the case was still awaiting trial. "Chinese Telecommunications Conglomerate Huawei and Subsidiaries Charged in Racketeering Conspiracy and Conspiracy to Steal Trade Secrets," *United States Department of Justice Office of Public Affairs*, February 13, 2020, https://www.justice.gov/opa/pr/chinese-telecommunications-conglomerate-huawei-and-subsidiaries-charged-racketeering.
157. Adam Segal, "China's Move to Greater Self Reliance," *China Leadership*, December 2, 2021, https://www.prcleader.org/post/china-s-move-to-greater-self-reliance.
158. Margaret M. Pearson, Meg Rithmire, and Kellee Sing Tsai, "China's Party-State Capitalism and International Backlash: From Interdependence to Insecurity," *International Security* 47, no. 2: 135–76, https://doi.org/10.1162/isec_a_00447.
159. "The Clean Network—United States Department of State," *United States Department of State*, January 17, 2021, https://2017-2021.state.gov/the-clean-network/.
160. Adam Satariano, Stephen Castle, and David Sanger, "U.K. Bars Huawei for 5G as Tech Battle Between China and the West Escalates," *The New York Times*, July 14, 2020, https://www.nytimes.com/2020/07/14/business/huawei-uk-5g.html.

161. "European Countries Who Put Curbs on Huawei 5G Equipment," *Reuters*, September 29, 2023, https://www.reuters.com/technology/european-countries-who-put-curbs-huawei-5g-equipment-2023-09-28/.
162. Sarah Marsh, Andreas Rinke, and Hakan Ersen, "German Proposal for Huawei Curbs Triggers Telecom Operator Backlash," *Reuters*, September 20, 2023, https://www.reuters.com/business/media-telecom/german-interior-ministry-wants-force-5g-operators-slash-huawei-use-official-2023-09-19/.
163. Ethan Cramer-Flood and Briana Boland, "CCP Inc. in Malaysia: How State Capitalism Supports and Constrains China's Tech Giants," Center for Strategic and International Studies, December 2022, https://csis-website-prod.s3.amazonaws.com/s3fs-public/publication/221216_Cramer-Flood_CCPInc_Malaysia.pdf.
164. "Anchoring the Goal of Building a Financial Power, Solidly Promote the High-Quality Development of Finance (锚定建设金融强国目标 扎实推动金融高质量发展)," *People's Daily*, February 21, 2024, https://www.gov.cn/zhengce/202402/content_6932983.htm.
165. "Xi Stresses Boosting High-Quality Development of China's Financial Sector," *Xinhua*, January 16, 2024, https://english.news.cn/20240116/06fa0ce297f14cc49034aef158d3aaad/c.html.
166. "Establishment of a Sound, Autonomous, Controllable, Safe and Efficient Financial Infrastructure System (建立健全自主可控安全高效的金融基础设施体系)," *Qiushi*, January 30, 2024, http://www.qstheory.cn/qshyjx/2024-01/30/c_1130069350.htm.
167. "Shanghai-Hong Kong Stock Connect: Capital Market 'Prime Minister's Strategy' Will Be Realized as Expected (沪港通: 资本市场'总理战略' 将如期兑现)," *Central Government Portal*, November 10, 2014, https://www.gov.cn/zhengce/2014-11/10/content_2777057.htm.
168. Zoe Zongyuan Liu, "China's Attempts to Reduce Its Strategic Vulnerabilities to Financial Sanctions," *China Leadership*, February 29, 2024, https://www.prcleader.org/post/china-s-attempts-to-reduce-its-strategic-vulnerabilities-to-financial-sanctions.
169. "RMB Tracker April 2024," *Swift*, April 17, 2024, https://www.swift.com/swift-resource/252278/download. It is important to

note that SWIFT may not capture all international RMB transactions. One estimate suggests that 80% of CIPS transactions utilize SWIFT messaging. See Raymond Yeung and Khoon Goh, "Petroyuan Will Not Bring About a Regime Shift Soon," ANZ Research—China Insight, April 6, 2022.
170. "2023 RMB Internationalization Report," *The People's Bank of China*, December 8, 2023, http://www.pbc.gov.cn/en/3688241/3688636/3828468/4756463/5163932/202312081954 5781941.pdf.
171. "Why Is Xi Jinping Building Secret Commodity Stockpiles?," *The Economist*, July 23, 2024, https://www.economist.com/finance-and-economics/2024/07/23/why-is-xi-jinping-building-secret-commodity-stockpiles.
172. Grace Hearty and Mayaz Alam, "Rare Earths: Next Element in the Trade War?" *Center for Strategic and International Studies*, May 27, 2022, https://www.csis.org/analysis/rare-earths-next-element-trade-war.
173. Qian Zhou and Sofia Brooke, "China Merges Three Rare Earths State-Owned Entities to Increase Pricing Power and Efficiency," *China Briefing News*, January 12, 2022, https://www.china-briefing.com/news/china-merges-three-rare-earths-state-owned-entities-to-increase-pricing-power-and-efficiency/.
174. Wayne Morrison and Rachel Tang, "China's Rare Earth Industry and Export Regime: Economic and Trade Implications for the United States," *Congressional Research Service*, April 30, 2012, https://sgp.fas.org/crs/row/R42510.pdf.
175. Rodrigo Castillo and Caitlin Purdy, "China's Role in Supplying Critical Minerals for the Global Energy Transition: What Could the Future Hold?" *Brookings Institution*, July 2022, https://www.brookings.edu/wp-content/uploads/2022/08/LTRC_ChinaSupplyChain.pdf.
176. Edward Burrier and Thomas Sheehy, "Challenging China's Grip on Critical Minerals Can Be a Boon for Africa's Future," *United States Institute of Peace*, June 7, 2023, https://www.usip.org/publications/2023/06/challenging-chinas-grip-critical-minerals-can-be-boon-africas-future.
177. "Opinions of the State Council on Promoting the Sustainable and Healthy Development of the Rare Earth Industry (国务院关于促进稀土行业持续健康 发展的若干意见)," *People's Republic*

of *China Central People's Government* (中华人民共和国中央人民政府), May 19, 2011, https://www.gov.cn/zwgk/2011-05/19/content_1866997.htm.
178. Sun Yu and Tom Mitchell, "China Merges 3 Rare Earths Miners to Strengthen Dominance of Sector," *Financial Times*, December 23, 2021, https://www.ft.com/content/4dc538e8-c53e-41df-82e3-b70a1c5bae0c.
179. "China's Rare Earth 'Super Aircraft Carrier' Sailing to the World (中国稀土'超级航母'驶向全球)," *Xinhua*, January 7, 2022, http://www.news.cn/energy/20220107/c91f9663f7884ac4871024fce402cf1d/c.html.
180. "Group Introduction (集团简介)," *China Rare Earth Group*, n.d., Accessed May 9, 2024, https://www.regcc.cn/zgxtjt/gywm/guym.shtml.
181. "China Tightens Grip on Rare Earths to Ensure 'Industrial Security'," *Caixin Global*, July 1, 2024, https://www.caixinglobal.com/2024-07-01/china-tightens-grip-on-rare-earths-to-ensure-industrial-security-102211895.html.
182. Keith Bradsher, "Amid Tension, China Blocks Vital Exports to Japan," *The New York Times*, September 22, 2010, https://www.nytimes.com/2010/09/23/business/global/23rare.html.
183. Gracelin Baskaran, "What China's Ban on Rare Earths Processing Technology Exports Means," *The Center for Strategic and International Studies*, October 13, 2024, https://www.csis.org/analysis/what-chinas-ban-rare-earths-processing-technology-exports-means.
184. Amy Lv and Tony Munroe, "China Bans Export of Critical Minerals to US as Trade Tensions Escalate," *Reuters*, December 4, 2024, https://www.reuters.com/markets/commodities/china-bans-exports-gallium-germanium-antimony-us-2024-12-03/.
185. Castillo and Purdy, "China's Role," 2022.
186. "Minerals Security Partnership—United States Department of State," *United States Department of State*, March 27, 2024, https://www.state.gov/minerals-security-partnership.

CHAPTER 5

Conclusion

The Party's conflicted relationship with the market has profoundly shaped China's economic reforms. Since the late 1970s, the Party has alternated between selectively embracing market forces and curbing them to preserve its control over the economy. This cycle has created the ebb and flow of economic liberalization in China. The enduring symbolism of the bird and the cage remains a useful way to understand the shifts in Chinese economic policy. Over time the cage expanded as market forces began shaping industries and private companies emerged as the primary drivers of economic growth. Yet, the cage never disappeared. When the economy began to develop in ways the Party found threatening, it would tighten the cage through restrictive economic policies designed to reassert state control.

During the years immediately after Mao Zedong's death, the Party both promoted market reforms from the top and permitted grassroots economic experiments undertaken by provincial leaders and Chinese farmers. As economic liberalization spread across China, many of the edifices of the socialist economy were replaced by private enterprise. The large-scale agriculture undertaken by Chinese collective farms was transformed into private family farming. Tens of thousands of small-scale businesses—called town and village enterprises—proliferated across the country, engaging in services and light manufacturing. Foreign companies began setting up factories in China's coastal areas to manufacture goods and export them to the rest of the world.

While liberal-minded reformers in the Party welcomed these developments, conservatives viewed them with suspicion. Among China's top leaders, there was a view that the Party needed to make use of the productive potential unleashed by market forces while preventing them from overwhelming China's socialist system. Deng Xiaoping embodied this nuanced approach to the market, describing his approach as "capitalist tools in socialist hands." The market was an effective, and sometimes dangerous, tool to be used to achieve China's great national rejuvenation. It unlocked tremendous productive forces and had the potential to lift China out of poverty and restore its place among the world's great nations. However, if left unchecked, it could also unleash volatile forces that threatened to undermine the Party's rule.

These concerns came to a head in the late 1980s. The Party sought to liberalize prices for many key goods to promote economic efficiency. This process went awry, creating high levels of inflation for consumer goods and leading to growing levels of social disconnect. In response, the Party undertook an economic retrenchment, cutting spending and pausing reforms to bring prices back under control. Soon afterward, the Tiananmen Square Protests and their violent suppression further cooled the appetite for economic reform.

In the early 1990s, China's proponents of economic reform were in a weak position. Those in favor of constricting the cage had the upper hand. They argued that market forces had gotten out of control in China, creating social strife and political turmoil. Only with Deng Xiaoping's Southern Tour was support for economic reform revived. Deng believed China's long-term strength and prosperity depended on continuing market reforms. However, going forward, reforms would need to be carefully controlled to avoid any potential threats to the Party's authority or stability.

In the 1990s and early 2000s, private businesses became a significant force in the Chinese economy. With their greater efficiency and innovation, private companies started to displace state-owned enterprises in many sectors. While the Party permitted this shift to some extent, it was primarily driven by the private sector's ability to compete more effectively and to tap into new markets that state-owned enterprises had ignored because of a lack of market orientation.

The rise of the private sector paralleled the decline of the state sector, which was weighed down by deep structural issues. China had a plethora of low-productivity, heavily indebted, and loss-making state enterprises. Reliant on cheap bank loans, they monopolized the country's savings and relied on state support to remain operational. By the late 1990s, the business models of many state-owned enterprises were collapsing. Loss-making companies could not repay their loans, leading banks to roll over their debts rather than recognize losses. When the full extent of these bad loans was taken into account, the banks, and by extension, the entire Chinese financial system, were insolvent.

To save the economy in the late 1990s, the Party undertook a major clean-up of the state sector and launched a bailout of the banks. Thousands of smaller state-owned enterprises were closed, opening up opportunities for the private sector to expand and drive forward growth. However, the Party was unwilling to allow private companies to completely replace the state sector. At the same time that smaller state-owned enterprises were shut down, other state companies were restructured to become larger and more powerful. China embraced a strategy of granting additional room for the private sector while ensuring that state companies continued to occupy the commanding heights of the economy.

The Party's approach to managing the private sector crystallized during the late 2000s and early 2010s. A hybrid economy emerged, characterized by a strong state sector and a fast-growing private sector. While the Party permitted private companies to expand and make money, it also took careful steps to ensure they did not become too influential or grow beyond its control. This was accomplished through two primary strategies. First, the Party attempted to co-opt private entrepreneurs by allowing them to join the Party and establish Party committees within private companies. This gave the Party eyes and ears within private companies and levers of control if they started behaving in a manner which the Party disapproved. The second strategy was to strengthen state companies in strategic industries, providing them with additional support and subsidies. The Party's conception of strategic industries was linked to sectors it viewed as important for national security or control over vital economic resources.

1 Xi's Economic Evolution

When Xi Jinping entered office, his views and policies on the economy were largely in line with those of his predecessors. Xi believed that the market reforms of the past few decades had been essential to China's economic growth. At the same time, Xi shared the Party's prevailing view that strong state-owned enterprises were essential for stabilizing the economy during periods of volatility and for investing in key policy initiatives.

Xi's first round of economic policy reforms was proposed during the 2013 Third Plenum. The reforms proposed during that meeting were initially hailed as major breakthroughs in pushing the Chinese economy toward greater marketization. However, in retrospect, the Third Plenum was not as bold a departure as initially thought. While they did call for a greater role for the market, the Third Plenum did not represent a departure from the Party's desire for powerful state-owned enterprises and control of the economy.

Although the Third Plenum fell short of the lofty expectations set for it, Xi implemented several notable reforms during his early years in office. In this respect, he followed in the footsteps of predecessors by embracing selective and incremental reforms to drive forward the Chinese economy. However, Xi's reform agenda was derailed by a series of economic crises in 2015 and 2016. China experienced a significant downturn in the housing market, a stock market downturn, and a currency crisis, all in short succession.

In response to these events, Xi began to slow the pace of market reforms and shift back toward supporting state-owned enterprises. The volatility of market forces in the economy had become more disruptive than the Party was willing to tolerate. Xi undertook a crackdown on the financial sector, which he viewed as the locus of risk within the Chinese economy. Overlapping with the financial sector crackdown, the Party went after many influential private firms, jailing several entrepreneurs it viewed as threatening its control. This action would be a precursor to the larger private sector crackdown led by the Party a few years later.

Soon after Xi slowed reform, the U.S.-China relationship began to deteriorate sharply. Years of growing tensions between the two countries boiled over, and both sides increasingly viewed one another as adversaries. After Donald Trump's election in 2016, China and the United States entered into a trade war and conflict over technology. China's vulnerabilities to foreign economic pressure were made abundantly clear as the country found itself restricted from key export markets and critical technologies.

Faced with this new challenge, Xi leaned further into economic intervention. He orchestrated a national campaign to make China more resilient to economic pressure from foreign countries, especially the United States. Through the guidance of both the state sector and private companies, the Party sought to make the Chinese economy more self-reliant and less dependent on foreign technology. To do so, it began more aggressively intervening in a wide range of industries.

Heightened tensions with the United States also reduced the Party's tolerance of economic volatility and potential challenges to its control. From the Party's perspective, much of this was driven by private companies that had become too large and exerted excessive control over strategic parts of the economy. These tensions came to a head in 2020 and 2021 when the Party undertook large-scale interventions in many different industries. Payments, e-commerce, social media, ride-sharing, and tutoring, all industries dominated by private firms, were upended by draconian rule changes issued by the Chinese government.

2 China's Economic Trajectory

The metaphor of the bird and the cage remains as instructive as ever. As Chinese economic policy has become overly tilted toward the goals of stability, control, and self-reliance, it has hindered economic growth and damaged the private sector. The pursuit of these goals comes at a heavy cost for the economy. China cannot avoid the tradeoffs that result from pursuing contradictory economic policies. As discussed in Chapter 4, a quest for excessive economic stability often comes at the expense of rapid economic growth. The desire to control large parts of the economy reduces the dynamism and capacity to innovate of companies, especially private businesses. Finally, the pursuit of self-reliance damages China's efforts to integrate into the global economy and gain access to foreign markets and technology. The cage has become ever tighter, threatening to crush the bird.

Although these contradictions have been a feature throughout China's reform period, they have become particularly significant under Xi Jinping. Strategic competition with the United States has pushed Xi to intensify economic intervention. At the same time, these interventions have become more costly in economic terms. This is because China's private sector has become the most important driver of growth in the economy and the Party's policies are stifling its potential. If the Party wants to achieve its goal of national rejuvenation, the Chinese economy must continue to grow and converge with the world's developed economies. Yet the policies of the Party are putting this goal at risk.

What does this imply for China's future economic trajectory? As discussed above, China's policy toward the market has waxed and waned throughout the reform period. The Party embraced market forces when it felt doing so would further its goals of national rejuvenation. When those same market forces appeared to be growing beyond the Party's control, it reversed course and began restricting its scope and activities.

This cycle of liberalization and restriction recurred throughout the 1980s amid periods of inflation and political unrest. It resurfaced in the 1990s as the Party worked to restructure the state sector and co-opt private enterprises. In the 2000s, this pattern emerged once more, with the Party countering the rapid expansion of the private sector by strengthening and consolidating state-owned enterprises.

Xi's rule during the 2010s initially seemed to follow this pattern. After the financial and economic tumult in 2015 and 2016, the Party once again enacted a series of restrictive economic policies. The regulatory windstorm of 2017–2018 and the crackdown on private conglomerates were reflective of this shift in policy.

After several years of these restrictive policies, the economy began to slow. If history were any guide, one might have expected Xi to pivot, easing restrictions and reembracing reform to revive growth. Instead, Xi remained steadfast, making few adjustments to his approach. By 2020, he doubled down, launching an even broader crackdown on private companies.

What, then, has disrupted the usual cycle of market openings and restrictions, marking the end of China's forty-year reform period and resulting in the onset of a new chapter in China's economic history characterized by slower growth? Some have argued that it's a byproduct of Xi's ideological makeup and the fact that he now exercises uncontested power in China. However, Xi's stated views contain too much continuity with those of his predecessors to make that likely. Like the Chinese leaders before him, Xi has professed support for private businesses and market forces while also declaring that China will maintain a strong and influential state sector.

Another argument is that China has persisted with policies that restrict the market in response to the severe disruptions associated with the outbreak of the COVID-19 pandemic. Any recalibrations that the Party might have considered in 2018 and 2019 were suspended after the virus outbreak. While COVID-19 was historically disruptive, this fails to explain why China would lean further into tight control over the economy after the worst of the pandemic had subsided.

Instead, the most likely explanation is that U.S.-China strategic rivalry has reshaped the Party's calculus. As a result, Xi is reacting to a perceived increase in threats to the Party's rule and control over the economy. While China has gone through periods of tension with other great powers, including the United States, the current period is fundamentally different. China and the United States are locked in an intense and large-scale economic conflict with no end in sight.

Blame for the deterioration in the relationship is shared on both sides. Xi has pushed China to play a more aggressive role on the global stage, leading to growing concerns in the United States. He has built up the Chinese military, made expansive territorial claims in the South China Sea, and has drawn China closer to American adversaries such as Russia and North Korea. Whereas previous Chinese leaders pursued foreign policies that generally tried to avoid provoking U.S. backlash, Xi is comfortable doing so if he thinks it furthers China's interests.

At the same time, U.S. leaders have done little to find common ground with China and have instead resorted to demagoguery for political gain, exaggerating the dangers presented by China's economic development. Trade and investment, even when it is mutually beneficial, has been characterized as threatening U.S. national security and aiding China's global ambitions. China has also been blamed for a host of economic problems in the United States, such as deindustrialization, which has many causes and are not solely the fault of Chinese exports. In response to the perceived threat from China, the U.S. government has imposed sweeping tariffs on Chinese goods, restricted the transfer of key technologies to China, banned many Chinese firms from the U.S. market, and taken steps to curtail capital flows between the two countries. There is a bipartisan and durable consensus in Washington about the need to take a hard line on China and many politicians are competing to outdo each other on who can be the toughest on the country.

In reaction to the deterioration of the U.S.-China relationship, Xi Jinping has leaned more heavily into economic intervention. Faced with competition from a superpower, the Party has prioritized stability, control, and self-reliance. Stability prevents the emergence of internal economic and social problems while the Party deals with a major external problem (i.e., U.S. pressure). Control allows the Party to head off internal challenges to its power and to direct the economy toward pursuing the political goals it views as necessary to compete with the United States Self-reliance is an overriding imperative to reduce the ability of the United States to pressure China or cripple its economy through sanctions.

The U.S.-China relationship is a critical explanatory factor behind the China's current economic policies. In an environment where China's leaders feel immense foreign pressure, their economic policies will be focused on helping China overcome that threat. Since the start of reforms in 1978 until the start of the trade war in 2018, China faced a mostly benign international economic environment. The capitalist world welcomed China back when it reopened its economy to trade and investment. The only period that echoes the challenges of today was in the aftermath of Tiananmen in 1989. After a violent crackdown on student protestors, China faced sanctions and trade restrictions from a variety of Western countries. That also coincided with a nadir of reform efforts. Faced with internal and external pressure, Chinese leaders shrunk the cage to the point of crushing the bird. As discussed in Chapter 2, Deng, believing the market was essential to achieving the Party's goals, embarked on the Southern Tour and pushed the policy pendulum back toward economic reform.

Chinese leaders may understand and even acknowledge some of the tradeoffs outlined in Chapter 4. However, Xi's words and actions suggest that he remains undeterred by these economic tradeoffs, viewing them as necessary in light of the perceived threats posed by competition with the US. Xi has undertaken no equivalent of a Southern Tour to alter the course of policymaking back toward market reform. Instead, his focus is on guiding the economy toward helping China overcome foreign economic pressure.

Unfortunately, this means that absent a change in U.S.-China relations, China is likely to remain focused on policies that strengthen the cage around the economy. There will be, of course, adjustments to policy in response to economic exigencies. The Party knows that if it crushes the bird, it will endanger social stability and derail China's national rejuvenation. Therefore, the Party will make the tactical adjustments necessary to keep the economy growing at a moderate rate. However, the Party's risk calculus has changed, making the bold and ambitious reform of the past unlikely.

This has many important implications for China's future trajectory. First, the Chinese economy is unlikely to return to its rapid growth rate of the past. The current slowdown in economic activity is likely to be a long-term structural shift toward lower growth. Fears that China would rapidly eclipse the United States in economic power and influence are likely to be unfounded. China may eventually surpass the United States in total GDP, but it will do so at a much slower pace as the difference in growth rates between the two countries is far smaller than a decade ago. China will remain economically important, but it will not be the unstoppable economic juggernaut that some analysts predicted in the past.

The Party's pursuit of cage tightening also means that China's ability to innovate will look very different than in the past. During looser periods of economic policy, China managed to spawn many innovative private companies in a variety of different industries. China produced such companies in payments, e-commerce, social media, robotics, electric vehicles, clean energy, and many other industries. These companies benefited from an environment where they had the space to compete, experiment, and expand into new areas of the economy. The policies of the Party have curtailed the space available to these companies. While China is likely to continue to produce some groundbreaking companies, it will do so at a much-reduced rate. Furthermore, the Party's efforts to centralize and guide technological advancement efforts, with state-owned enterprises on the front lines of innovation, are likely to produce weak results. Finally, China's efforts to achieve greater self-reliance will continue to invite backlash, threatening the global economic integration that has been essential to its growth.

3 How to Respond to China

The wide-ranging and interconnected economic relationship between the United States and China is at a critical juncture. While the two countries have never seen eye-to-eye on political issues, previously there was a widespread belief among many on both sides that the economic relationship could prove to be a stabilizing buttress against the inevitable political and economic disagreements that would arise. Commerce, trade, and investment would give each country a stake in the other's development and stability. Americans would not view China's rise in zero-sum terms if they stood to benefit from the growth of China's economy. Similarly, China would be reluctant to challenge the international economic system that had proved so amenable to its own development.

This optimistic assessment of the economic relationship has collapsed in recent years. Both countries see themselves as locked in long-term economic and geopolitical competition with each other. Many Americans now view China's economic growth as a threat to U.S. interests. They believe that if the Chinese economy eclipses America in size, exports, and industrial capacity, U.S. global influence will be weakened. Furthermore, they worry that the larger China's economy grows, the more resources the Party will have at its disposal to compete with the United States In this context, Xi's policies to increase the Party's control over the Chinese economy are even more concerning.

Historically, the US has had limited capacity to influence the direction of Chinese economic policy. American influence is even more constrained given that Xi and the Party believe China is locked in an intense geopolitical competition with America. De-escalation of tensions would be a lengthy and difficult process. As such, there is very little U.S. policymakers can do to change China's economic policies in the short run. Moreover, it is important to recognize that the Party's approach to economic management has persisted across decades and through successive generations of leaders. The Party will continue to seek a balance between the productive power of the market and private enterprise against its goal of establishing a modern, developed, and powerful socialist state. Within this ideological framework, there is little hope that the Party will ever let the Chinese economy become as market-determined and open as the Western capitalist countries.

How should American policymakers respond to China given the country's current trajectory? Understanding China's economic contradictions provides a guide for calibrating the policies necessary to protect American economic and national security interests. The Chinese economic policies Americans are most concerned with are also likely to be the most damaging to China's long-term economic prospects. The further Xi and the Party push for tight management of markets and strong SOEs, the less likely that China will be able to compete with American free market capitalism. This is because Xi's policies undermine the essential factor behind China's economic success over the past four decades, a cage large enough for the bird to continue to fly.

This inherent contradiction in China's approach argues for strategic prudence in dealing with China. Strategic prudence means that U.S. policymakers should continue to take steps to protect American interests. This involves taking countervailing trade actions to preserve U.S. industries, especially industries with strategic importance, from the negative impact of China's industrial policies. Protecting U.S. interests also involves safeguarding U.S. technology and intellectual property from state-sponsored theft. Additionally, a healthy skepticism of Chinese companies who seek to operate within the United States is warranted given the ability of the Party to control companies and direct their activities toward its own goals. All of these efforts are necessary in the face of an increasingly interventionist Party that is focused on directing the resources of the Chinese economy toward political goals.

However, strategic prudence also argues that U.S. policymakers should avoid the temptation to continually escalate tensions with China for domestic political gains. Economic demagoguery, such as exaggerating the threat from China or painting every Chinese action as a sinister plot, weakens the already frayed trust between the two countries and contributes to a cycle of ever-increasing tensions. The continuing deterioration in U.S.-China relations raises the possibility that the two sides may stumble into armed conflict. A war between the United States and China would be devastating for both sides and likely result in catastrophic losses in terms of lives and resources.

In light of these risks, the United States should focus on maintaining a stable relationship with China while allowing the strengths of its economic system to gradually compound to its advantage over time. It also requires a recognition that many types of trade and investment between the two countries can be mutually beneficial and stabilizing for the relationship. Overreaction and threat inflation are as dangerous as complacency in responding to the Chinese economic challenge. As long as China pursues that path of cage-tightening economic policies, time is on America's side.

Finally, strategic prudence also calls for remaining open to the possibility of change. Xi and the Party may eventually recognize that the pendulum of Chinese economic policy has swung too far. China might come to see that its actions to bolster its control over the economy have become a threat to its own goal of national rejuvenation. Rather than seeking self-reliance, China may come to see that economic interdependence serves its long-term interests. The Party might begin to reprioritize growth, openness, and global economic integration as the keys to its economic success. In doing so, China would become less threatening to U.S. interests and Americans might once again believe that China's economic development could be mutually beneficial. The path that leads China toward a stronger economy is also one that is less likely to bring it into conflict with the United States.

History and ideology argue that China is unlikely to make such a change. However, strategic prudence calls for remaining open to the possibility, even if it is improbable. During tumultuous periods between the two countries, trade and commerce have served as a ballast for the relationship. That stabilizing force has weakened significantly as the Party has tightened the cage around the Chinese economy. If the Party were to ease its grip on the Chinese economy, the two countries might once again find opportunities for mutually beneficial economic cooperation. In time, this might reshape views on both sides that the bilateral relationship need not be defined solely as a zero-sum competition. This is the best hope for a durable peace between the United States and China. The alternative is growing tensions, economic autarky, and the possibility of a disastrous conflict that would weaken China, the United States, and the rest of the world.

Index

0–9
15th Party Congress, 34
36 Articles, 46–48
1978 Third Plenum Communique, 17, 75
1994 Company Law, 31
2008 Global Financial Crisis, 52

A
advanced communications technology, 203
Aerospace, 107, 122, 203
Agricultural Development Bank of China, 36
Alibaba, 101, 118, 128–130, 187, 189, 190, 195
Alipay, 128, 130, 187–189
All-China Federation of Industry and Commerce, 116
Anbang Insurance Group, 95
Anhui, 17
Ant Group, 128–130
Anti-Rightist Campaign, 11
Argentina, 211
Artificial intelligence (AI), 122, 196, 203
A-share market, 41, 175
Asian Financial Crisis, 33, 34, 37, 38, 53, 64
Asset Management Agency, 49
Australia, 211
Aviation, 47, 122, 192, 203, 204

B
Backyard smelters, 11
Baidu, 101, 131, 132
Baihang Credit Services Platform, 189
Banco Delta Asia, 122
Bank of China (BOC), 40, 175
Bank of Kunlun, 122
Baoneng, 95–98
Baowu Steel Group, 35
Batteries, 200, 201
Beijing, 7, 9, 16, 17, 19, 20, 22–24, 30, 53, 78, 86, 116, 129, 176
Beijing E-Town, 108
Belt and Road Initiative (BRI), 110, 119, 191, 210

246 INDEX

biotechnology, 51, 203
Black swan, 85
Boxer Rebellion, 9
BYD, 200, 201
Bytedance, 118, 195

C
Cainiao, 192
Caixin, 194
Canada, 121
Capitalism, 2, 4, 11, 14–17, 25, 29, 31, 48, 76, 166, 242
CEFC China Energy, 95
Central Economic Work Conference, 77, 92, 166
Central Financial Work Commission, 39
Central Huijin, 39, 175, 176
Central Organization Department, 39
Central parity rate, 90, 91
Central planning, 8, 18
Chaebol system, 34
Chen, Duxiu, 9
Chengdu, 109
Chen, Yun, 3, 5, 15, 16, 19, 22, 24, 26–29, 73, 163
Chile, 211
China Banking Regulatory Commission, 39, 92, 129
China Chengtong Holdings, 193
China Construction Bank, 38, 40, 175
China Cosco Shipping, 193
China Development Bank (CDB), 36, 88, 108, 109
China Energy Investment Corporation, 103
China Guodian, 102, 103
China Insurance Regulatory Commission, 97
China Internet Investment Fund, 118
China Investment Corporation, 175
China Logistics Group, 193
China Merchants Group, 111, 192, 193
China Mobile, 41, 102
China National Tobacco Corp, 108
China Railway Materials Group, 193
China Rare Earth Group, 211, 212
China Reform Holdings and China Structural Adjustment Fund, 190
China Resources Group, 96, 97
China's Company Law, 115
China Securities Regulatory Commission, 113, 129, 130
China's Ministry of Industry and Information Technology's Whitelist, 167, 200
China Structural Reform Fund, 193
China Telecom, 41, 102
China Unicom, 101, 102
Chinese Academy of Engineering, 106
Chinese Communist Party (CCP), 2, 8–10, 27, 113, 114, 116
Chu, Shijian, 33
Cisco, 205
Clean Networks Initiative, 205
Clinton, Bill, 43
Coal, 76, 103, 168, 169
Cobalt, 211
Collective farms, 1, 233
Collectivization, 8, 10, 11
Commercial Banking Law, 37
Communes, 11, 18
Communique, 17
Communism, 25
Consumption tax, 200
Contract farming, 18
Contract Responsibility System, 20
Counter-cyclical, 90
Country Garden, 111, 112
Covid-19 pandemic, 125, 134, 168, 198, 239

Cross-Border Interbank Payments System (CIPS), 209
CSC Holding Company, 192
Cultural Revolution, 1, 11–13, 15, 20, 24, 75
Currency, 11, 33, 36, 90, 91, 207, 208, 210, 213, 236
Cyberspace Administration of China (CAC), 118, 194–196

D
Dai, Xianlong, 38, 186, 222
Dalian Wanda, 95
Decision on Accelerating the Development of Strategic Emerging Industries, 52
Defense Production Act, 212
Deleveraging, 131, 171
Democratic Republic of Congo (DRC), 211
Deng's Southern Tour, 30, 31
Deng, Xiaoping, 3, 4, 7, 11, 13, 14, 57, 73, 75, 81, 82, 211, 234
Denmark, 205
Depreciation, 33, 90
Didi Chuxing, 101, 131, 132
Document 9, 77
Double Reduction Policy, 173, 174
Douyu, 185
Draft Measures for the Management of Generative Artificial Intelligence Services, 196
Dual Circulation, 191
Dual-Track Pricing, 26

E
East Germany, 28
Economic Observer, 194
Economic reform, 2, 4, 7, 8, 13–17, 19, 24–30, 45, 49, 52, 53, 57, 81, 84, 85, 91, 134, 199, 233

EMS, 192
Entity List, 121, 205
Equity market, 90
Estonia, 205
Europe, 22, 78, 201
Evergrande, 97, 98, 170–172
Export-Import Bank of China (EXIM), 36
Ezubao, 90, 91

F
Facebook, 184
Fairchild Semiconductor, 109
Financial and Economic Affairs Group, 105
Financial Stability and Development Committee, 93
First Sino-Japanese War, 9
Fixing rate, 90
Foreign Entity of Concern, 201
Foreign joint ventures, 21
Forest City, 111, 112
Fosun, 95
Four Cardinal Principles, 82
Four Modernizations Campaign, 14
France, 205
Fujian, 24, 75
Full Truck Alliance, 118, 192

G
Gallium, 212
Gaotu, 174
Geely, 131
General Motors, 199
General secretary, 27, 57, 76, 81
Germanium, 212
Going Out Policy, 50, 210
Going Out Strategy, 110
Grasp the Large, Let go of the Small, 34, 45, 99
Great Leap Forward, 11, 14, 24

Grey Rhino, 85, 95, 128
Guangdong, 23, 24, 75, 96, 191
Guided capitalism, 34
Guizhou, 180
Guo, Shuqing, 92, 94

H
Hambantota Port, 111
Hangzhou, 89
Harmonious Society, 52
High-end Manufacturing, 52, 203
HiSilicon, 121
HNA Group, 95
Honda, 199
Hong Kong, 23, 39–41, 103, 117, 122, 129, 191, 208
Hongta Group, 33
Household businesses, 19, 20
Household farming, 18, 19, 45
Hua Capital Management, 109
Hua, Guofeng, 13–15, 22
Huawei, 121–123, 205–207
Hubei, 109
Hu, Jintao, 4, 7, 45, 46, 52, 57, 73, 76, 106, 110
Huya, 185
Hu, Yaobang, 15

I
Ideology, 7, 9, 10, 16, 22, 32, 56, 127, 244
Ifeng News, 195
India, 212
Indonesia, 33
Industrial and Commercial Bank of China, 38, 40
Inflation, 3, 15, 26, 27, 78, 167, 234, 238, 243
Inflation Reduction Act, 201
Initial public offerings (IPO), 41, 89, 129, 131, 176, 189

Integrated Circuit Fund, 108, 109
Integrated circuits, 107, 203, 205
Interim Ordinances on State-Owned Enterprises, 21
International Monetary Fund, 33
Internet of Things (IoT), 101
Iran, 120, 121, 209
Italy, 205

J
JAC Capital, 110
Japan, 9, 10, 13, 22, 41, 130, 207, 212
JD.Com, 101, 131
JDL, 192
Jiang, Zemin, 7, 30, 31, 34, 42, 44, 45, 52, 73, 113
Jinri Toutiao, 195
Juren Education, 174

K
Khruschev, Nikita, 25
Korean War, 197
Kuaishou, 118, 195

L
Landlords, 10
Land reform, 10
Lardy, Nicholas, 55
Large Enterprise Working Committee, 36
Lattice Semiconductor, 109
Latvia, 205
Li, Dazhao, 9
Lifeline industries, 48
Linxens, 109
Li, Peng, 28
Li, Rongrong, 50, 54
Lithuania, 205
Liu, He, 95, 99
Liu, Shaoqi, 11, 14

INDEX 249

Local Government Financing Vehicles (LGFVs), 80, 179, 180

M
Macao, 23, 191
Made in China 2025, 105–108, 110, 119, 198, 203, 205
Ma, Huateng, 186
Ma, Jack, 128–130, 189
Malaysia, 33, 112, 206
Mao, Zedong, 1, 7, 9, 11, 17, 233
Market economy, 3, 15, 81, 83
Marxism, 2, 8, 9, 127
Marxism-Leninism, 16
May Fourth Movement, 8
Mediatek, 109
Medium to Long-Term Plan for the Development of Science and Technology (MLP), 51
Megaprojects, 51
Meng, Wanzhou, 121
Mexico, 76, 182
Micron, 109
Middle East, 211
Middle-income trap, 182
Mid-to-Long-Term Automotive Industry Plan, 200
Ministry of Finance (MoF), 38, 39, 42, 108, 178
Ministry of Industry and Information Technology, 106
Mixed Ownership Economy, 100

N
Nanjing, 109
National Audit Office, 80
National Development and Reform Commission (NDRC), 105, 167–169, 194
National Integrated Circuit Fund, 108, 110

Nationalists, 8–10, 26
Negative List for Market Access, 194
Netease News, 195
NetsUnion Clearing Corporation (NetsUnion), 189
New 36 Articles, 47, 48
New Development Philosophy (NDP), 125
New Oriental, 174
New Socialist Countryside, 52
North Korea, 120, 239
Notice Concerning Deepening Financial Reform, Rectifying Financial Order, and Preventing Financial Risks, 37

O
Omnivision, 109
Opinions on Promoting the Sustainable and Healthy Development of the Rare Earth Industry, 211
Opium War, 9
Outbound investment, 90, 122

P
P2P lending, 90
Party committees, 32, 38, 41, 93, 112–117, 183, 186, 235
Paulson, Hank, 53
Peasants, 10, 13, 18
Peking University, 9
People's Bank of China (PBOC), 85, 94, 178
People's Daily, 29, 112, 133
People's Liberation Army (PLA), 117, 203
Platform economy, 132
Politburo Standing Committee, 76
Portugal, 205
Powertech Technology, 109

Princeling, 74, 75
Private enterprise, 2, 4, 18, 20, 32, 36, 48, 55, 85, 114, 132, 238, 242
Property Law, 48

Q
Qing Dynasty, 9
Qiushi, 126
QQ, 184
Quota, 18, 20, 26, 94

R
RDA Microelectronics, 108
Reform and Opening Era, 56
Reform and Opening Up, 5
Regulations on the Administration of Internet Information Service Recommendation Algorithms, 195
Rehabilitations, 13–15
Resolution on Financial System Reform, 36
Romania, 205

S
Section 301, 119
Securities Association of China, 94
Semiconductor Manufacturing International Corporation (SMIC), 109
SF, 192
Shadow banking, 78, 88, 93, 95
Shanghai, 9, 24, 29, 75, 94, 101, 201, 208
Shantou, 23
Shenhua Group, 102, 103
Shenzhen, 23, 24, 75, 201, 208
Shenzhen Metro, 97, 98
Singapore, 104, 111
Sino-Soviet split, 197
Sinotrans, 192
Six Stabilities, 165
SK Hynix, 109
Small-scale enterprises, 19
SME lending, 94
Socialism, 2, 19, 21, 25, 27, 31, 56, 77, 82, 103, 127
Socialism with Chinese Characteristics, 25, 103, 193, 212
Socialist Market Economy, 31, 81, 83, 133
South Africa, 182
South Korea, 33, 34
Sovereign wealth fund, 39, 175
Soviet Union (USSR), 9, 28
Speadtrum Communications, 108
Special economic zones (SEZs), 22–24, 28, 29, 42
Sri Lanka, 111
State Administration and Regulation, 131
State Council, 36, 37, 42, 46, 47, 50, 52, 103–106, 116, 118, 130, 211
State-Owned Assets Supervision and Administration Commission (SASAC), 49, 70, 190
State-owned Capital Investment Companies (SOCIC), 104
State-owned enterprise, 1, 2, 10, 16, 20, 47, 50, 96, 99, 108, 127, 175, 179, 210, 211, 234–236, 238, 241
State-Owned Enterprise Reform, 190
Stock Connect, 208, 209
Stock market, 1, 85, 88, 90, 99, 166, 174, 175, 177, 236
Sub-Saharan African countries, 13
Suharto, 33
Sultan of Johor, 111
Suning, 101
Sweden, 205

SWIFT, 209

T
Taiwan, 9, 23
Taiwan Strait, 23
TAL Group, 174
Tariffs, 43, 46, 120, 201, 239
Temasek Model, 104
Tencent, 101, 102, 131, 132, 184–190, 195
Tesla, 200, 201
Thailand, 33, 38, 182
Third Plenum, 74, 81, 82, 85, 91, 99, 100, 117, 236
Three Red Lines, 131, 171, 180
Three Represents, 44
Tiananmen Square, 8, 27, 234
Tomorrow Holding Group, 95
Town and Village Enterprises (TVE), 18–20, 28, 30, 32, 233
Toyota, 199
Trade war, 119, 236, 240
Treaty of Versailles, 8
Trump, Donald, 117, 119, 122, 129, 201, 236
Tsinghua Unigroup, 108–110
Tsinghua University, 75, 108
Two Whatevers, 13

U
UnionPay, 128, 186–188, 190
United States (U.S), 4, 11, 22, 28, 34, 53, 74, 77, 78, 119, 122, 123, 125, 164, 179, 201, 203, 204, 207, 208, 212, 237, 239, 241
United States Trade Representative, 119
U.S.-China Trade War, 51, 198, 204

V
Vanke, 96–98
Vehicle purchase tax, 200
Volkswagen, 199

W
Wall Street English, 174
Wang, Qishan, 53
Wang, Shi, 96, 97
"Wearing a Red Hat", 19
WeChat, 84, 184
Wen, Jiabao, 45, 46, 53
Western Digital, 109
Western powers, 9, 11
World Economic Forum Annual Meeting, 53
World Trade Organization (WTO), 42, 198
World War II, 10

X
Xiang, Junbo, 97
Xiaomi, 116, 117
Xi, Jinping, 1, 2, 4, 7, 73, 75, 91, 92, 99, 103, 113, 115, 119, 126, 133, 164, 177, 191, 193, 196, 198, 207, 208, 212, 236, 237, 239
Xi, Zhongxun, 1, 74, 75
Xu, Jiayin, 172
Xu, Xiang, 89

Y
Yao, Zhenhua, 97
Yi, Gang, 188
Yue, Kong-Pao, 23

Z
Zhao, Weiguo, 108

Zhao, Ziyang, 21, 26–28
Zhejiang Province, 75, 76
Zhima Credit, 189
Zhou, Bin, 76
Zhou, Enlai, 14
Zhou, Yongkang, 76
Zhuhai, 23

Zhu, Rongji, 33, 37, 42, 45, 49
Zimbabwe, 211
ZTE Corporation, 120
ZTO Express, 192
Zunyi Road and Bridge Construction Group, 180